WHAT ABOUT MOZART?
WHAT ABOUT MURDER?

REASONING FROM CASES

What About Mozart? What About Murder?

HOWARD S. BECKER

The University of Chicago Press Chicago and London

HOWARD S. BECKER is the author of several
books, including *Writing for Social Scientists*, *Telling
About Society*, *Tricks of the Trade*, and *Art Worlds*. He
currently lives and works in San Francisco.

The University of Chicago Press, Chicago 60637
The University of Chicago Press, Ltd., London
© 2014 by The University of Chicago
All rights reserved. Published 2014.
Printed in the United States of America

23 22 21 20 19 18 17 16 15   2 3 4 5

ISBN-13: 978-0-226-16635-3 (cloth)
ISBN-13: 978-0-226-16649-0 (paper)
ISBN-13: 978-0-226-16652-0 (e-book)
DOI: 10.7208/chicago/9780226166520.001.0001

Becker, Howard Saul, 1928– author.
What about Mozart? What about murder? :
reasoning from cases / Howard S. Becker.
pages cm
Includes bibliographical references and index.
ISBN 978-0-226-16635-3 (cloth : alkaline paper) —
ISBN 978-0-226-16649-0 (paperback : alkaline paper) —
ISBN 978-0-226-16652-0 (e-book) 1. Sociology—
Methodology. 2. Case-based reasoning. I. Title.
HM511.B435 2014
301.01—dc23

                                        2013048791

♾ This paper meets the requirements of
ANSI/NISO Z39.48-1992 (Permanence of Paper).

To the memory of
STAN COHEN,
LEIGH STAR, *and*
GILBERTO VELHO,
old friends and
intellectual companions

Some books are premeditated, others not. This one has grown by itself and discovered by its own movement its form and its end, constantly baffling in the course of its growth the intentions that I naively strove, again and again mistaking a branch or twig for a stem, to impose upon it.

MARC FUMAROLI, *When the World Spoke French* (translated by Richard Howard)

Contents

Acknowledgments

I have been thinking about these topics ever since I started studying sociology at the University of Chicago in the 1940s. I could not in any reasonable way thank all the people who helped shape my thinking over all these years, so I won't try. Some of my debts are obvious in the references and remarks in the text. Those that aren't recognized there—well, just know that I'm grateful even to the people whose help I don't remember.

I am, however, very mindful of what my long friendship and professional association with Douglas Mitchell has done for me in such a variety of ways. So, one more once, thanks, Doug.

Dianne Hagaman and I share our lives and I know how lucky I am to have that life with her. She read every word of this book and helped me in more ways than I can say.

I'm grateful for Matt Avery's laid-back design, which welcomes readers and makes them at home in my world.

Donald Westlake's novels helped me finish this book. In troubled moments, I turned to them for solace and refreshment.

I've been writing about these topics for at least thirty years, often for special occasions. Portions of the following publications have been altered to a greater or lesser degree for inclusion in this book.

"Distributing Modern Art," *New Art Examiner*, December 1983, 5–6.

"E di Mozart che ne dici? E dell'omicidio?" in *Rassegna Italiana di Sociologia* 44, no. 4 (October–December 2003): 483–92. Reprinted with the permission of the publisher, Il Mulino.

"History, Culture, and Subjective Experience: An Exploration of the Social Bases of Drug-Induced Experiences," *Journal of Health and Social Behavior* 8 (September 1967): 163–76.

"How Much Is Enough?" originally published in *Public Culture* 25, no. 3 (2013): 375–86. Reprinted with the permission of the publisher, Duke University Press.

"How We Deal with the People We Study," in *Crime, Social Control, and*

Human Rights: From Moral Panics to Denial: Essays in Honour of Stanley Cohen, ed. Christine Chinkin, David Downes, Conor Gearty, and Paul Rock (Cullompton, UK: Willan, 2007). Reprinted with the permission of the publisher.

"La Confusion de Valeurs," in *L'art de la recherche: Melanges*, ed. Pierre-Michel Menger and Jean-Claude Passeron, 11–28 (Paris: La Documentation Française, 1994). Reprinted with the permission of the publisher.

"The Lay Referral System: The Problem of Professional Power," *Knowledge, Work, and Society* 4, no. 2 (2006): 63–76. © Editions l'Harmattan. Reprinted with the permission of the publisher.

"Lessons from the Master, Everett C. Hughes," *Sociologica* 2 (2010): 1–11. Reprinted with the permission of the publisher, Il Mulino.

"The Power of Inertia," *Qualitative Sociology* 18 (1995): 301–9.

1 First Look

After the Civil War in the United States, after Abraham Lincoln proclaimed the emancipation of black slaves and the Congress and the several states passed the Fourteenth Amendment to the Constitution, guaranteeing full civil rights to all Americans, regardless of race—after those things happened, as soon as African Americans were able to vote, they voted overwhelmingly for candidates of the Republican Party and continued to vote that way for many years. Everyone knew the reason: Abraham Lincoln had been a Republican, and the Democrats had opposed him and his forward-looking policies with respect to race, so no African American person in his (women didn't have the vote for a lot of this time) right mind would vote otherwise. That relationship between race and voting for Republicans persisted for a long time. Until it didn't.

Until Franklin D. Roosevelt brought the Democratic party to power in 1932 and kept it there long enough to pass major legislation that changed the social and economic position of poorer people, a group that included most black citizens. The resulting relationship between race and voting for Democrats has persisted for a long time and looks as if it will be as permanent as the relationship between race and voting Republican once looked. Or will be until it isn't.

Similarly, after the post–World War II boom subsided, the United States changed in many ways. Factory and other blue-collar workers, who Roosevelt had also converted into persistent Democratic voters, stopped voting for the party in such large numbers, and the relation between class and party, which had seemed so permanent, stopped being so, and in a few years blue-collar voters started voting Republican in large numbers and the Reagan years began.

These correlations exhibited all the strength anyone could require to use them as building blocks of sociological thinking. But they disappeared and their opposites replaced them in a relatively short time. Were the research methods and theoretical strategies that produced those so-quickly falsified causal connections wrong? Were political scientists using bad data or faulty analytic techniques? More likely, were these supposedly invincible conclusions about race and class and voting so tied to historical circumstances that you couldn't be sure their validity would last until the next election? Was there something wrong with the way of thinking that supposed that specific, for the most part isolated, facts about people could predict with such certainty what they would do in a specific situation like an election?

Yes. Something was wrong. I think about these things because, as a working social scientist, doing research on specific questions that interest me and I hope will interest others, they bring up practical problems I have to solve. (Discussion of related, more abstract questions relevant to the philosophy of science, epistemology, or more abstract versions of sociological theory can easily be found elsewhere, for instance Hedström and Swedberg 1998; Hedström and Ylikoski 2010; Hedström and Bearman 2009; and Ragin 1987). Many things that I study change over time—people's experiences with drugs, for instance, which I take up in chapter 3, or how ordinary musicians, the kind who play in bars and for parties, can play together competently without any written music before them or any prior rehearsal (Faulkner and Becker 2009)—and I study them in an inclusive way, trying to learn as much as I can about what affects what I'm interested in, seeking the detailed understanding of social phenomena that results from studying them close up, finding out as much as I can about them. Close observation invariably shows that, even in the most ordinary situations, more than a few easily measured variables are at work and that everything in the situation has some effect on what happens next. If any one of those things isn't there or, better put, is there in a different degree or in a different form, the result (the next events that happen) will differ. As a corollary, everything left out of the analysis or data-gathering, perhaps because you aren't aware it's present, perhaps because it's too hard to find out about, let alone measure, is still there, at work, having its effects. I want to avoid the fate of researchers who relied too heavily on a relatively few easily observed facts to do their explanatory work, so I have to not only learn about all these other elements (or variables; the name isn't important) but incorporate them, systematically, into my explanations of what I've studied.

That insistence doesn't fit well with much contemporary thinking about how social facts or events occur and develop, which instead works by measuring the connections between measured things rather than explaining how those connections produce the results we want to understand. So I rely on what have often been called case studies, in-depth studies of particular situations, organizations, or kinds of events. (The essays Charles Ragin and I collected in *What Is A Case?* [1992] contain important discussions of these matters; I won't summarize them here.) Many experts have explained the logic of reasoning from collections of correlations between variables (see, especially, the illuminating essay by Passeron and Revel [2005]). This book offers explanations, arising from my own research experiences and those of others, of the logic of *reasoning from cases*. How do you get from the detailed knowledge of one case to more general ideas about how society, or some part of it, works? To explain that, I have to introduce a few more, not very complicated, ideas.

First, a simple observation. Everything present in or connected to a situation I want to understand should be taken account of and made use of. If it's there, it's doing something, however unimportant that thing seems, no matter how unobtrusive it is. Focusing on a sharply defined and narrowly delimited research question leads us to ignore everything else, or write it off as random error, or in some other way stop paying attention to it. I think that's a mistake and instead look for a way to build what might otherwise be left out into my thinking about what I'm studying.

Another simple observation. The things I study don't happen all at once, so I build the idea of change or process into my thinking about them. When some hitherto stable relationship turns up missing in what I'm studying, I don't treat that as the unfortunate failure of a theory I'm testing, but rather as an opportunity to learn about some parts of the process I hadn't seen until then. Not, as computer people say, a bug, but a feature.

I also know that what I'm studying at the moment connects to other things outside the framework I've built for my work and that, seen from another vantage point, the things I've left out could well be the center of my analysis. I try not to mistake my deliberate choices of focus for ineluctable aspects of reality.

As a result, my work doesn't produce timeless generalizations about relations between variables. It results instead in the identification of new elements of a situation, new things that can vary in ways that will affect the outcome I'm interested in, or new steps in a process I thought I'd understood until a result different from what I expected occurred. I can use these new elements of organization and process to direct my next inquiry. For me, that's the way social science works. I use the in-depth study of specific cases to produce new questions whose answers, in particular cases, can help me and others understand what's going on in the social world. (For a somewhat different, but related, view of how this works, see Vaughan's essays [2004, 2006, 2009] on analogical reasoning).

Many people think the object of sociological research and theorizing is to simplify our understanding of social life by finding the underlying laws that govern its operation. I think, contrariwise, that the object is to find out the nature of, and make a place in our thinking for, everything that observably contributes to producing the results I'm interested in. I want my analysis, my theory, to contain everything I need to describe and account for what my case study has forced me to see.

Many social scientists take nuclear physics as the model of the kind of theory they want their own work to resemble. I find a more realistic and useful model in some of the life sciences. In physiology, for instance, the reality we have to explain contains innumerable cases of the things that interest us (e.g., human bodies and their components), but, unlike the things physicists or chemists study, none of them are just alike, the way samples of copper or oxygen are or can be made to be. We have to explain how an underlying mechanism, like a circulatory system (whose fundamental design doesn't vary much among individual specimens), produces widely differing results (blood pressure, for instance) depending on the activity of all the other systems feeding into it (that's the substance of the input-output machines, or black boxes, I discuss in chapter 3 and again in chapter 6).

Like physiology, sociology explains how an underlying mechanism produces a great variety of experiences, depending on all the other processes whose results feed into the process producing those results (the way, for instance, drug users' ideas about what will happen affect what does happen when they take a drug).

If you think sociology should produce a simple model that explains everything, you won't find this way of working attractive. If you think a functioning scientific community thrives less on piling up conclusions than on creating a continuous flow of new problems to solve (which I take to be one of the messages of Thomas Kuhn's [1970] description of scientific activity), this approach will keep us busy long into the future. It's not just the complexity of social life that guarantees that, but also the fact of historical change, which keeps producing new forms of collective activity that provoke new ideas, new research problems, and new categories of elements whose variation will be at work in these new forms.

The chapters that follow take up a variety of questions that arise when you work this way, always looking for new elements to add to the explanatory scheme and finding them in the careful inspection of the details of specific cases, reasoning from the details of a case to a more general idea. Each chapter uses specific cases, mostly work I've done and reported on in the past, which exemplify one or another way of doing that, and explain how I did it. The specific cases have an interest of their own, but the emphasis is on what's to be learned from them about this way of working, and how to do it fruitfully.

2 *What's Happening Elsewhere: Reasoning from a Case to the World*

Empirical cases, studied in depth, lead us (if we pay attention to their details), to important social processes and the details of social organization that produce them. A few illustrative cases from my own experience introduce a detailed analysis of Everett Hughes's classic article (1949), which linked race, ethnicity and the processes involved in industrialization in a general account of social change in the modern world, based on his own intensive study (1943) of a town in Quebec. International comparisons play an important role in theories of industrialization and elsewhere, and his 1949 article embodies a useful analytic strategy.

When sociologists look at other countries, they hope to see something different from what they see at home. But they also want to use what they see elsewhere to enlarge their understanding of events and organizations at home. Sometimes, more ambitiously, they hope to learn something about all countries, about countries in general, so they compile data on all the countries there are, relying for the most part on statistical data gathered by international organizations and polls. They compare countries to one other and to international averages and ranges, seeing which ones score high or low on such variables as health, wealth, political freedom, and other topics of major theoretical and political concern. Other researchers hope to learn about the generic character of certain forms of life through intensive studies of several relevant cases.

Comparing countries has a long history in sociology and related social sciences. Historically oriented social scientists have traditionally used what's conventionally called the comparative (or comparative-historical) method to understand societies and social change at the "macro [i.e., macroscopic or large-scale] level." They have compared, as in Edwards's pioneering *The Natural History of Revolution* (1927), societies that experienced a violent revolution, to see what is common to that kind of event. More recently, Skocpol's *States and Social Revolutions* (1979) compared revolutionary events and outcomes in Russia, China, and France and became a model for a succeeding generation of such studies, using archival and secondary materials to produce historical interpretations oriented toward distinctively sociological comparisons.

After World War II, the United Nations and its ancillary organizations (UNESCO, WHO, FAO, and many others) made possible and gave impetus to a new kind of cross-national research when they collected, archived, summarized, and analyzed information and then distributed the data and results widely. Sociologists, economists, political scientists, and others suddenly had massive amounts of quantitative data, useful not only for the administrative purposes for which they were gathered but also for research focused on topics of interest in their disciplines. This produced the field of "development," the study of how countries that had not yet industrialized and modernized along Western European and North American lines fared as that process moved forward. United Nations statistics made possible, for perhaps the first time, large-scale research on a variety of topics in that general area.

So comparative sociology often takes the form of cross-national comparisons, comparing the kinds of things that happen to, and in, whole societies. Researchers who envision society as operating according to laws that specify how things like revolutions are caused by antecedent conditions, deduce possible solutions to these problems from theories, themselves deduced from more general principles or by induction from a mass of already studied cases. They try to establish, with modern statistical techniques, relations between variables describing whole societies, mostly numerically—demographic data on years of school completed, as a proxy for education; percentages of the population belonging to various religious communities; age and income distributions; political party affiliations; data on aspects of governmental forms; share of the vote political cal parties of differing orientations got in the last election; the incidence of various medical conditions—which might account for variation in the variables they've used to measure the development and modernization they want to explain.

Some anthropologists hoped that similarly testing hypotheses on larger samples would help them escape the problem of the inevitable specificity of their findings and the consequent lack of general laws that had always plagued their field. Studies of individual societies produced provocative and interesting findings. But did such findings occur universally? Margaret Mead's research in Samoa had exploded the theory that the hormonal changes of adolescence necessarily produced the stormy emotional lives of Western adolescents, by showing that Samoan adolescents, who experienced the same hormonal changes, didn't have those problems. But maybe one case didn't count for so much. Wouldn't it be better to test her idea on a larger number of societies? Such concerns led

George Peter Murdock to create the Human Relations Area Files (HRAF), a heroic effort to summarize and catalog everything anthropologists had discovered and published about all the societies they had studied over the years, so that generalizations linking variables in a variety of topical areas could be checked against real data on a much larger number of societies than was possible with the single case studies that characterized almost all anthropological research (Lemov 2006, 147–69).

Political scientists and sociologists who worked on problems in societal development, and anthropologists seeking universal laws with the help of the HRAF, modeled their work on the quasi-experimental methods that dominated both psychology and economics, comparing the values of quantified variables in a large sample of societies. Though such procedures were a second-best substitute for the rigorous experimental controls of the sciences they wanted to emulate, no one knew any better way to do it, so that's what researchers did. If their research produced the numbers the theory said it should, they took that to prove that the hypothesis they wanted to test was correct. In the anthropological cases, the variables might be quite simple, something like the presence or absence of a trait like cross-cousin marriage. With the more complex data available for nation-states, researchers used correlation coefficients or still more sophisticated measures computed from the primitive numbers. Researchers wanted to accept or reject ideas about the co-occurrence of variables, correlations that would provide evidence in favor of one hypothesis or another.

As the work progressed, these scholars thought, they would eventually be able to formulate laws modeled on what they took (not necessarily accurately) to be the kind of general laws developed by physical scientists, operating in the same way everywhere, not subject to local variation. In principle, they hoped to arrive at a social scientific "theory of everything," like the one physicists seemed always on the verge of creating, which explained all the variation in the social world being studied. They knew—all scientists know this, though they don't always say so—that this goal, in principle reachable, couldn't really be reached. Everyone expected to be happy with successively more accurate approximations.

But these social scientists had a big problem. The world contains a very small number of countries, so any attempt to use standard statistical techniques immediately began to "run out of cases," to end up with tables in which many cells were empty or contained very small numbers, and in which the small numbers made it difficult to find statistically significant correlations, since that technique is heavily influenced by the number of cases available for analysis. There weren't enough countries to use the techniques that worked well with survey data, where the more easily gathered larger numbers of cases allowed testing relatively complex hypotheses. (Ragin [1987, 2000, 2008; see also Becker 1998, 183–89] later developed set-theoretic methods that provided a different mathematical basis for making such tests, substituting Boolean algebraic techniques for the more traditional procedures based on probability theory. But that's another story.)

We can look for understanding of cross-national differences in a different way, and I'm going to use some personal experiences that sensitized me to cross-national differences and what you could make of them sociologically to introduce the use of specific cases to do the same kind of analytic work. I found a model for these casual exercises in Everett Hughes's remarkable elaboration of a casual conversation he had with two Germans after World War II. This case furnished the empirical seed for his later investigations, theoretical and empirical, of the topic he called "dirty work":

The architect: "I am ashamed for my people whenever I think of it [the Holocaust]. But we didn't know about it. We only learned about all that later. You just remember the pressure we were under; we had to join the party. We had to keep our mouths shut and do as we were told. It was a terrible pressure. Still, I am ashamed. But you see, we had lost our values and our national honor was hurt. And these Nazis exploited that feeling. And the Jews, they *were* a problem. They came from the east. You should see them in Poland; the lowest class of people, full of lice, dirty and poor, running about in their Ghettoes in filthy caftans. They came here, and got rich by unbelievable methods after the first war. They occupied all the good places. Why, they were in the proportion of ten to one in medicine and law and government posts!" He then fell silent and forgot what he had been talking about.

I [Hughes] said firmly, "You were talking about loss of national honor and how the Jews had got hold of everything."

The architect: "Oh yes! That was it! Well, of course that was no way to settle the Jewish problem. But there *was* a problem and it had to be settled someway." (Hughes 1971, 90–91)

Hughes made an analytic gem from this conversation and says that what he made of it was later verified by more formal studies and other conversations he had. The important point for him was not the particular details about Germany, as important as they were, but the general phenomenon this simple case alerted him to, what he later called "the moral division of labor," a phenomenon he thought common to all societies. Societies, he said, defined some kinds of work as "dirty," soiling the person who did them physically (like collecting garbage), morally (like being cruel to innocent people), or both. People whose own work their society defined as clean wanted the dirty work done (just as the German architect wanted the "Jewish problem settled") but didn't want to do it themselves. Other people, who had less choice of how to make a living, did the dirty work and the people who wanted it done could benefit from its doing while they themselves stayed clean.

That gave Hughes, and us, an analytic tool to use in other situations, as when he used the idea of a moral division of labor to understand medicine and law better (Hughes 1971, 306–10). I learned from that example a way of working that I knew how to do before I realized I was doing it. I've devoted this book to following that clue, and this chapter to thinking back on some simple examples of what Hughes did, to see how he extracted such a general idea from such a simple case.

The simple exercises I'm going to describe embody for me the big lesson Hughes taught: how to work from a small observation to a large possibility. This chapter uses some small experiences of my own—experiences, not research findings—as raw material pointing to how to find and work with the kinds of clues Hughes used as guides when he constructed his profound analysis of the relations between industry, race, and ethnicity.

GETTING A VISTO IN RIO DE JANEIRO

My first international comparative experience arose out of differences in common activities I knew only in the ethnocentric way I had experienced them in my own home country. I got a rude lesson in that kind of national variation when I went to Brazil to teach for two months in 1976, in the full bloom of the Brazilian military dictatorship (which lasted from 1964 to 1985). A Brazilian anthropologist, Gilberto Velho, had read some of my work on deviance and persuaded people in the Rio de Janeiro branch of the Ford Foundation to put up the money for my stay, so that he and I could teach a class together.

I learned many lessons about living in another country—it was the first time I'd done that—but I've never forgotten the scariest one. I had to get a visa to go to Brazil (I hadn't needed such a thing to go to England) and learned, when I arrived in Rio, ready to go to work, that I also needed a work permit. To get a work permit, I had to fill out many forms and provide a photograph. I went to a recommended photographer, who made the picture. But when I took the picture to the office that dispensed work permits, an employee ignored me for fifteen or twenty minutes and then told me I had the wrong kind of photograph. Mine had a white background but the photograph for a work permit required a gray background. I went back and got another one and finally got the permit.

That didn't scare me, but it softened me up for the problem of the *visto*, which did. Someone told me that to be in the country and work, as I was doing, I needed this special document, but, not to worry, it would come one of these days. It didn't, but people in the Ford Foundation office and at the department of anthropology, where I was teaching, kept telling me it didn't matter. After all, I was working, wasn't I? Stop worrying.

But then I learned that I not only needed the *visto* to work, I also wouldn't be allowed to leave the country without having it. My limited permit to stay in the country required me to leave at the end of two months, so I began to see a potentially impossible situation. After two months I would have to leave, but I wouldn't be able to leave without the document I didn't have. What would happen to me? (Remember, this was the era of the military dictatorship, a governmental form I had no previous experience with.)

I knew, realistically, that the Ford Foundation and the school would not let me go to jail for this infraction and would find a way to save me. But realistically wasn't how I started looking at things. I worried, seriously, and Gilberto told me that now I was learning what it meant to be a Brazilian in that period, how it felt to be the possible victim of a capricious and cruel government.

When I started to obsess about my *visto*, the kindly staff of the Ford Foundation told me to stop worrying. Cesar, they said, would take care of it. And who was Cesar? "You don't have to worry, Cesar is the best *despachante* in Rio de Janeiro." What was a *despachante*? Possible translations into English are "expediter" or "middleman," the guy who knows how to get impossible things done, how to speed up action on your passport application, how to get your application for a driver's license approved, how to get a visa for a foreign country—who, in short, knows how to get unresponsive bureaucrats to do what they should do cheerfully and willingly as a matter of course but seldom do. I never understood whether the *despachante* simply knew how to bribe people who insisted on a bribe to do the job they were already supposed to do, or whether there were further and more complex layers of mutual obligations involved.

All the talk about Cesar told me what I might have thought just from knowing I had the protection of a big player, the Ford Foundation. But Cesar was not delivering the goods, the *visto*. Day after day I called or went to the Foundation office and was told Cesar was on the case. In the end, having been reduced to a nervous wreck, I got the *visto* on the day of my departure, when everyone said, "We told you Cesar would take care of it!"

I thought about this experience often and began to connect it to other things I had learned in Brazil. For instance, the concept of *jeito*. Telephones didn't work very well in Rio at that time (they may still not work very well, but have been mostly replaced by portable phones that do) and you might have to dial a number several times before it would connect to the other line and start to ring. When this happened to me, Gilberto (who loved making jokes like this) told me that I just didn't have the *jeito*, I didn't dial with the correct physical motion, there was some little knack that Brazilians had that I didn't. I knew this was nonsense but began to hear the word more and more often, applied to all sorts of things, both physical and intangible. It sometimes implied grace or physical mastery but just as often implied social know-how, those little bits of knowledge you had to have to make things come out the way you wanted them to, the things a *despachante* might know that an ordinary person wouldn't that would get a bureaucrat to cough up a needed *visto*.

HOW DO FRENCH PROFESSORS GET A RAISE?

A second case added to my personal international database. In 1999, somewhat to my surprise, Alain Pessin, of the Université Pierre Mendes-France in Grenoble, France, invited me to come to his university to receive an honorary doctorate. I was very pleased. Who wouldn't be? But a stiff price was attached. I had to come for ten days and participate in two big conferences, one on my classmate in graduate school Erving Goffman, and the other on the sociology of art, giving a paper (in French!) at each of them.

Dianne and I had been studying French for some years by then and, thinking this would be a real test for us, decided to go for it. We knew a little about France, but I still didn't understand the academic system: what the ranks were, how people moved from one university to another, who set their salaries, and what a professor's responsibilities were, all the grubby details of daily academic life. I didn't understand many other things the French did differently, like at what stage of a career you got a PhD, and things that didn't exist in North America at all, like an *habilitation* and what it meant to get through that career stage. Still, we thought we knew enough to survive such an event (we knew, for instance, that *conference*, which in America meant the kind of event we would be involved in in Grenoble, meant something quite different in France, referring to what we would call "giving a talk." The kind of large event we would attend was a *colloque*).

We could understand and handle differences like that, but we weren't ready for what happened one night when, after a day of listening to papers, several of the participants, professors from various universities, invited me to have a *verre*, a drink, with them. They could hardly wait to sit down to pop the question they had been dying to ask: "When you look for another academic job in the States, can you bargain about salary?" I said of course you could, what else was there to bargain about? They said that in their country they couldn't do that because—something I had sort of known but whose implications I hadn't understood—they all worked for the same boss. Almost all French universities (except a few Catholic and private universities, which aren't important for most academic careers) operate under the jurisdiction of a central agency, the Ministère de l'Enseignement Supérieur et de la Recherche. Whichever public university you work for, you work for this ministry and they set your salary. No one competes with them. So you have no one to bargain with, the way an American professor could bargain with a dean at a private university or one in another state.

A professor who works in the United States has trouble grasping this. I certainly did. But it taught me something I half knew already. University teachers in France are *fonctionnaires*, what we in the United States would call civil service employees. Once they complete a probationary period of a few years, they have a job (barring gross misbehavior, I suppose) for life. It's not the same as North American academic tenure. *Fonctionnaires* are guaranteed some government job, although not necessarily a teaching or research position in a university. They can look for jobs in other universities, and they often find ways to make deals that get them some kind of raise in their pay, usually through a shift in rank. But the systems of rank aren't divided into a large number of "steps" or "grades" the way, say, the position of full professor in the University of California is. They mostly get a salary based on typical civil service criteria: rank in the system, seniority, and so forth. They can't do what American professors, if they have something other universities want, can do: ask for a sizable raise. American universities have policies about this, but those policies vary widely. A professor who has something another university (especially a university of comparable stature) wants—a distinguished record of scholarly publications, a track record of raising sizable amounts of research funds that the university gets some percentage of in overhead—can ask for a lot and no national authority can forbid the university to pay what's asked. Which is, by the way, one important reason scholars from other countries take jobs in the United States.

"WHAT KIND OF CROSS-NATIONAL COMPARISON IS THAT?"

What kind indeed? Am I trying to prove that Brazil or France are different from the United States? Am I trying to establish some believable propositions about the social organization of those countries? What kind of sample of what universe would I need to do that? What variables would

I have to measure, and how would I measure them in order to establish the differences I announced so cavalierly in the preceding paragraphs? I hadn't measured anything or brought any data to bear on the questions I've been talking about, other than my own highly suspect recollections, so I can't offer any conclusions about general characteristics of the societies involved in these comparisons. Why should anyone believe what I say?

An important prior question, however, is: believe what? If I'd tried to prove that Brazil and the United States and France differ in these crucial ways, those would all be important criticisms. Shouldn't I be worried about these questions? Not really.

Because I didn't intend to prove anything about these countries. I was doing something very different. I wasn't *measuring* variables. I was *looking for* variables, using my casual experiences to identify interesting ways these countries seemed to differ, using the differences history had created among them to learn about the way social life in them differed from what I was used to. I wasn't trying to establish how specific countries like France and Brazil *actually* vary but just how they *could* vary, from which I *might* learn what we *could* be looking for, what we *might* want to take into account, in assessing any particular situation of collective human activity, wherever it occurred.

The glimpses I caught of daily life in the two countries told me something about how governments might behave. In the most extreme case, it's possible that my observations were just wrong: I misunderstood what people said; I didn't grasp some subtleties that longer immersion in the country would have made clear to me. Maybe what I noticed were things that were true of the few people I talked to but not true of the millions of others who lived there.

None of that is unlikely, since most ordinary reasoning (including the reasoning that interprets the results of larger numerical studies) relies on just such evidence. My observations took no precautions about sampling. But the way everyone I talked to in Brazil, people of a variety of social positions, took for granted the necessity of having a *despachante*, the way no one reacted to such talk as odd or as anything but the most obvious commonplace, made it likely that this was a ubiquitous form of collective activity in Brazil. The French professors who asked me the Big Question about bargaining for salaries might, similarly, not be representative of the French professoriate as a whole, but all of them (coming as they did from a variety of posts in a variety of places) thought it really was a Big Question, one they really wanted to know the answer to. That "proves" that this is at least a possible feature of some part of French academia.

What's accomplished by proving that something has occurred at least once and maybe, but not necessarily, more often? That takes us to the heart of what you can learn from studying a single case. If a conventional comparative analytic model aims to establish laws governing the relation between variables, what does this kind of informal, seemingly unmethodical, model try to do? Let's compare them, using each to illuminate features of the other.

The standard model, the law-seeking model, taking experimental science as its model, supposes that social organization exhibits deep regularities, that certain forms of collective action take the same basic form, and that careful measurement of indices of those regularities will reveal the laws that produce them. It isolates variables, measures them, and demonstrates their regular association with each other, expecting that a *small number* of variables will suffice to explain most of the variation in the independent variables being investigated.

My informal exploration followed a different model, based on a different logic. This model recognizes that there will never be enough variables to explain all the variation in any specific situation, but it doesn't want to miss any that operate in the situation we're interested in and affect what happens there. It uses cases to find *more* variables. It tries to do two things more or less simultaneously: understand the specific case well enough to know how it ended up happening the way it did, and at the same time find things to look for in other cases that resemble it in some ways, even though they differ in others. There's some overlap with the standard model but a very different emphasis. Instead of testing conclusions, this "looking-for-complications" model wants to use the unfamiliar elements of each new case to improve generalizations by identifying new things to add to the grid of variable elements that helps us understand any case of that kind.

Working this way envisions (without being frightened by it) the social world as infinitely complicated. It takes as a working principle that everything—everything!—present in the situation you want to understand contributes to its being what it is and events turning out the way they do. I made this the basis for my understanding of the social character of art (Becker 1982), insisting that everything and everybody that contributed to the making and experiencing of a work of art was a necessary component of it, something a full analysis should include and account for. And I meant everything: not just the musicians who performed a composer's music, but also the copyist who wrote out the parts they played from; the instrument makers and repairers who made playing physically possible; the ticket sellers and everyone else who contributed to the concert's financial feasibility; the audience who listened; and even (I said this to be provocative but meant it seriously) the parking attendants who found room for your car.

Put more abstractly, a vast number of things affect the course and result of any given individual or collective action; each of these things in turn has been affected by a similarly vast number of things, each of them in turn. . . . You get the idea. Unlike what I'm calling the standard model, this defines the job as, in principle, never-ending, since the world continues to move and change and the possible combinations continue to multiply.

Think of it arithmetically. Two elements, each capable of taking two values, can combine to make four combinations or, said another way, 2^2 possibilities. Three elements, each capable of two values, create 2^3 or eight combinations. For the case of a concert, imagine that composers can work in only one of two ways, that musicians can play in only one of two ways, that repairers can work in only one of two ways, and that the parking attendants can work in only one of two ways. Each pair of possibilities raises the number of possible combinations by a power of 2 (two kinds of composers multiplied by two kinds of performers, and so on). And, of course, I said there were only two values for each of these variables when, in fact, there are all kinds of composers and performers and the rest. The numbers quickly become unmanageable by conventional procedures aimed at testing general propositions.

Researchers who follow the looking-for-complications model don't throw up their hands in despair. They welcome all the variation the world shows them. They try to identify and understand everything at work in a situation that contributes to the result they want to understand, the composer *and* the performer *and* the copyist *and* the parking attendant.

This explains why my little "discoveries" (discoveries to me but not discoveries at all to people who lived in those countries) about Brazil and France interested me so much. Analysts often don't notice everything that's operating in a situation they're studying, because some of those things work in the background. We don't notice them because they're always there, and so they're not worth commenting on. Mostly, they become visible only when we study some approximately similar situation where that very thing makes its importance known by taking a different form or, in the most noticeable case, not being there at all. That's why I was so interested in the case sociologist Richard Emerson (1966) described. Studying a team (of which he was a member) trying to climb Mount Everest, he reported that, because the air at the altitudes the team encountered didn't contain as much oxygen as air at lower levels, climbers' ability to overcome that physiological problem was a major condition affecting their success or failure in reaching the summit. We don't ordinarily measure the oxygen content of the air people breathe as a variable affecting what they do and how well they do it. But Emerson's analysis alerted the rest of us, if we were paying attention, to air quality as a potential contributor to other situations we studied where we hadn't thought of it as a variable at all. His study offered a framework for thinking about, for instance, the effect of air quality on people's satisfaction with the city they lived in, which might seriously affect their decisions to stay or move and thus exert an appreciable effect on long-term large-scale population movements.

What I learned from the *despachantes* and the French professors played exactly that role in my thinking, provoking some ideas I might never have had otherwise, ones that don't automatically and immediately offer themselves as candidates for attention in any conventional assessment of the literature on the problems social scientists study.

FINDING GENERAL RESULTS IN THE UNEXPECTED AND UNFAMILIAR: BRAZIL

I more or less forgot about *despachantes* after I returned from Brazil. The phenomenon didn't show up in my life in Chicago or San Francisco, though those cities also have lazy bureaucrats who are reluctant to put themselves out for a mere citizen. But I read a lot of things about Brazil, including the work of Antônio Cândido, a great social scientist and literary scholar (some of whose work I ended up translating [Cândido 1995]), who had written an essay on another peculiarly Brazilian concept, the *malandro*, usually translated in English as "scamp" or "trickster" or something like that, English words that hardly convey the wealth of its connotations (the best contemporary translation, I think, would be "hustler"). It's one of those words (and *despachante* is obviously another) about which people say, correctly, "You just can't translate it."

You can't translate words like this because the thing the word refers to doesn't exist in the same way in the country whose language you want to translate it into. We don't have *malandros* in the United States or Europe. We do have hustlers and crooks and a lot of other things, but not *malandros*. We have people a Brazilian might recognize as such a thing—a Brazilian version of Brecht's *Three Penny Opera* was called *Opera do malandro*, and Marlon Brando's portrayal of Sky Masterson in *Guys and Dolls* probably would be recognizable. But we don't have the word and the concept because by and large we don't have the thing, defined and embodied as it is in Brazil.

And not just the thing, but the whole organized setting in which the thing makes sense. North Americans don't have *despachantes*—the word or the concept—because they don't as often deal with bureaucrats who won't do anything unless someone who has the *jeito* comes to deal with them. Many of us know how to threaten to call the lazy bureaucrat's boss or a local politician, as I learned, dealing with an incompetent San Francisco city department, that the way to get action was to call the mayor's office. But we don't have a full repertoire of the kinds of tricks the *despachante* knows.

I was trying to understand something unfamiliar in Brazil by comparing it to something I did know in my own country, and as a result I found a dimension of activity and organization that applied to both countries, though in different ways. I might never have thought of what I eventually made of this without having the category that made the comparison available. To be explicit: Brazilians routinely have to deal with officials who won't do the work they are supposed to do unless you send someone to take care of the matter who knows how to do things their way, a way ordinary citizens don't know or don't want to spend time learning. We in the United States don't have people who need that, so we don't have the specific job title or formal specialization. We don't have to hire a specialist to help us get a passport.

But, once we see that such a thing can happen, we recognize that some of us sometimes do have such needs, and that some people take advantage of the possibility and do that work. And now we can look at earlier research and begin to identify some possible variants of the same phenomenon: some people and activities that resemble, sort of, though not point for point, the Brazilian situation. They add new dimensions and variations to my primitive analysis. This is what Hughes did in searching for analogues of the Germans who didn't know what the Nazis were doing but nevertheless saw their actions as things that "solved a problem" that needed solving.

For example. Larry Felt (1971) did research in a poor black neighborhood of Chicago. He didn't know what he wanted to study, just that he wanted to see how poor people managed their lives when they didn't have much money. Part of the answer, he thought, correctly, was welfare, the system of financial support provided by various governmental agencies. But many would-be recipients of welfare found the agencies that administered it a maze as impenetrable as government bureaucracy was for everyone in Brazil.

Felt found that out by sitting around a laundromat (the least threatening place he could think of for a white man to sit in this all-black neighborhood), where he began to meet neighborhood women who came there to consult a somewhat older woman (she had made it her place of business) who helped them manipulate the bureaucratic maze. When a clerk in a welfare agency told you that you needed a form 2132 and you didn't know what that was . . . she knew. And told you where to go to get it and had you bring it back to her so that she could show you how to fill it out "correctly," the way the welfare people liked to see it filled out. She knew what auxiliary papers you needed to get the money you were after— a birth certificate for this kind of aid, a death certificate for that kind, a school record, the stub from a paycheck—and where and how to get them, and which person you had to go see to get through the succeeding steps on the way to the money. Many people just could not do that by themselves. Which was understandable: the complicated procedures used unfamiliar bureaucratic language and shorthand and presumed that you knew things and had skills you probably didn't know or have.

When this lady helped you solve these problems, it was only reasonable and neighborly to give her a little present, some of the first money you got now that you had all your papers in order. She was running a regular business, sitting in the corner of the laundromat helping people fill out papers, a sort of H&R Block for poor black women, who were the people in this society who needed this kind of *jeito*. They didn't have that word to refer to what this woman knew, but they knew she was the one who knew how they could get what they needed. She was something very much like a *despachante*, though the details were different: different clients, different bureaucrats, different procedures and papers, and different tricks.

If you combine the two cases, making small abstractions to get rid of some detail, you have a new category, one we don't have a name for: someone who serves as your messenger/advocate/adviser in dealing with a difficult-to-deal-with bureaucracy. With that definition in mind, we can easily locate some other examples more familiar to North Americans and Europeans. Medical patients now know that it helps to have a "patient advocate," maybe a relative or close friend, maybe someone furnished by an organization devoted to making life easier for people with medical problems, especially when their illness makes it hard for them to deal those problems themselves. Office workers lucky enough to have such a colleague know the one person in their office who knows both the rules that govern "the way things are done" in that organization and who to call to facilitate getting those things done. And who probably has in turn done some favors for that person in the other office and so can invoke the obligations that go with continued interaction in such a network of mutual assistance. (Professors preparing a research proposal for a government agency are lucky if they have someone like that to guide them through the numerous pitfalls of that highly bureaucratic procedure.)

Comparing two or more such cases really pays off when you use this rule of thumb: if you find it, whatever *it* is, in one place, you'll find some version of it in other places like it too. Maybe not going by the same name, or dealing with exactly the same problem, but similar enough to let you know where to look, what to look for to understand the case you're investigating, and what new things might be worth looking for in the old case, which you thought you knew all about.

How, for instance, do these experts know the tricks that open bureaucratic doors? I don't know how the *despachantes* learn their trade, but Felt learned how the woman in the laundromat learned hers. Nothing complicated. She learned on the job. She may not have known the answer the first time someone asked her a question, but she had learned how to learn from solving some of her own problems early on, and she was analytic enough to distill some general lessons about what kind of people would know the answer to a particular kind of question. So she could make a good guess about what to do when you came to her with a paper she hadn't seen before and didn't know for sure how to fill out. She didn't just know answers; she knew how to find answers to questions she hadn't heard before. After she solved your problem, she could add that solution to the stock of specific problems she knew how to solve. She got a reputation in the neighborhood as someone who knew stuff like that, so more people brought her their problems. She solved them and so learned more. After a while she knew a lot and had a pretty good business. (In chapter 3, I'll discuss other versions of this phenomenon described in, and suggested by, Eliot Freidson's studies of medical practice.)

To generalize the point, Felt's work gives us what we need to guess that these experts and advocates in similar situations (like *despachantes*) might learn some of what they know through some kind of training, but also (very likely) by dealing with specific instances of the problem and filing away what they learned in an ever-growing and adapting body of knowledge. And we can see that this might be a version of the more general category sometimes called "expertise," distinguishing it from mere guesswork on the one hand and verified scientific or scholarly knowledge on the other, often what you have to know to apply generalized principles to specific situations (something like the kind of know-how engineers and artisans need to apply whatever general principles they've been taught to the concrete situations they work in).

I first learned this tactic when Everett C. Hughes told me about consulting for the American Nurses Association. Wanting to take one of the obligatory steps for nursing to "become a profession," they had decided they should sponsor some research. They called Hughes in to discuss the kind of research they might do. As the meeting went on, he realized that they were avoiding what seemed to him likely to be a major issue, one he said he had been alerted to by my master's thesis research (reported in Becker 1963, 79–100) on musicians who played in bars, for parties, and so forth. These men openly and frequently denounced the people they played for, both those who hired them and those who consumed their music, as "squares," ignorant and unworthy of respect. But nevertheless they had to please those people. So, assuming that what occurred in that case occurred in other service occupations—why not?—he interrupted the nurses' consideration of respectable research topics and asked, "Why don't you do some research on a problem that really worries you, which is why nurses hate their patients?" He said they looked at him in horror, and then someone said, "How did you know that?" Not a lucky guess, but a shrewd and imaginative example of the method of reasoning from cases.

We learn from the small comparison between Brazil and the United States that some dimensions of the problem of expert knowledge pop up in other countries in a different form than they take in the country we're most familiar with. An American notices the *despachante* immediately: it's so unlike anything we know, and we might be tempted to think the need for such a service indicates some kind of Latin American failing and decide it's not worth thinking about. But Brazilians don't notice the thing right on the surface that calls an American visitor's attention to itself, because it's "natural": how else could you ever get anything done? We learn something about both countries when we take the unfamiliar phenomenon seriously and decide to investigate further.

Looking into it teaches the American (this American, anyway) that we can look for something like this in places where we hadn't noticed it or thought it would exist, and then use the differences between the two cases to deepen our understanding of the general class of things both cases belong to. And the Brazilian social scientist might learn—from an American friend's reactions, or from reading about Felt's research—to see the *despachante* as more than a necessary evil when you deal with bureaucracy. The cross-national comparison gives us something important and useful: a more general category that the case we're familiar with belongs in.

To be clear, reasoning from a case this way won't tell us what the correlation (speaking somewhat metaphorically) is between some feature of a country and the presence or absence of *despachantes* or something like them, allowing for national variation in the form this possibility takes. Instead it tells us that when we find a service like this being offered, we should look for a situation in which some people need knowledge that's hard to get and others make a business of providing it. And, further, that the knowledge that's hard to get is knowledge of how to manipulate something complicated, something that requires a special understanding or skill. That's not a universal generalization, but it could well be a help when we're trying to understand a situation we'd like to learn more about.

LEARNING FROM THE UNEXPECTED
AND UNFAMILIAR: FRANCE

We can reason in the same way from my case of the French professors.

After the conversation in a Grenoble bar taught me how much less control over their own fate French professors had than at least some Americans, I began to see both the fact and the implications of what I hadn't noticed before in my own milieu: the extreme (from a North American point of view) centralization of French academic life. (Yes, many other people, more worldly than me, knew all about this centralization. I don't know how they learned this fact, but this is how I learned it.) I had read, in Pierre-Michel Menger's (1983) detailed description and analysis of the way Pierre Boulez dominated the world of contemporary French musical composition (in his heyday, he controlled the bulk of government funding for musical composition, either directly or indirectly), that France was centralized in areas I wouldn't have expected. There weren't many private sources of support for scholarly or artistic work. You got it from some ministry of the national government or you didn't get it at all. Well, I exaggerate. People I knew got money from municipal or regional government agencies for various small projects, and some people learned to work the European Community system for multicountry projects. On the other hand, the once somewhat diffuse set of subunits scattered through the state apparatus had eventually been consolidated into the Agence Nationale de Recherche, which I suppose was the centralized bureaucracy's way of attempting to assert control over what they almost surely saw as some kind of dangerously "uncontrolled" behavior.

And I had begun to understand that the large network of private and state universities and colleges, denominational schools, and municipal colleges, all administered by different bosses and all with different sources of financial support, including gifts from alumni and grants from foundations and government research agencies, and sometimes football, that we North Americans take for granted as the way things just are— nothing like that existed in France. France has many fewer higher educational institutions. It's harder for students to get into them. The same ministry runs all of them (and that includes setting salaries). And universities don't have sports teams for whose support successful alumni make donations. A professor who wanted to bargain couldn't find anyone or anything to bargain with.

I had also come to realize, not quite consciously but increasingly so, the enormous difference in scale between the two countries. Yes, the United States had a larger population and area than France—but not *that* much larger. Whereas the United States at the time of my conversation in the Grenoble bar had perhaps twenty thousand people who made their living as sociologists (some in full-time research outside universities, but mostly as university employees), there were maybe two thousand (counting generously) professional French sociologists. Considering how few of them there are, relatively speaking, they produce an amazing amount of scholarship, published in a large number of journals; a quite varied book industry publishes an equally large number of books; and this small number of sociologists provides the personnel for an incredible number of two- and three-day *colloques* on a great variety of topics. But still, there aren't so many of them.

Once I grasped these differences in scale, certain features of French sociology (and this applies to British sociology as well, because the same differences in scale appear there) became less mysterious. I suppose I'd thought, unreflectively, that the sharp and often bitter factionalism of French sociology grew out of the Gallic temperament or some equally mysterious force, but now I saw it as the more-or-less understandable competition of a small number of people for a slice of a small pie of jobs, research money, and other valuables, in which the head of a powerful team of loyal and devoted colleagues and former and present students had a considerable advantage. It also explained how a specialized intellectual pursuit like ethnomethodology or small-group research or symbolic interaction—which in the United States could easily accumulate enough followers to have an organization, a journal, an annual meeting, a presidential address, and all that, but never succeed in dominating the national scene—could in France or England take over a substantial chunk of the intellectual territory: there wasn't that much territory to get control of. French sociologists, of course, had the same kind of trouble understanding why no Bourdieu-like figure can dominate the American sociological scene as I had come to understand Bourdieu's quasi-dominance in France. Americans didn't know how little it would take to dominate French sociology, organizationally speaking. And the French didn't understand that no one could possibly have that sort of hegemony (a concept from Europe that really didn't have an empirical embodiment in the internal organizational life of American sociology) over anything as sprawling and seeded with independent power centers as American sociology: too many places to get research grants, too many departments to get your tentacles around, and so forth. You can freeze some tendencies out of places in France, but no tendency in American sociology is so eccentric or unusual that it can't find a home somewhere.

FINDING YOUR WAY AROUND THE BIG CITY: REASONING FROM "BLOCKS"

People usually know their way around the place where they live: where things are, how you get from one place to the other, how you tell someone how they can get from here to there. They learn all those things as children or when they move to a new place. They learn the system people before them have created to accomplish those tasks, things that we can think of as part of "culture." As cultural artifacts, these systems of geographical representation vary from place to place. I had occasion, some years ago, to think about these matters in an exploratory way. Though my explorations never resulted in any serious research, they might have if things had turned out differently, so here they are as an example of how reasoning from small incidents, treated as "cases" of something more general, can lead to elaborate constructions that might well inform serious research.

Years ago, an American sociologist visiting Paris for the first time asked me and my friend Henri Peretz how many "blocks" we were, at the moment, from someplace he wanted to go. We explained that Paris didn't really have "blocks," not the way he understood that idea from American cities. A little irritated, he said that was ridiculous, of course Paris has blocks, every city has blocks, and besides he could see the blocks from where he stood. What he saw were places where two or more streets intersected and where there were, therefore, "corners," as they are called in English, or *carrefours*, *coins*, or *angles* in French. For him, those intersections, with their familiar angles and streets shooting off in various directions, implied the existence of a system of blocks, laid out in a regular grid—one set of streets running east and west, parallel to one another and equally far apart, the other similarly arranged but running north and south. It makes sense, in cities laid out that way, to say that someplace is eight blocks from someplace else, and that's the kind of answer our friend expected, probably accompanied by instructions that said "Go four blocks this way, turn left, go four more blocks, and you'll be there."

It makes sense for North Americans to expect that kind of answer because so many American cities are laid out that way. Salt Lake City, Utah, is organized around the ten-acre Temple Square in the center of the city, where the Mormon Temple stands. On each side, numbered streets run parallel to the side of the square, equidistant from one another: 1st Street

West, 2nd Street West, and so on. And similarly on the east, north, and south sides of the square. So addresses in Salt Lake City read like this: 234 South 2nd Street West. To find where you are and how to get to where you want to be is as simple as looking up a word in a dictionary.

Few American cities have such a pure form. So, though most cities have a generally gridlike structure, each city has to be learned as a variation on a grid. What Chicagoans, for example, learn and use in order to find their way around its variant of the grid seems both simple and complicated. It's what a child or visitor or immigrant has to learn, but once it's learned you don't have to think about it any more; it won't change.

Let's look at the complications of this simple pattern in Chicago, which begins not from a square, but from the place in the city center where State Street (a straight line north and south) and Madison Street (a straight line east and west) cross. Every street in Chicago is numbered from that point.

The numbering system for individual addresses in Chicago conforms to this grid. Every eighth-of-a-mile segment of a street contains (potentially) one hundred numbers, not all of them necessarily used. So the first block east of State Street will contain addresses numbered between 0 and 99, the second block between 100 and 199, and so on. This implies that any two or more streets equidistant from State or Madison Streets will be numbered in the same range. The blocks of two parallel streets—for example, Monroe and Adams—will contain the same one hundred numbers: if a block on Adams contains addresses from 1200 to 1299, so will the parallel block on Monroe, one block away. Even-numbered addresses are always on the north or west side of a street, odd-numbered addresses on the south or east side.

Furthermore, with some exceptions, there is a "major" street every half mile (every fourth street), that is, a wider street containing businesses, as opposed to the "side streets," which are almost purely residential. Major streets usually have public transportation lines. When two major streets cross, they produce a "major intersection," and these become reference points. So you can say that an address is "near Ashland and Belmont," which is such a major intersection (1600 west and 3200 north).

Any location can be specified by its place in this grid: An address like 777 North Michigan Avenue indicates that the building referred to is in the 8th block north of Madison Street, and we could consult a map to learn that Michigan Avenue is two streets east of State Street. Similarly, if we say that Howie Becker lived at 5430 Monroe Street as a child, any competent Chicagoan would immediately understand that he lived in the 55th block west of State Street and (consulting the map to locate Monroe Street, if necessary) one block south of Madison Street. Addresses on the city's South Side, where east-west streets (following a system like Salt

Lake City's) have names that are consecutive numbers, require even less calculation. A knowledgeable Chicagoan immediately knows that 1250 East 54th Street is in the 12th block east of State Street, in the 54th block south of Madison Street. (The streets are actually laid out in accordance with the true directions of north, south, east, and west.) Another important difference when we make international comparisons of street systems is that American streets seldom change their names. Some Chicago streets go for twenty-five or thirty miles with the same name.

To summarize this basic urban cultural knowledge, Chicago streets almost always intersect at right angles and are equidistant, and houses are numbered in a pattern whose coherence comes from that design. Every intersection (those that include the few diagonal streets are something of an exception) presents a standardized appearance: four square corners at an intersection of two streets. A piece of land surrounded by four such intersecting streets, a "block," has four corners. Almost always perfectly regular, it permits easy standardized calculations (of, for instance, how far it is from point A to point B), the kind of answer our friend asked Peretz and me for.

Finally, Chicagoans see the city proper as divided into four great sections (a fifth consists of what is called, generically, "the suburbs"): the North, South, and West Sides, which surround "Downtown." The grid system furnishes the raw materials out of which inhabitants construct their own more limited local versions; they don't all draw the boundaries in the same way, but they coincide well enough to avoid confusion. Within those segments, finer distinctions based on street numbers get more important.

So competent Chicago residents, given a few clues, know precisely where a given address is located. That is why our friend (who was from Chicago) assumed that distances in Paris could be communicated in blocks.

All of this laboriously spelled out detail is second nature to the mythical "competent" Chicago resident I've invoked. But this Chicagoan is actually not so mythical. If you grow up in Chicago (or somewhere else with a similar street system) you learn all this as a small child. You learn the cardinal directions with reference to the street system.

Competent adults use this set of idealized coordinates to relate spatially to their surroundings, orient themselves to specific geographic locations, and give and receive instructions about where things are and how to get from here to there. When they find themselves in a place that doesn't meet these specifications, they don't treat this as a potentially different (and therefore interesting) system of organizing space, but as a deformed, incomplete, and deviant version of the grid system, "just like" Chicago, with certain unfortunate exceptions.

Can I use this minutiae about Chicago streets to understand something beyond my friend's transient troubles? Yes. I can ask a question, inspired by the ones I answered for Chicago: how do Parisians learn to get around their city, given that they don't have the simplicity of Chicago's quasi-mathematical system to work with? And, as a preliminary to that, what system of organizing space does Paris have, and how did it get it? The answers give us some more general categories we can apply to any city.

Like most cities in long-urbanized parts of the world (and thus very different from the North American cities I know well and on which so much urban theorizing has been based), Paris antedates the development of modern, "rational" methods of laying cities out. Its street patterns result instead from incremental growth: the gradual incorporation of small adjacent hamlets—each with its own pattern of streets, with different names, often not running in quite the same directions, depending on local geography and the choices early settlers made—into larger agglomerations. Because these old cities antedated the development of modern systems of water distribution and waste disposal, people sited homes and small buildings housing tanneries, stables, and other polluting activities along natural waterways, so that inhabitants could wash waste down streets that sloped toward a nearby river. Streets and settlements grew up along the route the water followed seeking that low point. (Gagneux et al. 2002, 8–28, describe the history of the Bièvre, a river that now runs underground in the heavily populated 5th arrondissement of Paris.) Once a few buildings set a pattern, inertia weighed heavily in later siting decisions. No central authority decreed that an overall pattern should dominate.

Paris rebuilt itself many times, as the city expanded toward what had been suburbs or farm areas and also (what has been the subject of innumerable studies) by being torn down and rebuilt, most notably by Baron Haussmann, who, between 1853 and 1870, destroyed large areas of old Paris to make way for the broad boulevards, parks, and other features that now characterize the city. (The story is told in many places; I read it in Jordan 1996). Some of the avenues and boulevards were built to make it easier for troops to reach centers of insurrection by marching down wide, uncluttered roads, instead of having to fight their way through mazes of small, twisting, easily barricaded streets. But much of the rebuilding consisted of replacing housing that was barely habitable, whose only virtue lay in its antiquity (an early version of what's now called "gentrification"). (Eric Hazan's book [2002], among many others, on Parisian geography tells the story of the growth and rebuildings of Paris in detail. Thézy's [1998] collection of the photographs by Charles Marville of Paris before, during, and after Haussmann's activities in the mid-nineteenth century gives some sense of the convoluted character of the older Paris.)

So Paris, because of these gradual unplanned developments, has none of the quasi-mathematical order of a city planned all at once, like Chicago, where inhabitants can rely on the system to find their way. Now we have a new question: how do Parisians, without such a resource as a system of blocks, find a place whose location they don't already know? Peretz and I discussed this for weeks, looking for Parisian analogues of the methods Chicagoans use.

Is there an equivalent to the Chicago system in Paris? How do Parisians tell you where the place you're looking for is, concisely and without ambiguity?

There is a Parisian equivalent to the "Chicago system" that makes the communication of geographic information possible, though it's different in many ways and much less obviously "efficient." Parisians recognize two main sections, more or less equivalent to Chicago's big geographic divisions: Rive Droite and Rive Gauche (Right Bank and Left Bank), plus the ill-defined *banlieue*, the suburbs lying beyond the city border, which is defined by the *périphérique* (the limited-access highway system that more or less encloses the city proper). These furnish a general orientation, telling me which side of the River Seine contains the place I'm looking for. But that covers too much territory to be much help.

Suppose I want to locate a specific address. Someone might tell me that it's in the 5th *arrondissement*. Paris is divided into twenty of these administrative units (each with its own mayor), but they're also too big to be much help.

Many people use stops on the Parisian subway, the Metro, as a way to tell you more precisely how to find where you want to go. You might say, as we did for years to tell people where we lived, that it was "Metro Censier-Daubenton," a stop on Line 7, one of the fourteen subway lines that criss-cross the city. Or someone might say that it's near a well-known landmark you can find on any map: "It's near the Eiffel Tower" or "Père Lachaise Cemetery" or "the Bon Marché department store." All ways that might work in any large city.

The exact street address won't help you until you've found the street. In Chicago people will tell you that such-and-such a street is "2100 west" or "1600 north," but that's not possible in gridless Paris. It's easier just to learn the name of the street, because, in Chicago terms, many streets are only one or two blocks long. Once you find the street, you'll have no trouble locating a specific number on it. So people say, "It's in Rue la Vieuville," which runs for a short distance between Place des Abbesses and Cité de la Mairie, and perhaps they will add that it's quite near Place Pigalle. With that information, you won't have much trouble.

But, of course, you have to know where Rue la Vieuville is. How do you find that out? The largest difference between finding your way in Chicago and Paris appears here. Many Parisians, and knowledgeable tourists, have carried with them at all times (at least until the advent of smartphone maps) a small book, usually called a *Plan* [map] *de Paris*, some eighty pages of complete street maps of small sections of the city in which every street (*rue*), boulevard, avenue, dead end (*impasse*), and so forth is clearly marked and which contains occasional numbers so that you can tell where a particular building whose number you know can likely be found. The book also contains an alphabetical index of names of streets, places, squares, and the like, which specifies the book page and where on that page to look. You find the name of the street you're searching for, turn to that page, and use the numbers on the margins to locate it.

Then you go to the place you found on the map and can reenact the very meaningful (once you've grasped all this) photograph in Bruno Latour and Emilie Hermant's *Paris ville invisible* (1998, 26.), in which Mme Lagoutte, trying to find an address on rue de la Vieuville, looks first at her *plan* to locate the street, then at the blue and white enamel sign on the wall of the building in front of her that says "Rue la Vieuville," to see that it verifies what the book says. Then, and only then, she knows she's in the right place, with only the number of the building left to discover. (Street signs don't automatically appear on walls. Latour and Hermant go on to describe the kinds of work and workers necessary to make the sign and to verify that it's where it should be.)

One further complication. Street names change from time to time, or part of a street is renamed for someone found to deserve such recognition, and people who knew the street under its "old name" have to learn that it is now called by a new one. The *plans* are updated frequently enough that this causes only minimal confusion.

Because no system really delivers all the needed information reliably, many other systems find users. Daniel Cefai, another Parisian, read this and remarked:

> I have never used a Plan de Paris. I usually orient myself knowing which is the nearest subway station, getting there and checking on the map of the neighborhood you have at every station exit where to go [they indicate the names of streets in an index and on the map, numbers help you choose the right segment]. If you need more info, you can ask the agent at the desk in the subway (this is part of their job and they usually do it, checking on the Plan de Paris they do not lend you because they are afraid you will steal it). You can ask. Once you are out in the street, you can ask the newspaper seller in his "kiosque," if he's in a good humor, he will answer you, if not he will tell you to go to hell!

In short, no general, mistake-proof system is possible, because there is no general system governing the assignment of descriptive data to places. Parisians have to learn by trial and error over the course of a lifetime.

Peretz and I both had many other professional commitments, so this exploration went no further. Though we wouldn't present such unfinished thoughts to a journal as a finished article or to an audience of colleagues at a meeting, they aren't useless ramblings. We knew we had a researchable idea. We'd identified some things to read, had some ideas about what earlier works might serve as models for us, and could anticipate the kinds of conclusions we might come to well enough to know the kinds of data we'd need. We accomplished that by reasoning from two cases we knew well enough to see where fruitful questions and answers might lie.

The work I do go on with and finish always begins with exploration like this. Working researchers play these games often—for me, it's a kind of mental exercise that keeps some important mental skills in working order. Most of the things I think about never go beyond a daydream. But the results stay with me as a reservoir of possibilities I might have started serious work on, if it had worked out that way.

(The same exercises work well in later stages of research. People who do fieldwork often recommend what they call "memo writing," which usually consists of doing this kind of exploration, more or less just to see where it leads. You can see that exercise in action in Becker and Faulkner 2013, a complete record of the thinking Robert Faulkner and I did together while we wrote a book about musicians [Faulkner and Becker 2009].)

INDUSTRIALIZATION: EVERETT C. HUGHES'S CLASSIC DEMONSTRATION OF REASONING FROM A CASE TO A GENERAL PROCESS

The examples I've given so far are simple: you find two or more things that are alike in some important way and different in some other ways, and look for the further differences that create the ones you first noticed, searching for the deeper processes those surface differences embody. These operations give us concrete sociological knowledge of the world and, at the same time, more abstract theories that tell us what to look for the next time, when we look at a similar situation.

Finding things that are alike sounds easier than it is. We usually think two things are alike because they have the same name: all things called schools must be alike, all things called families are the same in all important respects. Why else would we call them by the same name? In fact, schools differ in crucial ways and especially in what they actually do. Some may be doing something that could charitably be called "education," but many others are more like prisons (see the description of such a school in Nolan 2011). And other organizations that go by different names—prisons, for example—can easily be seen to do a great deal of educating, both the kind prison officials organize to teach inmates a useful trade and the kind inmates organize to teach each other potentially more useful trades.

If we can't take names at face value, how do we find similar things to compare? We can do what Goffman did in his famous essay on total institutions (1961, 1–124): choose a trait that defines the category to be investigated and stick with it, no matter how counterintuitive a collection of cases it produces. Goffman chose an identifying trait that varies in sociologically interesting ways: "Every institution captures something of the time and interest of its members and provides something of a world for them; in brief, every institution has encompassing tendencies. . . . [Some] are encompassing to a degree discontinuously greater than the ones next in line. Their encompassing or total character is symbolized by the barrier to social intercourse with the outside and to departure that is often built right into the physical plant, such as locked doors, high walls, barbed wire, cliffs, water, forests, or moors" (4). This separation from the outside world constrains social interaction: total institutions, so defined, prevent inmates and staff who live and work in them from interacting with the outside world and strictly regulate and minimize interaction between these two categories of inhabitants. Those characteristics, easy to discover and "measure," provoke no definitional arguments.

We don't argue about Goffman's definition of a total institution, even though it doesn't coincide with our conventional categories of moral judgment, which typically put "incongruous cases" in a morally relevant slot. We routinely make moral judgments, one way or another, about prisons and mental hospitals, which we conventionally know as wicked places filled with wicked or flawed people (whether we mean the inmates or the custodians), and about places like convents or military training centers, which we conventionally know as respectable organizations, filled for the most part with people morally better than average. But we have no such ready-made judgments about a category that includes those four organizations, as well as submarines, ships at sea, and all the other varied phenomena that Goffman's definition assembles. The morally disparate character (from a conventional point of view) of these organizations, so clearly alike in their limitation of interaction, frees the analysis from having to conform to conventional ideas of good and bad.

Having found a category whose interactional similarities promise to produce sociological insight, we then look for other interactionally interesting differences between them. And we look for the conditions that create such differences and for their consequences. Goffman's example doesn't help here, because he didn't make a differentiated analysis of kinds of total institutions, pursuing the differences between convents, submarines, mental hospitals, and jails. We find this more complicated form of comparative analysis in Everett Hughes's (1949) probing dissection of industrialization, in which he reasons from the specifics of a variety of cases to understand its characteristic processes.

Some Background

Everett Hughes—student of Robert E. Park, a sociologist with a truly global perspective when that was rare—went to Germany after he finished his dissertation on real estate salesmen, and there he studied ethnic and religious variations in the industrial labor force (Hughes 1935). Then he went to teach in Canada and soon interested himself in similar problems there, first in the larger economic setting of the country, then in the province of Quebec (Hughes 1941), and finally during a year of intensive fieldwork, done with his wife Helen MacGill Hughes (also a Park student) in the small city of Drummondville, which had recently welcomed two textile factories. This research produced what is probably the first major sociological study of industrialization (Hughes 1943), though it is seldom mentioned in the history of that subdiscipline.

He became a professor at the University of Chicago, and then World War II arrived. He was immediately interested in the general question of how a war (or any other major historical event) would affect institutions, a word he used synonymously with organizations (Hughes 1942). This overlapped with a practical problem University of Chicago researchers had been asked to investigate: how to deal with an industrial labor force that managers, desperate for workers, had integrated racially, over the objections of white workers. Hughes collaborated with other researchers at the university on several studies of race relations in the various war industries operating in and around Chicago (Hughes 1946). These studies, enriched by his wide reading on a variety of related topics, provided the basis for the specific and detailed analysis begun in his book on French Canada, and for the broader investigation I'm concerned with here, which generalized his findings in this area.

The Basic Analysis

In 1949 Hughes published a paper with an accurate but unconventionally, for the time, long title: "Queries concerning Industry and Society Growing out of Study of Ethnic Relations in Industry," which integrates the findings of his field studies with his extensive reading in a comparative analysis of processes of industrialization around the world.

He first identifies two related questions, superficially different, but similar in the underlying structures they refer to. The first is factual: what is the ethnic division of labor in former colonies that have been penetrated by European- and North-American-based industry?

The second question arises in the context of a more practical and parochial concern: how to make the fullest possible use of the total American labor force? More bluntly, how can you get rid of inequities and inefficiencies produced by ethnic and racial prejudice and discrimination?

He connects these specifics, vaguely (but not for long), to the most general possible theoretical perspective, saying: "Whenever one scratches a problem of racial and ethnic relations, he uncovers problems concerning society itself; and in this case, concerning industry and society." Fair warning. He will look for the most general phenomena in the specifics of individual cases.

To that end, he makes three sweeping generalizations, factual statements he asserts as indisputably true, which serve as the major premises of the argument that orients the rest of the paper. Though few people recognize it, Hughes thought in an essentially mathematical way, frequently reasoning from a few basic premises to a variety of interesting, unexpected, but logically connected consequences. Of course, he chose premises his knowledge of this area of human activity ensured would prove analytically fruitful. I don't mean that he simply deduced logical results and then tested them empirically. Nothing like that. Instead, he created a structure of argument from which these results followed logically. Induction as much as deduction, nourished by an intimate knowledge of the phenomenon.

The first generalization is "Industry is always and everywhere a grand mixer of peoples." He explains that when a local area first acquires industrial organizations and forms of work, an inevitable result is ethnic and racial mixing. This seemingly innocuous observation motivates all the following analysis and puts the specific examples he refers to in a framework in which they stand for more than what they at first seem superficially to be.

The generalization is supported by its own chain of reasoning. Industry always precipitates a grand mixing of peoples because the indigenous population, working in a preindustrial agricultural economy, cannot provide enough workers for the arriving factories. Land used for agriculture can't support the number of people an industrial plant needs, so the factory managers have to import the workforce from elsewhere. Geographically separated populations almost always differ from one another racially or ethnically, or both, so the imported workers inevitably differ from the local inhabitants in culture as well. Small geographical distances produce noticeable cultural differences in understandings and practices with respect to work, money, and other things that affect industrial operations (even in ethnically similar populations).

Hughes then makes a crucial distinction: between industrialization as it occurred in the mother countries of industry (the countries where the industrial revolution first occurred) and in their colonial outposts, to which the mother countries have exported industrial patterns of organization and work with which the indigenous population has no experience at all. He immediately finds a characteristic organizational difference between the two situations in the patterns of ethnic recruitment to the industrial ranks in them.

The mother countries already have the matrix of law, customs, and institutions necessary to the operation of industry. All that apparatus is already there and working. Managers, technicians, and core skilled workers, who occupy the top positions of the industrial hierarchy, live where the factories are and so are immediately available when a new one is built. Native to the area, and originally from the same ethnic stock, they share cultural understandings about work and, especially, about the discipline of wage work. However, often enough the new factories have to import the lower echelons of the labor force, the people who do the actual factory work, from elsewhere. These imported workers at first come from nearby, and cultural and ethnic differences, though real enough, are essentially those between various European nations. Older, preindustrial elites (landed, commercial, and professional) may be jealous of the new industries' leaders, especially if they differ ethnically. The ethnically different industrial workers may be successfully mobile, perhaps in a second generation; or they may be more or less permanently locked into a lower position. In the latter case, politics can take on an ethnic flavor. But mobility in the factory's ranks is usually some kind of possibility.

In colonies and ex-colonies, on the other hand, the people who will make up an industrial labor force already live there, but they require training in the skills and discipline of industrial work. Or similarly untrained people will be imported from a third country. The upper echelons of technical and managerial people have to be imported as well, since no indigenous people have the training or attitudes that owners and top managers think necessary for these positions. The distinction between mother country and colony is embodied in such pairs as England and Africa, the Netherlands and the Dutch East Indies, the United States and the Philippines. A minor variant occurs when rural people from the same country are imported to an urban setting to do industrial work (the situation Hughes encountered in his research in Quebec).

This distinction gives Hughes, as we will see, what he needs to understand many phenomena of industry in the colonies and then, working the comparison in both directions, in the mother countries as well. How do you pick a difference that is so analytically productive? Goffman looked for traits that affected possibilities of interaction. Hughes focuses on differences between these basic situations of industrialization that affected patterns of interaction, in this case differing patterns of ethnic recruitment and their immediate consequences in the distribution of ethnicities among organizational ranks.

His second generalization says, "Modern industry, by virtue of being the great mixer, has inevitably been a colossal agent of racial, ethnic and religious segregation." He defines segregation statistically: wherever the ethnic distribution among ranks and kinds of work differs from what might have occurred through a random assignment of people to these categories, you have segregation. Note that this makes the term a technical rather than a moral category; in this understanding of segregation, it is not by definition a "bad" thing. Using a technical statistical definition lets Hughes note something of interest and importance, something that ordinarily carries a moral charge, without having to engage in polemics about it. We shouldn't be diverted by the feeling that we must make immediate moral judgments. Time enough for those judgments when we fully understand the dynamics of the situation and of the possibilities for action of all the participants.

Many kinds of distributions can result. At an extreme, people of differing ethnicity and culture fill each rank and specialty in the industrial organization. And they remain that way, because industries seldom provide opportunities for mobility to the racially and ethnically different occupants of lower ranks. Although some may occasionally allow or even encourage such mobility, these organizations more often resemble caste systems, allowing no mobility beyond the ethnically assigned limits. Hughes flags the degree of ethnic segregation and the rate of interposition mobility as questions that need answers, general forms that need specification, when you study such situations.

In the relations between industrial ranks, marked by potential and (often enough) actual trouble, industrial, political, religious, and ethnic conflicts can and often do merge. The empirical possibilities for misunderstandings range from simple confusions about the meaning of words to open warfare and the development of racially and ethnically based politics, with many in-between steps that Hughes makes good analytic use of.

His third generalization is "Industry is almost universally an agent of racial and ethnic discrimination. People who hire industrial workers almost always have to choose from an ethnically differentiated applicant pool, so any choice they make is inevitably an ethnic choice." If segregation is a deviation from a chance distribution, discrimination produces a deviation because the chooser considers ethnic traits even though they are irrelevant to work behavior. But segregation is not in itself evidence of discrimination. The industrial experience and training of people varies with their ethnicity, and a choice based on ethnicity may result from taking into account relevant traits that are in fact correlated with ethnicity. This makes it difficult to know when discrimination occurs. Even the people who make the choice may not know whether they are discriminating or not. (Similar confusions about one's own motives furnishes a major theme in chapter 5.)

The distinction between mother countries and colonial situations is the right comparison to make, because it emphasizes striking differences in the organization of what are essentially the same industrial activities. Ethnic distribution among industrial ranks is the right choice for the major dimension of analysis because it affects all the other features of interaction in the factories and communities where industrialization occurs. Hughes adds one more crucial feature: the political and social organization of the community the new factory's owners plant it in.

What We Get from Comparing Cases of Industrialization

Having laid the groundwork, Hughes now produces—like a magician taking flowers and rabbits out of an empty hat—a complex analysis of the relations between industrial ranks, work organization, and community structure, covering such questions as mobility, ambition, sponsorship, nepotism, trust, and the role of government. The basic operation is simple: suppose that whatever you find in the one case will be present in the others, probably in a form different enough that we wouldn't notice it if its presence in the first case hadn't alerted us to the possibility. It's what Goffman did in his essay "On Cooling the Mark Out" (1952): if confidence men need a special member of the team to quiet the potentially destructive actions of an angry mark whose sense of himself has been rudely disappointed, other situations in which people experience that kind of disappointment will display similar personnel and similar operations. He finds such analogues, for instance, in greeters in restaurants (who calm patrons who aren't going to get the special treatment they think they deserve) and in the activity of psychiatrists, who, he suggests, do the cooling out of people society has disappointed in

a more general way. Hughes works his comparisons between industrial settings in both directions, letting phenomena in the colonies tell him what
to look for in the mother countries, and vice versa. A good example is his
analysis of the practice and meaning of mobility between ranks in industry.

Although all Western countries have ethnically differentiated hierarchies of power, skill, and prestige (in some the ethnic differences may
have withered away over the years), the generally more open class systems
of the mother countries encourage mobility, so rising through the ranks
is, at least in principle, possible. Management encourages workers to be
ambitious, and there is perhaps just enough mobility to make that not
quite foolish.

Not so in colonies, where no indigenes gain entry into the inner circles
of industrial prestige and control. That has several consequences, most
importantly that neither group can grasp the other's meanings and intentions. And this produces the anomalous position of the "straw boss": a
management person marginal to both indigenes and the ethnically different bosses, perhaps a person of mixed ancestry, but in any case someone
who knows and understands the ideas and thinking of both groups. The
bosses tell him what to tell the workers, and he does that, just as he lets
the bosses know what the workers are thinking and saying. "Such a person will know the peculiar ways of the workers, and will deal with them
accordingly. He is a liaison man, a go-between. And wherever there are
workers of some kind extremely alien to industry and to the managers
of industry, someone is given this function. He documents, in effect, the
gap between the higher positions and the lower; and symbolizes the fact
that there is no easy ladder of mobility from the lower position to the
higher" (Hughes 1949, 218). The straw boss is bilingual both literally and
culturally, translating the meanings industry takes for granted into language understandable to people of a different culture. Does that job, that
function, exist in the mother countries? Not by that name, but it does.
Looking for it, Hughes uncovers a web of connections between ethnicity,
mobility, ambition, and trust that appears, in one form or another, in both
kinds of settings.

[In the colonial situation] the straw-boss symbolizes limited mobility.
He is himself mobile, and ambitious. But the nature of his job rests on
the lack of mobility of the masses. In the mother-countries, the straw-
boss turns up, too. He is found wherever some new and strange element is introduced into the labor force in number. The Negro personnel man [in U.S. industry in the 1940s] is one of the latest straw-bosses;
he acts as a liaison man between management and Negro help. He can-

not himself be considered a candidate for any higher position or for any line position in industry; his is a staff position which exists only so long as Negroes are hired in fairly large numbers, and so long as Negro help is considered sufficiently different from other help to require special liaison. If the race line disappeared, or tended to disappear in industry, there would be no need of the Negro personnel man. (ibid.)

Hughes transforms "straw-boss" from a term of industrial argot into an analytic concept applicable in all industrial settings where people of differing cultures meet—and, remember, his first big generalization was that industry always produces cultural mixing.

Hughes compared examples from his own research in Chicago industry in wartime (the example of the Negro personnel man) and from his work in the textile factories of quasi-colonial Quebec to generate a new concept for understanding industrial organization, a new "telltale" that alerts us to basic organizational phenomena. In addition, he surely relied on what he learned from the work of his students (e.g., Melville Dalton's [1959, 199] research on the kinds of ethnic loyalties or lack thereof required in U.S. business organizations) as well as on his voluminous reading in the literature of colonialism.

The straw boss provokes questions about ambition: just how ambitious is it appropriate for workers to be? Industry thinks workers should be ambitious—sometimes. But industry (like society more generally) is ambivalent about ambition (a topic Hughes returned to repeatedly), complaining when it's absent and also complaining when people are too ambitious (Hughes 1947). Does industry really want the ambition it claims to look for in everyone? What proportion of ambitious people can an organization absorb without trouble? He notes an organization in which managers speak of the "Thank-God-for people," who are content, thank God, to remain where they are.

Controlling groups want to be able to trust their members.

In the colonial or semi-colonial industrial regions, management often quite frankly talks of the necessity of keeping management in loyal hands; that is, in the hands of people closely identified with one another by national sentiment as well as by general cultural background. In the mother-countries of industry, one does not hear such talk, but it is possible that the mechanism operates without people being aware of it. It may operate through the mechanism of sponsoring, by which promising young people are picked and encouraged in their mobility efforts by their superiors. In the course of their rise, they are not merely given a technical training, but also are initiated into the ways and sentiments of the managerial group and are judged by their internal acceptance of them. (Hughes 1949, 219)

The highest, most powerful ranks in industry confine power in the hands of people thought to be loyal not merely to the particular organization but to the managerial class and its culture. They take ethnicity to be an accurate indicator of that cultural loyalty.

Having raised the question of sponsoring power, Hughes looks for it elsewhere and, sure enough, points out the sponsoring power of lower ranks, who often control recruitment to their own ranks by suggesting "trustworthy" people from their village or family as recruits when openings at their own level occur. Stereotypes about what different groups are "good at" grow and persist.

Hughes covers other topics in this short paper, though by no means all those dealt with at length in the monograph on Quebec, which also analyzes religion, family structure, class structure, community organization in and between ethnic groups, and politics. All of these are amenable to the same kind of comparative development (and in fact many are dealt with in some of the other papers in his comprehensive collection *The Sociological Eye* [1971]).

Questions of Method

I've identified some of the crucial steps in the process of reasoning from specific, detailed cases but haven't begun to answer all the questions raised by Hughes's practice, and won't here; it's a big topic and some of them reappear elsewhere in this book. The chief operations calling for further exploration and specification are these:

· How do we choose the right cases to compare? How do we find oppositions as fruitful as "mother country of industry" and "colonial setting?"
· How do we choose the right dimensions to compare, dimensions as fruitful as the ethnic division of labor?
· Most difficult, perhaps, how do we find the sometimes seemingly insignificant events or social types that connect a variety of general phenomena fruitfully, something the phenomenon of the straw boss did for Hughes?

It's clear, when you read Hughes or Goffman, both masters of this kind of analytic operation, that they knew all sorts of odd facts, esoteric

stories, historical oddities—things we didn't have to know for the examinations we took when we were students, things we don't have to know to
set examinations for students now, and definitely not among the things
we think "every sociologist ought to know." Those conventional requirements, while no doubt necessary for some purposes, mirror the limited
range of things sociologists already think important, and they probably
won't contain the kinds of references that not only enlivened the prose of
these masters but also gave them the theoretical purchase that produced
new ideas and connections. Departmental requirements often force students to spend so much time learning what they "must know," it's no surprise that they don't have time to read widely in other areas (particularly
as the professional "literature" of conventional sociology continues to increase exponentially).

As Harvey Molotch (1994) has pointed out, sociologists (students and
professors alike) would profit from venturing more often outside the walls
of their own quasi-total institution, the university, perhaps finding the
breadth of examples fruitful comparisons demand.

Not only do sociologists often lack the breadth of experience and
knowledge it takes to produce unconventional comparisons capable of
feeding theoretical reasoning. Worse yet, they have usually learned to
ignore the random impulses that might lead them to unconventional
forms of comparative reasoning. It's hard to imagine many sociologists
today who would compare, as Hughes loved to do, prostitutes, priests,
and psychiatrists, so discovering the dimension of "guilty knowledge"
(knowledge of their client's secrets and possibly illicit behavior) he found
so interesting. I think, rather, that most contemporary sociologists would
consult the literature on professions and come up with a list of conventionally defined professions as the basis for a comparative analysis.

No formula solves these problems automatically. The requirements for
making good comparisons are irreducibly idiosyncratic, time-consuming,
and dependent on possessing a sort of random array of knowledge that
conventional training doesn't give us.

It does help, however, to have models of kinds of reasoning that lead in
such directions. The next two chapters go into more detail about reasoning by analogy with cases we already know about and, especially, about
the theory-building metaphor of the "black box," whose exploration and
understanding produces new things to look at and to look for.

3 *Reasoning from Analogy*

THE LOGIC OF ANALOGY

In David Lodge's *Small World* (2011), a comic novel about university life, one of the many subplots concerns a British professor named Philip Swallow, whose small book in pale blue covers about William Hazlitt, *Hazlitt and the Amateur Reader*, has not sold very well, perhaps because it has gotten no reviews. Swallow calls his publisher, Felix Skinner, of the firm of Lecky, Windrush, and Bernstein, to complain that a friend of his has not received the complimentary copy that should have been sent to him. But he can't speak to Skinner because at 2:45, the receptionist tells him, both Mr. Skinner and his secretary are still at lunch. Not true. They are in the basement storeroom of the firm, making love on a pile of cardboard boxes. As they approach climax, she suddenly says she's falling. And then they do fall, in a pile of broken cardboard boxes. She complains, but

> [Skinner's] attention had been diverted by the books that had fallen out of the broken boxes. He was on all fours, his trousers still fettering his ankles, staring at the books with astonishment. They were identical copies, in pale blue jackets. Felix opened one and extracted a small printed slip.
> "My God," he said. "No wonder poor old Swallow never got a single review." (Lodge 2011, 362–63)

Whoever should have sent out the complimentary copy and, more importantly, all the review copies, of Professor Swallow's book had just never done it. How could anyone fail to do such an elementary but important job?

One of the simplest ways to use specific cases to explain other, more puzzling cases is to reason from analogy, treating one case you know well as a model that will explain what you don't understand about another one, or at least point you in the right direction, and put you on the road to discovering a general mechanism common to both. Lodge's anecdote combined with some experiences of my own to make a perfect body of material to do that with, reasoning from one situation to another one, on the surface quite different, to uncover a mechanism common to both.

Analogical reasoning works like this. You know a lot about some phenomenon. You understand how it occurs. You have a good idea what processes produce it, what influences those processes, what difference their results make to still other processes, and so on. In the case that concerns me here, you know all this because someone's research has uncovered it all and made it clear.

And then you run across a new phenomenon, not at all intending to "study" it or even think about it analytically, it's just something that pops up in your reading or your own experience, at work or in your neighborhood . . . or, really, anywhere at all (the way the topic of urbanites' methods of spatial orientation did for Peretz and me). You experience the "shock of recognition" that Herman Melville described having when he first read Hawthorne, and you say to yourself, mundanely enough, "That's just like that thing I read about the other day."

Everyone has these experiences. Since I'm a sociologist, I often find useful analogies in books, but sometimes in real life too. I knew about the causes of Professor Swallow's problem before I read *Small World*. The story especially amuses many of its university-situated readers because, as people who occasionally write books, they know very well the many slip-ups and failures that get in the way of getting their books into print and into the hands of the public they'd like to think waits for them. I had in mind, as the analogical case to reason from, embezzlement, what Donald Cressey wrote a classic book (1953) about. Cressey had alerted me to a process that sounded a lot like Lodge's story and my own experiences.

Some years ago I had a connection to a start-up publishing company that, riding on the rising tide of opportunity created by the baby boomers just beginning to enter college, found a niche publishing social science books written by the first wave of post–World War II PhDs and representing new approaches to research in those fields. Sociology had a major part in this development, and I agreed with the president of the company to create a series of books reporting on observational studies of contemporary social problems of one kind or another. The series did well and I had a warm and profitable connection with the firm and its president, Marvin (I've changed the names because they aren't important). We published good books, people bought them, reviewers for the most part praised them, the authors rejoiced, the firm prospered.

The operation owed part of its success to Sally, the incredibly efficient production manager, who made sure that manuscripts, when they arrived for evaluation, promptly went out to reviewers who (with her urging, not to say nagging) got them back with a useful judgment and recommendation in a reasonably short time. When I recommended a book to Marvin, he looked at the readers' reviews and decided quickly whether to do the book. As a result, our authors seldom had the all-too-common experience of waiting several months for a decision about publication.

Once a book was accepted, Sally sent it to a copyeditor, who wasted no time preparing the manuscript for publication, checking the dozens of things an author might do wrong (from misspellings to improperly formatted citations of works referred to) and doing what could be done to improve the writing, always a consideration with academic prose. She also sent the book to a designer, who selected typefaces, created the page layout, and chose the jacket art. In a larger organization she might also have sent it to someone who estimated its cost of production, but in this relatively small firm she did that herself. She sent the edited manuscript to the author for final approval and, when that arrived, sent it to the printer, made sure that the author and everyone else got page proofs as they became available, and took care of any last-minute questions or snags that came up. Every one of these steps was a potential trouble spot, a place where the train of production could get derailed, delaying production of the book involved. These delays happened often in academic publishing then, and still do. Not when Sally was running the show. She was, you could honestly say, a phenomenon!

In the small world of publishing, Sally's reputation grew and soon reached larger and more important companies in bigger and more interesting cities, who paid a lot more, and it didn't surprise any of us when she accepted a more responsible and better-paying job in New York. She left production in the hands of her capable assistant, Shirley, who she had personally trained and who had had the benefit of watching Sally operate for several years.

In a short time, unpleasant things started happening. Authors whose books I had recruited wrote me, wondering why they hadn't heard about the fate of their book yet—why were the readers taking so long?—or asking why the copyedited manuscript they'd been told would arrive weeks earlier still hadn't appeared. When Marvin or I asked Shirley, she said she'd take care of it, and eventually whatever was supposed to happen finally happened. Then that magic stopped working, and things no longer eventually happened. They didn't happen at all.

The mystery cleared up one day when Marvin asked her about a long-overdue set of proofs. Shirley said she was going out to lunch but would take care of things as soon as she got back. She never came back. She just disappeared, even leaving a paycheck behind, and no one ever heard from her again. Marvin went into her office and discovered manuscripts and proofs and all the other missing things squirreled away behind filing cabinets, under her desk, behind rows of books on the shelves—everything missing reappeared because it had never left her office, never been sent to where it was supposed to go.

Marvin, shocked, realized he'd have to work hard to undo the damage, get production back on schedule, and regain the trust of his authors. Shocked, but not surprised. Not because he'd suspected Shirley wasn't doing the job, but because he'd heard the same story before, about other people in responsible positions at other publishing houses. Production people who hid their failure to get the job done by pretending they really had done it. The head of a small but well-thought-of university press who had gone home for six months to care for an ailing relative, leaving behind all the work that should have been done, undone and unreported to the people it concerned, especially authors (real life, not-so-funny examples of David Lodge's comic story).

Shirley's flight surprised me too. But the story sounded familiar, not because I had much experience in publishing but because it sounded, in somewhat different form, like Donald Cressey's (1953) description of what embezzlers did. These bank tellers and other financially responsible people siphoned money from people's accounts into one they'd created under a fictitious name, or sent checks to nonexistent companies, checks that they then cashed themselves. They stole money. Shirley didn't steal money, but she was stealing, in a similar way, time.

Cressey described a characteristic process of becoming an embezzler, one he learned about by doing long interviews with embezzlers, people who had, as he put it, "violated a position of financial trust." Everyone he interviewed had taken a job in good faith—they didn't intend to steal when they took the job—that gave them access to large amounts of money. But, as Cressey told the story, they all developed, after they took the job, financial problems they couldn't tell anyone else about. A bank teller had a girlfriend his wife didn't know about, whose existence cost him money he didn't have; a company bookkeeper became addicted to playing the horses, made some bad selections from *The Racing Form* and owed money to people who wouldn't take no for an answer. Since being financially responsible was a condition of holding their job in the first place, these people couldn't tell anyone who might be able to help them manage their problem. For someone who had another kind of job, these difficulties would have been troublesome, but no more than that.

So these folks had a problem. And they also knew how to solve it. When they learned the mechanics of doing their job honestly, they learned

skills they could use to do it dishonestly, manipulating the financial records they routinely kept and hiding what they were doing with the same
methods they had used to work with those records honestly.

Since they had been ordinarily honest people, they didn't begin stealing without serious consideration of the moral issues involved. Professional thieves think of taking other people's money as the work they do.
But these embezzlers had shared the conventional low opinion of theft,
and they had to explain to themselves why it was, after all, OK for them
to take cash out of the till or manipulate the books, supposedly for the
benefit of their employer but really for their own profit. They found the
solution relatively easily, in a conventionally available rhetoric that describes all employers as thieves themselves, out to cheat employees and
customers any way they can (especially so in the case of large, impersonal
employers like banks).

Shirley, the production manager, wasn't that kind of embezzler. She
didn't steal the company's money. She stole time. She wasn't as competent as Sally, hadn't mastered the skills of managing the routine work
flow of a production manager, and couldn't meet her responsibilities on
time. So she "borrowed" the time she needed (just as embezzlers "borrow"
the money they take) by pretending she'd already done things she hadn't
done yet. She hadn't sent all those books to reviewers. She hadn't sent accepted manuscripts to copyeditors and to printers, hadn't sent finished
page proofs to authors, and couldn't explain to anyone why the finished
manuscripts and proofs and review copies they expected didn't appear on
schedule. All she could do was hide them—on the top shelf of her book-
case, behind her desk, in a closet, getting farther behind, farther from
making up the lost time and repaying what she had stolen. When she realized the boss was finally going to discover her deception, she disappeared.

I tried to understand what Shirley did by pretending she was "just like"
the embezzlers, so that I could transpose the process Cressey had discovered to explain what embezzlers did to what Shirley had done, which
seemed so similar. That's what you do when you reason by analogy. You see
a phenomenon in one setting that looks like something you know more
about from another setting. You pretend that the Case of the Disappear-
ing Production Manager is just like the Case of the Thieving Bank Teller,
and you look for the things that explained what the bank teller did that
can help you understand what the hapless production manager had done,
with suitable alteration for differences between the two situations.

What did I do? Intuiting a similarity between the two cases, I then
looked for the analogues in Shirley's case of the elements Cressey had
identified as crucial for the embezzlers. If my intuition was going to help
me understand her behavior, it would do that by suggesting that I ask,

for instance, what Shirley's "non-shareable" problem was. It seemed like a promising question, because it had a clear answer, which made it likely that there would be other similar elements. She didn't have the skills she'd pretended to have when she accepted the promotion; more charitably, she thought she could learn them and found that she couldn't. And the problem couldn't be shared. It wasn't as nonshareable as a bank employee addicted to horse racing stealing to cover his losses, but it was bad enough. She didn't see how she could tell anyone that she didn't know how to do her job. So she just kept that to herself and stole time.

She couldn't carry the deception off, because she wasn't skilled enough to do what Sally had been able to do. She wasn't like the embezzlers in that way—although most embezzlers eventually get caught, showing that they don't have the necessary skills either. That's why those embezzlers were in jail for Cressey to interview; they could fool their colleagues and bosses, but they weren't good enough to fool the auditors who checked the books every year, whose superior investigative skills and routine suspicion of everything uncovered what the till-then successful-embezzlers had kept out of sight.

I had no idea (and still don't) what Shirley, and others like her in the publishing business, use to convince themselves that what they're doing is "alright." I suppose, but it's something to investigate if we really want the answer, that they use some version of "I'm just borrowing it [the time] for the time being." And probably justify what they're doing by telling themselves that their superiors are asking them to do more than is humanly possible in the available time.

The real utility of the analogy lies in giving us things to look for. Suppose I wanted to study what we might call "time embezzlement." How would I begin? Ordinarily, we don't know as much about what lies behind cases like Shirley's. We only know about her case because it showed up in a dramatic disappearance that came to the attention of a curious sociologist. Usually, when such events happen in a publishing milieu, the time embezzler's colleagues know only that a manuscript or a proof isn't arriving where it should be. And, almost invariably, they "explain" what happened, to themselves and to others, as a personal failing, an odd circumstance. Certainly not as the to-be-expected result of the social organization of work in that place. In a case I heard about recently, a contract that was supposed to have been sent somewhere (I'm leaving out all the details for obvious reasons) didn't arrive. The person waiting for it asked where it was, but none of the people he'd negotiated it with answered his e-mails. He was, after all, just another complaining author, and these people spent a lot of their time listening to complaining authors. Another party to the negotiation, in a more powerful position vis-à-vis the offenders, intervened with a peremptory question that produced almost instantaneous action. But no one involved knew or knows why the contract hadn't been processed more promptly. As far as anyone knew, it was just one of those things, someone falling down on the job.

If I had the embezzling analogy in mind, I could begin my investigation or analysis by thinking about it as "just like" the instances of financial crime Cressey had analyzed and by looking for some thing like, some analogy to, a nonshareable problem. Presumably, most (or at least some) people working in publishing who fail to send things out that should have gone out have been doing their jobs for years and probably know how to do them reasonably well. But what would produce the problem causing the time theft? If someone in a publishing house is playing the horses unwisely, or has an expensive lover, who cares? What changes in their situation make them start stealing time?

You don't have to do a lengthy study to find out that time is a scarce commodity in publishing. From time to time, events overwhelm the normal work process. More manuscripts arrive that absolutely *must* be attended to *now*. But they can't be, because there aren't enough people to handle them, given the normal work routines of the house. So something has to give. Or, another version (which happens often enough): a new management team, armed with new theories about how to improve the organization's efficiency, now requires more forms to be filled out, more reports to be submitted to higher-ups, more meetings to prepare for and attend. All of which cut into the time available to do the work that had been doable before the bosses added all these new tasks to the workload. "We used to have enough time, now we don't, even though we work just as hard as we ever did." It's what industrial workers call a "speed-up." The bosses speed up the assembly line, leaving individual workers less time to do the same operations. We may not know the exact reason for the change, but, being sociologists, we might guess, in a general way, that something changed in the organization of work, in relations between workers and bosses, and people now have less time to do the work they know how to do (this time using analogy to reason from industry to white-collar work).

Do I know this about publishing? No. Or maybe I should say, "Not yet." Because my argument by analogy doesn't tell me anything for sure; it just suggests a likely place to start. If I really were going to study this phenomenon (and it would be, as we say, a good topic for a dissertation), I wouldn't spend time looking for personal weaknesses of the workers who commit time theft. Instead, I'd look for some change in the conditions of work that created a problem of time management for personnel that they couldn't complain about. Is this guaranteed to be the right thing for me to be looking for? No, no guarantees. But it gives me a place to start, a way to get my investigation off the ground.

So reasoning by analogy consists in using what we know about one thing to tell us what to look for somewhere else, assuming that two things that look alike in some way may be alike in related ways. This is the kind of reasoning Everett Hughes used to create the analysis of industrialization and ethnic relations chapter 2 dealt with.

From here on, I'm going to proceed in two ways. First, an account of a classic use of analogical reasoning, Eliot Freidson's elegant account of lay and professional referral systems, which works by finding similarities, and differences within those similarities, between the ways lay people and medical professionals gather and distribute information about possible ways of dealing with sickness. Then I'll apply what we learn from that analysis to another social phenomenon we might use the same analogies for, the way ordinary people and experts deal with information about what makes their computers work and how to deal with the problems they present, treating computer problems as analogous to health problems and looking to see how we can use what we know about the one to help us understand the other.

THE ANALOGY BETWEEN LAY AND
MEDICAL REFERRAL STRUCTURES

Eliot Freidson's classic article "Client Control and Medical Practice" (1960) presented the novel idea of the *lay referral system*, which people turn to when they first suspect they have a medical problem, treating it as another version of the referral system physicians use when they send their patients to specialists. This analogy between the two kinds of information and help for medical problems shaped his analysis of the careers of illnesses (another analogy, this time between the conventional notion of an occupational career and its generalization to processes of other kinds) and his investigation of how sick people look for information and help before they get involved with doctors and hospitals and how their search changes once they get into that world. Freidson's concern was less abstract than mine is here. I'm using his work to illuminate some analytic possibilities. He was mainly concerned with a serious political problem—how to keep professional power under lay control, a policy issue that occupied him throughout his career—and used the analytic techniques that interest me as a means to that end.

Freidson based his argument on interviews he did with medical patients about their experiences with their diseases and with the system of professional medical practice those diseases had involved them in; and also on his studies of doctors in various situations of practice. He started with the simple idea that we should study medical patients in the communities they live and participate in and medical doctors in the professional communities they work in; and also study the system of relations both groups participate in, as these relations cross and recross the lines that separate the two communities. In this situation, doctors claim—it's the basic assumption that legitimates the professional dominance Freidson worried about—that laymen can't understand or evaluate their skills; only the evaluations of fellow professionals, who share their esoteric knowledge, count. If and when others accept that proposition, doctors and the others in their professional community get power over a variety of auxiliary medical personnel (nurses, laboratory technicians, and the full array of helpers we see wherever professionals work with sick people) and, above all, over their patients, who they tell how many pills to take when, what treatments to submit to, what surgery to have, and whatever else they think important for getting rid of the patient's disease, as they have diagnosed it.

If you, the doctor, know why I, the patient, am sick, and I don't know that, if you know what to do so that I'll get better and I don't know that either—then you have the upper hand, the power, in our relationship. If I want to achieve my goal of getting rid of my disease, I have to do what you say, whatever that is and whatever I think about it. Freidson saw that, in this situation as in others, power corrupts and that doctors' prescriptions for their patients sometimes reflected interests beyond the simple desire to effect a cure, interests having to do with their obligations to colleagues, hospitals, and other people and organizations in the medical world that might at times conflict with their obligations to their patients. As he saw it, fighting the tendency for complete power to lie in the profession's hands would preserve some freedom of action for sick people, who were in danger of being pushed around by professionals pursuing their own private, even selfish, interests.

Where do people get their ideas about what makes them sick, what's making them sick right now, and what might get rid of their sickness? Freidson noted a fundamental similarity: members of communities, both the residential and familial communities patients lived in and the professional communities doctors practiced in, share some cultural understandings about disease, treatment, and cure. Following this analogy closely, he noted the differences between these two "medical cultures," particularly the differing rationales that members of the two communities found for their beliefs. Professional communities justify their ideas by referring to a body of scientific knowledge and professional experience. Lay people operate on the basis of common knowledge, what "everyone knows," and haphazard, but close-up, knowledge of the diseases of people they know. When the culture of the lay (i.e., non-medical-professional) community provides answers to questions about how and why people get sick that differ substantially from those the professional medical community accepts, lay community members feel they have a basis to do something other than what their doctor tells them to do. When the two cultures resemble each other closely—when doctors and lay people share the same ideas about causes and cures of disease, and especially when lay people accept medical definitions without questioning them—members of the lay community have a reduced margin of freedom of interpretation and action.

But, Freidson insisted, the analogy only goes so far. The two communities, and especially their methods of referring patients, resemble one another because they are, after all, connected. Doctors don't practice exclusively in a professional milieu. Their practice is embedded in a community of laypeople, on which they depend for their patients and, therefore, for their livelihood. Their patients evaluate them on the nonprofessional criteria current in their local, lay community.

Though the two systems of value touch, they're different: "The local physician may be seen as the 'hinge' between a local lay system and an 'outside' professional system. Structurally, the practitioner's support theoretically lies outside the community in which he practices, in the hands of his colleagues, while his prospective clientele are organized by the community itself. Culturally, the professional's referent is by definition 'the great tradition' of his supralocal profession, while his prospective clientele's referent is the 'little tradition' of the local community or neighborhood" (Freidson 1960, 376).

Laymen have to decide that they need better help than their family, friends, and neighbors provide, that they need to get it from a doctor, and then they decide which doctor is a "good" doctor. Freidson describes how people did that in the community he studied, how they moved from self-diagnosis to canvassing the opinions and ideas of friends, fellow workers, and neighbors. He found the categories for his analysis by analogy to the way doctors form their opinions: the same underlying process (this similarity makes the analogy work) of canvassing the opinions and ideas of people who might know something useful, but taking a different form:

Conceiving the need for "outside" help for a physical disorder seems to be initiated by purely personal, tentative self-diagnoses that stress the temporary character of the symptoms and to end by the prescribing of delay to see what happens. If the symptoms persist, simple home remedies such as rest, aspirin, antacids, laxatives, and change of diet will be tried. At the point of trying some remedy, however, the potential patient attracts the attention of his household, if he has not asked for attention already. Diagnosis then is shared, and new remedies may be suggested, or a visit to a physician. If a practitioner is not seen, but the symptoms continue (and in most cases the symptoms do not continue), the diagnostic resources of friends, neighbors, relatives, and fellow workers may be explored. This is rarely very deliberate; it takes place in daily intercourse, initiated first by inquiries about health and only afterward about the weather.

He introduces the term "consultant," borrowed from the analogical medical practice, to name all these people in the local community a sick person turns to for advice and help. The analogy points to how people trying to deal with their own sickness rely on others for specific knowledge that they don't have, how the pharmacist or the family member or the neighbor does what a medical practitioner's consultants do. In the professional medical community, a doctor calls in another doctor with specialized expertise, a consultant, to assist in the diagnosis and treatment of a case ("orders a consult"). Freidson looked for the analogue of this professional practice in the lay community, using the idea more generally to refer to anyone a sick person called on for advice or treatment, whatever their professional status. He treated lay people as though they were doctors and, since doctors had consultants they relied on for information they didn't have, he decided to look analogically to see whether lay people had consultants too. Of course, his interviews had already told him they did. He thought it likely that when sick people had a large number of "lay consultants" they could ask about their medical problems (how to establish that number is a serious research problem), they could far more easily preserve their independence from professional controls.

This casual exploring of diagnoses, when it is drawn out and not stopped early by the cessation of symptoms or by resort to a physician, typically takes the form of referrals through a hierarchy of authority. Discussion of symptoms and their remedies is referral as much as prescription—referral to some other layman who himself had and cured the same symptoms, to someone who was once a nurse and therefore knows about such things, to a druggist who once fixed someone up with a wonderful brown tonic, and, of course, to a marvelous doctor who treated the very same thing successfully. Indeed, the whole process of seeking help involves a network of potential consultants, from the intimate and informal confines of the nuclear family through successively more select, distant, and authoritative laymen, until the "professional" is reached. This network of consultants, which is part of the structure of the local lay community and which imposes form on the seeking of help, might be called the "lay referral structure." Taken together with the cultural understandings involved in the process, we may speak of it as the "lay referral system" (Freidson 1960, 376–77).

These analogies gave Freidson two dimensions of difference to explore: "the degree of congruence between the culture of the clientele and that of the profession and the relative number of lay consultants who are interposed between the first perception of symptoms and the decision to see a professional. Considerations of culture have relevance to the diagnoses and prescriptions that are meaningful to the client and to the kinds of consultants considered authoritative" (Freidson 1960, 377).

He then used a well-known sociological technique, popularized by Paul Lazarsfeld, to create a four-celled table by combining two such variables and systematizing their possible combinations. Combining these two conditions—"the degree of congruence between the culture of the clientele and that of the profession and the relative number of lay consultants who are interposed between the first perception of symptoms and the decision to see a professional"—gave him new possibilities: "These variables may be combined so as to yield four types of lay referral system, of which only two need be discussed here—first, a system in which the prospective clients participate primarily in an indigenous lay culture and in which there is a highly extended lay referral structure and, second, a system in which the prospective clients participate in a culture of maximum congruence with that of the profession in which there is a severely truncated referral structure or none at all." He used the analogy to generate a typology, whose importance for his problem he made clear:

The indigenous, extended system is an extreme instance in which the clientele of a community may be expected to show a high degree of resistance to using medical services. Insofar as the idea of diagnostic authority is based on an assumed hereditary or divine "gift" or intrinsically personal knowledge of one's "own" health, necessary for effective treatment, professional authority is unlikely to be recognized at all. And, insofar as the cultural definitions of illness contradict those of professional culture, the referral process will not often lead to the professional practitioner. In turn, with an extended lay referral structure, lay definitions are supported by a variety of lay consultants, when the sick man looks about for help. Obviously, here the folk practitioner will be used by most, the professional practitioner being called for minor illnesses only, or, in illness considered critical, called only by the socially isolated deviate, and by the sick man desperately snatching at straws.

The opposite extreme of the indigenous extended system is found when the lay culture and the professional culture are much alike and when the lay referral system is truncated or there is none at all. Here, the prospective client is pretty much on his own, guided more or less by cultural understandings and his own experience, with few lay consultants to support or discourage his search for help. Since his knowledge and understandings are much like the physician's, he may take a great deal of time trying to treat himself, but nonetheless will go directly from self-treatment to a physician.

Of these extreme cases, the former is exemplified by the behavior of primitive people and the latter by the behavior of physicians or nurses when taken ill. (Paradoxically, they are notoriously "uncooperative" patients, given to diagnosing and treating themselves.) Between these two extremes, in the United States at least, members of the lower class participate in lay referral systems resembling the indigenous case, and members of the professional class tending toward the other pole, with the remaining classes, taking their places in the middle ranges of the continuum. (Freidson 1960, 377–78)

Formalizing the analogy, he made its details explicit:

Beyond these measures, however, we must note an additional important source of strength: Insofar as there are two "traditions" and two structures in a community, the lay referral system is one, and what we might call the "professional referral system" is the other. The professional referral system is a structure or network of relationships with colleagues that often extends beyond the local community and tends to converge upon professionally controlled organizations such as hospitals and medical schools. Professional prestige and power radiate out from the latter and diminish with distance from them. The authoritative source of professional culture—that is, medical knowledge—also lies in these organizations, partly created by them and partly flowing to them from the outside. The farther this professional referral system is penetrated, the more free it is of any particular local community of patients. A layman seeking help finds that, the farther within it he goes, the fewer choices can he make and the less can he control what is done to him. Indeed, it is not unknown for the "client" to be a petitioner, asking to be chosen: the organizations and practitioners who stand well within the professional referral system may or may not "take the case," according to their judgment of its interest.

This fundamental symmetry, in which the client chooses his professional services when they are in the lay referral system and in which the physician chooses the patient to whom to give his services when he is in the professional referral system, demonstrates additional circumstances of the seeking of help. When he first feels ill, the patient thinks he is competent to judge whether he is actually ill and what general class of illness it is. On this basis he treats himself. Failure of his initial prescriptions leads him into the lay referral structure, and the failure of other lay prescriptions leads him to the physician. Upon this preliminary career of failures the practical authority of the physician rests, though it must be remembered that the client may still think he knows what is wrong with him. (Freidson 1960, 379–80)

Having created two types of referral structures through analogical reasoning, Freidson considered how they influenced the career of an illness, the usual stages of its development.

When people first feel that something is wrong with their bodies and consider the possibility that they may be "sick," they look for interpretations of what they're feeling, first, in their own experiences and understandings: "I suppose it's an allergy that's making me sneeze and cough"; "My stomach upset is probably due to something I ate that didn't agree with me"; "I've got this headache because of that extra drink I had last night." These interpretations, common in almost any American community, suffice to explain a large number of the transient incidents of malaise that affect us all. The headache and the stomach upset go away; the sneezing continues but I don't develop a fever and the newspaper reports that the pollen count is high this spring. Reports like that confirm my initial self-diagnosis.

But sometimes the symptoms don't go away, and the newspaper tells me that the pollen count is exceptionally low. The next stop for most people is their circle of relatives, friends, and fellow workers. If I report my symptoms to these people and many of them tell me that they, or someone they know, has had the same thing and it goes away after a few days, I stop worrying: I have the very common disease called "something that's going around," and anything that's affecting so many people probably isn't serious enough to worry about—unless my symptoms don't go away as other people's have.

Many find, in their circle of intimates, people who have (usually because of their own medical histories) more extensive experience to draw on and more detailed interpretations of symptoms and possible courses of action to take. Maybe they're a little hypochondriacal and have had occasion to consult a variety of sources of medical knowledge. My father was like that; I often accused him of being an amateur doctor. He read such medical literature as he could find (most of it, to tell the truth, in the *Reader's Digest*) and collected information from doctors he knew and from a pharmacist friend, who also gave him pills he couldn't have otherwise gotten without a prescription. He used his knowledge and his hoard of pills (augmented by a large collection of over-the-counter medications) to "treat" friends and relatives, who were ready to take his "expert" advice.

When people's diseases continue to bother them, and their ordinary resources of home remedies, self-medication, and consultation with their normal lay consultants don't produce results, they may just ignore the problems and wait to see what happens. Or they may finally turn to the professional system. Remember, for Freidson, that's where the lay and professional systems intersect: "The local physician may be seen as the 'hinge' between a local lay system and an 'outside' professional system" (1960, 376).

In making this argument, Freidson continued to work by analogy. He knew from his own work, in which he had studied how the members of a medical group practice judged one another (Freidson 1975), that doctors were very circumspect, seldom actually criticizing anyone's way of working (though they spoke frankly to Freidson about their occasionally low opinions of one another's knowledge and skills). And he knew, too, what these professionals did when they thought one of their colleagues was not fully competent or ethical (not much). So he asked the same question, analogically, about how lay people made similar judgments of competence about both lay and professional consultants, judgments that shaped the way they looked for help.

He concluded that patients and prospective patients, when they rely on the lay referral system, use lay systems of thought and evaluation to judge physicians and the results of their work. Professional power, and the ideas and standards that underlie it, don't come into play until patients leave the lay system behind and enter a world organized and run by medical people, dominated by professional understandings and judgments. Physicians may be sensitive to patient evaluations when they think about how to get new patients from the community, but they are generally much more sensitive to the judgments of their fellow professionals in the course of their everyday medical practice. That's why they're more powerful than patients in setting the terms of lay-professional engagement. They don't care what patients think and needn't care as long as their colleagues think well of them. That's especially true of specialists, who patients usually don't choose themselves, instead going to the ones some other doctor, sometimes but not always a general practitioner, sends them to.

This is an elegant argument, the terms clear, the links between them described in empirically observed detail and intuitively believable. It is, of course, too good to be true, and in the latter part of his paper Freidson shows how empirical reality exhibits all kinds of mixtures, some medical practitioners being very much dependent on patient judgments while others are practically immune. The reasoning by analogy doesn't prove that anything happens the way the analysis says it does. But it gives a road map that tells investigators where to look and what to look for in understanding how illness gets treated.

LAY REFERRALS AS A GENERAL PHENOMENON

The distinction between lay and professional understandings of an area of professional practice makes sense in many areas besides the medical arena Freidson focused on. Here's an example of how Freidson's analogical method can lead to new discoveries about other kinds of social behavior, in this case the problem of getting and learning how to use a computer.

Many, perhaps most, people who use computers don't really understand how the machines they depend on actually work. Business people know just enough to start up "their program," whether it is for bookkeeping or medical appointments or library withdrawals or art gallery inventory, and fill in the boxes the screens present them with. Most people have figured out how to get and answer e-mail and how to consult the Internet for information they want. But if something goes wrong, if they press the accustomed key and "it doesn't work," or the machine just stops working altogether, they don't know what to do. They then engage in something like the search Freidson described in the medical case. They rely on folklore or on common sense, which is of very little use in the totally artificial and arbitrary, though logical, environment of computing. If they're lucky, they have someone to turn to who knows more than they do—a "guru"— who can tell them what they did wrong.

An example: a friend of mine had typed his way into a crash; the computer responded to no command that he knew how to give. So he called the friend who had advised him when he bought the computer and had set up the programs he used for writing and for e-mail. The friend came, like an emergency physician, asked some questions, fiddled with the keyboard, and fixed whatever was wrong. My friend wanted to know how this disaster had occurred, and his savior explained that computers are stupid, literal machines that do whatever you tell them to do. In this case, he explained, my friend had given it two contradictory commands and the dumb machine couldn't decide which one to obey. My friend got testy and said: "It knew what I meant!" The machine didn't. But his savior did.

These relations of guruship (to coin an ugly word) go quite far up the ladder of knowledge. My wife and I act as consultants (or gurus) to more than a few friends who use far less of a computer's possibilities than we do and who are lost when they venture beyond simple word processing, net surfing, and e-mail. We advise them on what computer to buy and what software to use, how to solve simple hangups and do things they didn't know were possible. But each of us had to learn what we know from someone, and we each quickly reach our limits.

An early computer user (early, that is, for a social scientist who did not routinely engage in statistical work), I began to use an Apple II sometime in the 1980s, heavily influenced by my own guru, Andy Gordon, a fellow professor at Northwestern who had extensive experience programming mainframe computers and was a serious proselytizer for the not-yet-popular cause of personal computing. He recruited me easily, taught me with great patience the somewhat arcane procedures necessary in those early days, and even persuaded me to try my hand at programming: under his guidance, I created, after many weeks and hundreds (probably thousands) of mistakes, a small program that opened a file of U.S. Census data and used it to create a population pyramid (essentially two bar charts back to back) that displayed a population's age and sex composition. Andy was a model guru. He saw what I didn't understand and nudged me along so that I discovered what I needed to know for myself. The experience left me with no desire to write any more programs, but with a rudimentary understanding of what was making the programs I routinely used work. And that was good enough to make me, in turn, a guru to people who understood less than I did and who got hung up on more elementary points.

After Andy and I both moved to the University of Washington in Seattle, I acquired a new guru (who, I think, served in that capacity for Andy as well), the head of social science computing there, Fred Nick, a genial man with a deceptively simple manner that hid an encyclopedic knowledge of what was available in hardware and software, what could go wrong with it, how you could fix what might go wrong, and who you could consult in the rare case when he didn't have the answers. (His knowledge went so far as to allow him to tell you that something you wanted to do couldn't be done, not now anyway.)

When my wife, Dianne Hagaman, wanted to construct a visual work that required doing something the complex application called Macromedia Director didn't have available as an already programmed option, she had to take classes in that software. But that wasn't enough, and she finally found that creating the effect she wanted would require more study than she (a photographer who had no ambition to become a programmer) wanted to do. So she hired a guru, a programmer who was expert with that software and had in fact worked on its development. But this guru, though he knew a lot, could not solve the problem either. He appealed to a community of programmers more expert than he was—his gurus—who gave him the clues and suggestions that eventually led to a solution.

Gurus tell you what you need to know when you need to know it. They are usually part of your own community: friends, and friends of friends, who will take on this responsibility. Such services have been somewhat regularized now, with the advent of experts for hire, who come to your house or office, set up your equipment (avoiding the intense anxiety that accompanies that procedure for people who aren't experienced in the troubles it invariably produces), and tell you what to do when things go wrong. This has been further regularized in the Genius Bar, which is an important feature of the Apple Store, and in such services as the Geek Squad.

What I've just described is an analogue of the lay referral system Freidson described in the case of disease and medicine: people with varying degrees of knowledge relevant to the common problems that affect computer users, to whom users with trouble can turn for help, just as people who feel sick can ask themselves, their families, friends, co-workers, pharmacists, and all the other non-medical-professionals available to them for advice about what to do. It's not the same as the lay referral system available to sick people: the problems aren't so potentially important. But the example also points us to some qualifications and additions we might make to the Freidson model and thus to an important use for analogical thinking.

For instance. Computer users often have problems—I might better say that they suffer from problems they don't know they have—because they only use a tiny fraction of their computer's abilities, having no idea that ten minutes' learning would simplify their work appreciably. A colleague of mine once watched me make some changes in a document displayed on the screen of my computer. When I "made" a word disappear and another word take its place, she asked, with fascination and a little jealousy, "How did you do that?" She thought you had to delete the word a letter at a time and then type in the replacement and was astounded when I copied a word from somewhere else on the page, selected the word I wanted to replace, and then, in one operation, got rid of the word I wanted to change and pasted in its place the word I had copied. "How did you do that?" I showed her how. Which provoked another and deeper question, "How did you learn to do that?" In this case, I said, I had read it in the user's manual. She said, unhappily, that she couldn't make head or tail out of that book, but she did understand when I explained it to her. I became her guru (one of her gurus, no doubt) on the spot.

Compared to medical problems, computer problems are generally not very critical or dangerous. People often use their computers very inefficiently and don't know that they could have a lot less trouble. We can use that observation analogically to point up a feature of the medical system that Freidson didn't make much of: how seriously people need the kind of help that trained professionals can provide. If I suffer a life-threatening medical emergency, I really need the highly skilled help doctors and other health professionals can provide, just as I need it, though not so urgently, if I have a low-level chronic condition that keeps me tired and irritable and unhappy most of the time. But I don't need a computer guru's help, ordinarily, in situations like that. Instead I need it when I decide I want to do something I've never been able to do before or only at a great expense of time and effort but that I now imagine I can do much more easily if I can get the machine to cooperate. I might never have imagined such a thing was possible before, but now I suspect or have heard that it's possible. I don't know how to relieve this new itch, but maybe I know someone who does. In my case, it was Andy Gordon and, if that failed, Fred Nick. And if that failed—I gave up. Dianne, whose need was much greater because what she didn't know was more central to the work she was doing, had to look further.

Gurus don't learn what they teach their "clients" so much by going to school as by helping others solve problems (in this resembling the woman who helped her poor neighbors deal with the forms and procedures necessary to get their welfare checks and other things from government agencies, described in chapter 2; she expanded her skills by solving their problems). You, the client, just get your problem solved. But if your guru didn't know how to solve it but learns by working on it, he has added a new entry to the list of solvable problems he's ready to deal with. Every inquiry is a potential source of new knowledge and new problem-solving ability. That was why Andy Gordon once told me he liked helping me: "You have such interesting problems," he said. (And here we've added something new to the list of things we can reason from in cases like this, something we can apply to the next one that comes along.)

"Guru" is not the name of a social type. In some respects, it's a generalization of the idea of referral system. Instead of treating relations characterized by differences in knowledge and skill as a division between a world of experts and a world of lay people, it describes a social relationship between a more knowledgeable person and one who knows less. The person you call when you don't know what to do with a computer problem is your "computer guru." Your guru may not know a lot about computers, but knows more than you do and can solve the problem you've experienced. The person who is a guru to you probably has a guru of his or her own, who solves the problems your guru can't solve. (Shapiro 1988 contains much case material relevant to this discussion; see also Barley and Kunda 2004.)

SOME COMPARATIVE THOUGHTS

Freidson's paper on lay referral systems concerns, ultimately, the power professionals exercise by virtue of a perhaps real, perhaps imagined, in any case claimed, monopoly of knowledge about some esoteric field of activity. We do what doctors tell us to do because we think they know more than we do and thus can help us achieve our goal (in the medical case, the goal of health) when we otherwise couldn't. But we can't judge what they do for us, and they may not always be as competent as they proclaim themselves and may at times act to further interests of their own that might not coincide completely with ours.

Freidson described the medical case, in which professionals are licensed by the state and so empowered to exercise a monopoly over activities in their arena of supposed expertise. There's a clear line between professionals and lay people, and once you've crossed that line, you're in the hands of the professional monopoly. His research suggests that a countervailing force, which protects us from this kind of exploitation, is the existence of a system of lay opinion, which tells us when professionals act against our interests and gives us alternatives.

The case of recreational drug use, taken up in the next chapter, shows that the relation between lay and professional isn't always defined that way, that taking medical practice as the archetypal situation can be misleading. In the case of recreational drugs, professional experts do exist, but their expertise is very limited, extending only to the "bad effects" of the drugs they investigate. Having no knowledge helpful to interested users of these drugs, they can't function as knowledgeable experts. Users rely instead on a network of amateur investigators like themselves, whose pooled knowledge, based on personal experiences and distributed through an alternate system of communication, replaces that of the experts. In that case lay people evade the control of knowledgeable and "legitimate" experts by creating an alternate source of knowledge based in their shared experience.

The case of computer expertise shows us features of lay referral systems that the medical case displays only when we look at it comparatively. For instance, the state isn't interested enough in the area of computer knowledge to license experts and monitor their training and activity. So, there is no clear division between licensed professionals and amateurs; knowledge is distributed along a chain of increasingly experienced and competent experts, who can function as gurus for those less knowledgeable than them but who turn to more knowledgeable people to serve as their own gurus. Everyone can be a guru and everyone can have a guru. Knowledge is widely distributed, but the degree of knowledge varies from one particular guru to another.

Freidson's analysis of the lay referral system thus opens up a large vista of research possibilities, focused on questions like these: How is knowledge that is not "common knowledge," more or less known to all members of a community (or at least all members of the appropriate age and sex groups), controlled? Who needs it? How do people who need that knowledge get access to it? What is the role of the state in controlling the accumulation of and access to such knowledge? What are the consequences of this distribution of knowledge for its ultimate users? How do all these things vary, and in response to what?

What reasoning by analogy from known cases gets you isn't guaranteed knowledge about an entire population of similar cases but something more valuable and less ephemeral: a collection of connected researchable questions about a family of related phenomena, ideas that can orient your next research from the first moments of aroused interest through the actual research.

Such a collection of questions and hints can confuse us. Chapter 4 uses the extended case of drug experiences to explore a device, the "black box" or input-output machine, that creates a more orderly way to think about these complications.

4 *Black Boxes: Using Cases to Study Input-Output Machines*

THE LOGIC OF INPUT-OUTPUT

Most social scientists, and many lay people as well, find the metaphor of "causation," the idea that A and B "cause" C to happen, appealing. Social scientists like the idea because it works well with the tools (and the descendants of those tools) they learned to use when they studied statistics. Although everyone also learned in those classes that "correlation is not causation," in fact most of us accept that equation unthinkingly. We know how to do correlation, we want to know if A causes B, correlations provide (or at least suggest) possible reasons for A to follow B. We should be able to use them to find causal connections. What's the problem?

An Empirical Example

The empirical problem shows up when A, which has always caused B in the past, suddenly stops working. B shows up though A didn't happen. A happens and B doesn't show up. An example I like concerns the causes of opiate drug addiction, though the failure of the connection occurred in the past, about which we usually know less than we do about the present. From roughly the 1920s until the present, opiate addiction has occurred mainly among young black men, and many people have concluded that if youth, gender, and race aren't causes, they are excellent indices of whatever does create the result of addiction. That thought leads to an easy acceptance of age, gender, and race as "causing" addiction. And all the available statistics (mainly records of police activity) support that causal analysis.

The empirical problem with this correlational approach arises because, in the late nineteenth and early twentieth centuries, in the United States, at least, opiate addiction occurred most prominently among middle-aged, middle- and upper-class white women. Age, gender, and race, statistically speaking, "caused" addiction in that segment of the population just as it now "causes" addiction among young black men.

How can that be? How can such a robust finding, replicated geographically, from one legal jurisdiction to another throughout the continent, and for the better part of a century, turn out not to operate only a few years before that period began?

In addition to that thorny empirical problem, saying that age, gender, and race cause opiate addiction poses a theoretical problem: it doesn't tell us how this effect occurs. Yes, young black males become addicted to opiates, and other drugs, far out of proportion to their numbers in the overall national population. But how does that happen? The usual "analyses"—I put the word in quotation marks because no one ever offers any serious empirical evidence for them—tell a story that seems plausible to the person who tells it, and maybe to some others. But not to me. For instance: young black men become addicts because they deal with the pain of their hard lives by getting high on drugs. Maybe, but no one shows us those young men suffering their hard lives and then deciding to get high and forget it all. Maybe it happens that way, but an analysis of correlations based on arrest records can't provide proof of that happening.

I'd like to know *how* A leads to B. In language made familiar by analysts of science, we sometimes call stories like that "black boxes," meaning that all we know is what goes into this mysterious device and what comes out. We don't know what we most want to know: how what goes in (usually called the inputs) becomes what comes out at the other end (the outputs). I want to open up the black box this effect occurs in and see what steps make that happen. The conventional analyses I've just described give us inputs (age, gender, and race) and outputs (people who have become addicts). But the intervening pieces of machinery stay stubbornly hidden.

Comparing the two contradictory cases can show us some of what goes on inside the black box. In this case, we can compare the case of middle-class middle-aged white women before the 1920s to young black men today and make a more informed guess about how those characteristics induce the machine to turn them into addicts or not, depending on the decade. Much of what I'm going to say now is somewhat speculative, a charge I just leveled against correlation-based analyses. But the analysis I will propose at least gives us some concrete steps that might verify it in historical and other records.

The new piece of evidence I've added to the story shows us some unlikely candidates becoming junkies. How did it happen? The general outlines of the story seem clear (only plausible, however, not proved). Middle-aged women eventually experience menopause, with physical and psychological experiences that many of them find unpleasant: hormonal changes that produce "hot flashes" and mood instability, for instance. In the nineteenth century, many of them learned from their doctors, their women friends, or maybe just from advertising, that they could deal with their "female complaints" (the usual term in the discrete advertising of the day) with patent medicines available without a prescription from their local pharmacists. The medicines usually contained substantial amounts of tincture of opium or related chemical products capable of producing physical habituation (a key component of addiction) so that, if they stopped using the medicine, they experienced unpleasant symptoms, including chills, muscular cramps, fluctuations in their heart rate, and a lot of psychological unpleasantness. If they complained to the doctor or pharmacist who had suggested the remedy, they learned that they had become addicted to the morphine or opium in the medicine. Many women, having become addicted that way, just made sure to always have their "medicine" available, and there was nothing to stop them from doing that, and from living a more or less normal life.

Then in 1914, the U.S. Congress passed the Harrison Narcotics Tax Act, which effectively made it illegal to buy, sell, possess, or use opiate or cocaine-derived drugs without a prescription written by a licensed physician. This happened when international organizations, set up eventually under the auspices of the League of Nations and, later, the United Nations undertook to manage the world supply of opiate drugs so as to preserve the monopoly of Britain, France, Germany, and the United States over the very large market for the uses of those drugs for medical purposes in doctors' offices and in hospitals, among other things by preventing the rise of an illicit market whose merchandise could be diverted in such a way as to threaten their captive market. (The story is told in Dudouet 2003 and 2009.) The United States signed international conventions that required it to outlaw any other uses of the drugs. Pharmacists stopped selling menopausal women their "medicine," and many of them found themselves kicking the habit more or less cold turkey. Middle-class female addicts more or less disappeared from the historical record, though some who belonged to the demimonde in large cities probably continued as users.

Once outlawed, these narcotic drugs (no longer available from legal suppliers) found, like other outlawed substances and activities, illegal suppliers who stepped in to provide the banned merchandise. But these businessmen couldn't sell their merchandise in a nice, clean drugstore with a window on Main Street. They found other sites of distribution, largely in urban neighborhoods whose inhabitants, having no political power, couldn't protect themselves against drug sellers setting up shop around the corner. These neighborhoods, largely inhabited by poor, mostly black, people, became the sites of drug-selling operations that used out-of-work young men in the neighborhood as personnel for the enterprise, becoming entrenched in these areas as major sources of employment and money for the local population. People who worked in the trade could take a little for themselves now and then and eventually become addicted too. The new generations of addicts came from the pool of young black men who staffed the lower ranks of this business and the young black women involved with them or active in related illegal activities.

So what? That long story makes a simple point. Historical events occur when a large number of events and conditions, each in turn historically contingent, converge in time and space. If those conditions aren't present, the event in question won't happen. In this case, the rate of opiate addiction in a population group depends in some part (the degree of dependence itself historically contingent) on whether that group has easy access to opiate drugs. Members of a group with no access at all can't become addicts. Simple as that. Something in the black box makes it easy for some people to get their hands on opiates, harder for some others, and altogether impossible for still others. (This story varies for other drugs, regulated through different laws, having different histories. LSD is not heroin, the most commonly used illegal opiate drug, and the story differs accordingly.)

The comparison I made, between middle-class white female addicts and lower-class black male addicts, shows that at least one thing in the black box is a distribution system for those drugs and, further, that the system of distribution changes from time to time. When the law lets any adult buy those drugs at the local pharmacy, respectable middle-class white women can easily get them. When the pharmacy no longer carries opiates in the form of patent medicines for "female troubles," they can't. When the law makes selling those drugs without a medical prescription a crime, neighborhoods that can't prevent criminal activity from going on in their midst can't prevent some young people, in search of income, from taking jobs in illicit trade, thus automatically getting access to drugs that weren't, before the appearance of this form of business, available to them. That means that, whatever else may be going in the black box that produces addicts, variation in access to drugs has to be part of the input-output machine.

Remember that access is only one of the things in that machine. Common observation tells us (we don't need a federally funded research project to find this out) that not all middle-class middle-aged white women got addicted to the "medicine" that helped them through menopause, and not all young black men in poor neighborhoods who are employed in the drug trade experiment with the merchandise they're moving and develop an addiction. That lets us know that our search for the way people become addicts isn't over.

Not yet. Other parts of the black box's machinery remain for us to discover. That's the lesson of this example for the way social scientists work. We often say, even insist, that social events have multiple causes. But standard methods don't contain mechanisms for searching for causes we don't know about yet. They're good for assessing the degree of the relation between A and B but much less good for investigating "the unexplained variance," which stays in the black box until we go looking for it.

How do you look for things you know must be there in the black box, but about which you know barely enough to recognize them when they turn up? They must be there, because so much still needs to be explained; so many cases of whatever you're studying don't fall into the subgroups that do exhibit the regularities you've found. Many researchers treat these "negative cases" as pesky critters they just wish would go away. Others, notably the great analyst of survey data Paul Lazarsfeld, point to them as sites of theoretical growth, sources of new variables whose effects we can investigate (Kendall and Wolf 1949).

This brief story about historical variation in addiction rates suggests that the way to understand such anomalies is not to get a bigger sample or improve your measurement techniques but instead to find another case that might point you in the right direction. Some years ago I went looking for cases like that, wanting to understand what was going on in the 1960s when lysergic acid diethylamide (LSD), a drug invented in Switzerland some years earlier and originally touted as useful in treating mental illness, became available in informal markets in the United States and elsewhere. Drug research, an area that had become a little stale and unexciting to the new researchers just leaving graduate school, once more looked pretty interesting, even cool. Among other things, reports began to circulate in the medical literature about LSD provoking serious mental breakdowns, and about unexpected and disconcerting reappearances of its effects ("flashbacks") long after it had been metabolized. In particular, reports circulated of people showing up in hospital emergency rooms, frightened by what had happened and continued to happen after they took LSD, and then being hospitalized, diagnosed as having a drug-induced psychotic break. Many people took this to mean that LSD use produced psychosis.

When I was writing about marijuana some years earlier, I had read some early medical papers describing, in almost the same words, cases of people seen in hospitals suffering psychotic breaks diagnosed as due to marijuana use. But no such reports had been published in many years, and my own casual knowledge of the worlds in which people smoked marijuana convinced me that that kind of thing didn't happen any more. People occasionally became upset when they got high on marijuana, but their companions usually "talked them down." (That anticipated what later became the preferred treatment for LSD-related psychological upsets.)

That, and other similarities between the earlier reports about marijuana and the 1960s reports about LSD, convinced me that some things at work in this area weren't accounted for by standard demographic or psychological variables. I wrote a paper about it and then later wrote a more comprehensive report that identified some of what was going on in the black box that produced what were usually called "drug effects." What follows is that paper, in much the same form as its original publication. I've added annotations (in italics), which point out just how I went about locating the additional inputs to the black box and generalizing the method I used to do that.

DRUG EFFECTS, KNOWLEDGE, AND SOCIAL STRUCTURE

I began the analysis with a premise I took from the work of psychologists who, having studied drugs and their effects in the laboratory, concluded that physiological processes alone couldn't account for what people who took drugs experienced. The basis for such an analysis needn't come from a verified scientific finding. It can just as easily come from chance observations, stories we hear, or things we just imagine, as other examples will show us.

In my analysis, I followed a simple principle: whatever question I ask about one example of drug use, I will ask about every example I use, and I will try very hard to find as wide a range and assortment of cases as possible. That could mean gathering a lot of cases, but in this instance it just meant ones that were very different in ways that became clear to me as the work proceeded.

Scientists no longer believe that a drug has a simple physiological action, essentially the same in all humans. Experimental, anthropological, and sociological evidence has convinced most observers that drug effects vary greatly, depending on variations in the physiology and psychology of the persons taking them, on the state they're in when they ingest the drug, and on the social situation they ingest it in. We can understand drug experiences better when we see how they depend on the amount and kind of knowledge available to the people taking the drug. Since the distribution of that knowledge depends on the social organization of the groups in which drugs are used, drug experiences vary with variations in social organization.

Then I proposed the main "variable" that informs the rest of the analysis: the differences in social organization that affect the distribution of knowledge people can use to interpret what happens when they take a drug.

I will explore three quite different settings of drug use: the illegal use of drugs for pleasure, the use of medically prescribed drugs by doctors' patients, and the involuntary ingestion of drugs by victims of chemical warfare.

Instead of assuming that "drug effects" result from biological processes more or less the same for all human beings, I let the psychologists show me that "set" (their word for what I called "expectations") and "setting" (the word they used to describe the social situation of drug-taking) created variations in experience that chemistry and physiology couldn't account for. This unexplained variation made me want to open the black box called "knowledge of drug effects influences those effects" and see what was inside producing the variation that puzzled me and others. I started by looking for what makes drug effects vary that way and found what I was looking for in a well-known but mostly ignored fact: the multiple effects of all drugs.

Drug effects have a protean character, varying from person to person and place to place. They can vary that way because drugs almost always have more than one effect on the organism. People who take them usually recognize and focus on only one or a few of these effects, ignoring everything else that happens as irrelevant. Most people think the effect of aspirin is to control pain; some know that it also reduces fever; few people who take it think of gastric irritation as a typical effect, though it is one. That suggests a possible generalization: users focus on "beneficial" effects and ignore those irrelevant to the benefit they seek. Because drugs have so many effects, users can interpret them variously, ignoring some and emphasizing others, responding to extremely subtle contextual influences, using ideas and beliefs they have acquired earlier to interpret what they feel (Becker 1967).

What they know, or think they know, about a drug influences the way they use it, the way they interpret those multiple effects and respond to them, and the way they deal with later phases of the experience. What they don't know affects their experience too, making some interpretations impossible, thereby ruling out actions based on that missing knowledge. I use "knowledge" in an extended sense to refer to any ideas or beliefs about the drug that any of the actors in the drug-use network (e.g., illicit drug sellers, physicians, researchers, or lay drug users) believe have been tested against experience and thus carry more warrant than mere assertions of faith. All people probably take knowledge they believe to have been tested against experience as a guide to their own interpretations and actions. Members of contemporary Western societies, who accept the value of science and scientific knowledge so uncritically, probably do so doubly.

I made an important move here by defining "knowledge" without requiring what we know to be verified in some reputable way (which usually means "scien-

tific," though it ordinarily can also be legitimated by being "religiously" or "logically" derived as well). I left room for what people know to be whatever they think is good enough for them to take seriously and act on. And now I go on to ask how what they know about a drug, in this extended sense of "know," affects specific parts of the activity of drug-taking. That opens the black box a little more and lets us see other inputs to the machinery inside that produces the variety of drug experiences that are the output.

DOSAGE AND ROUTES OF ADMINISTRATION. Many drug effects are dose-related. The drug has one set of effects if you take a certain amount and quite different effects if you take five times that amount. Similarly, drugs have different effects when taken orally, by inhalation, intramuscularly, or intravenously. How much of the drug you take and how you take it depend on what you understand to be the proper amount and route of use.

I noticed these dosage-related variations in drug effects as soon as I started reading about the medical uses of drugs. Normal curiosity leads to asking yourself what lies behind them, and that started me looking for relevant clues in what users knew or thought they knew about how they should take the drugs. Which in turn made me curious about how most people learn a lot about some drugs and nothing at all about others. That led me to ask how they judge the "legitimacy" of information, given whatever knowledge they have about its source.

Understandings about drug dosage depend on what you have learned from sources you consider knowledgeable and trustworthy. If I have a headache and ask how many aspirin I should take, almost anyone will tell me two; anyone can learn that from the directions printed on the package, or I can just ask any competent adult (it's lay medical folklore). In the same way, "everybody knows" (it's part of common culture) that I should swallow the aspirin rather than dissolving them in water and injecting them. Most people, however, know little or nothing about how to use a large variety of drugs, either those medically prescribed (e.g., cortisone) or those used without benefit of medical advice (e.g., LSD). To use them, would-be users develop some notions about how much to take and how to take it, either by trial-and-error experimentation or by adopting the ideas suggested by sources they consider reliable (scientists, physicians, or more experienced drug users). Those sources usually have recommendations. They can tell prospective users how much to take and how to take it to cure their colds, control their blood-clotting time, have a mystical experience, get high, or whatever other effect they desire. These same sources can also tell users how much will be too much to take, producing unwanted effects of overdose. They may say to take four pills of the kind the druggist will sell you, one after each meal and one before retiring; they may give more elaborate instructions, such as those given diabetics about controlling their metabolic balance with food and insulin; they may informally suggest that the novice has probably smoked enough hashish and ought to stop until it takes effect, or that most people find five hundred micrograms of "good acid" enough to induce an adequate amount of consciousness expansion.

Having acquired these understandings, users take amounts whose effect they can more or less accurately predict. They usually find their predictions confirmed (though the accuracy of conventional knowledge, as opposed to its confirmation by a retrospective adjustment of expectations, can't be taken as a given). In this way, users' access to knowledge exerts a direct influence on their experience, allowing them to control the physiological inputs to it.

Since what users know varies with how much control they have over their ingestion of the drugs in question, I next added that to the list of important inputs to the operations in the black box. Then I could make a list, from more or less common knowledge, of how those inputs of knowledge about doses varied and how they might affect such outputs as cure of a disease or discomfort, control of unwanted effects, and so on.

These speculations suppose that users have complete control over the amount they take, any variation being due to variations in their understanding of the consequences of taking different doses or taking the drug in different ways. But drug availability is often regulated by law, so that users can take only what they can get under given conditions of supply. I might want to take large amounts of cortisone, but I am restricted to what a doctor will prescribe for me and a pharmacist will sell me. Except in hospitals, doctors ordinarily prescribe and pharmacists sell amounts larger than recommended for one-time use, so that users can take more than they are "supposed to," as sometimes occurs with prescriptions for barbiturates. I can also purchase drugs illicitly or semilicitly (e.g., from a friendly neighborhood pharmacist) and so evade medical control of dosage.

Users also lose control over the amount they take when someone more powerful forces them to take more than they want or to take a drug they don't want to take at all. This occurs commonly in pediatric medicine, when doctors prescribe medicines adults can force children to take; in mental hospitals, when patients take their "meds" with a nurse standing by to make sure they swallow the pill; in tuberculosis hospitals when the medical staff gives patients drugs whose taste or effects they dislike; in chemical and biological warfare, when "enemies" can be given drugs harmful to them, sometimes when they don't even know that's happening; and in the addition of chlorine or fluorides to city water supplies (which most recipients think of, if they think of it at all, as a good thing).

In all these cases, the relevant knowledge for an understanding of the drug's effects, insofar as they depend on dosage, is knowledge about the people or organization powerful enough to force users to ingest the drug.

So far, I've taken "effects" to be more or less undifferentiated, the consequences, whatever they are, of getting the drug into your body. But now I want to take account of a common medical distinction, between main effects and side effects, realizing that Nature doesn't make such a distinction (so it's not a "scientific fact" waiting to be discovered), that only the people involved in the drama of drug use can or would want to do that.

MAIN EFFECTS. Social scientists have shown how the definitions drug users apply to their experience affect that experience. Persons suffering opiate withdrawal will respond as "typical" addicts if they interpret their distress as opiate withdrawal, but not if they blame the pain on some other cause like recovery from surgery (Lindesmith 1947). Similarly, marijuana users must learn to interpret its subtle effects as being different from ordinary experience and then as pleasurable before they "get high" (Becker 1953a). Native Americans and Caucasians interpret peyote experiences differently (Aberle 1966), and LSD "trips" have been experienced as consciousness expansion, transcendental religious experience, mock psychosis, or being high (Blum et al. 1964).

This begins the analysis of my tactics properly speaking. I've announced the main organizing idea—that what drug takers experience is shaped by what they know about what they've taken. Now I start by seeing what kinds of ideas they actually do apply (where they get those ideas will come afterward). The first distinction is between effects that are usually considered (who does the considering here is still an open question, but not for long) to be the ones that someone, usually the people doing the taking, want to occur, as opposed to the side effects, which are effects too, but ones the people taking the drug don't want to happen.

We get different answers to the question of what the main and side effects are, depending on whose point of view we take, what kinds of information those people have access to, and who they get it from.

Users bring to bear, in interpreting their experience, knowledge and definitions derived from participation in specific social groups. Native American culture teaches those who acquire it a different view of the peyote experience than non-Indians have available. Marijuana users learn to experience the drug's effects from more experienced users. LSD trips are interpreted according to the understandings available in the various settings in which it is taken.

These examples all come from situations in which the drug use hasn't been ordered by medical personnel but rather results from the user's own volition. But we can also consider medical use, looking again for main versus side effects. Doc-

tors who prescribe drugs are usually the main source of information for the drug-taker, though others (pharmacists, other patients with the same disease, books, etc.) might be available too.

The process has been studied largely in connection with nonmedical drug use, but it presumably occurs in medical use too. Here the chief sources of authoritative interpretations are the prescribing physician and, for many people, the pharmacist. Patients on maintenance regimes of a drug for a chronic disease like diabetes, epilepsy, or gout might develop a user's "drug culture," meeting in doctors' and hospital specialty clinic waiting rooms, or consulting the Internet, and trading information and generalizing from their common experiences, but no one has studied this extensively.

In both cases, the knowledge acquired from authoritative sources helps users identify the drug's main effect, know when it is occurring, and thus decide that what is occurring, even when it seems undesirable or frightening, is acceptable, if only because it is expected.

In either case, identifying a drug's "main effect" tells users what to look for, expect, and desire. Identifying a "side effect" tells them what they should be alert for and try to avoid.

SIDE EFFECTS. Side effects are not a medically or pharmacologically distinct category of reactions to drugs. Rather, they are effects not desired by either the user or the person administering the drug. Both side effects and main effects are thus socially defined categories. Whether an effect is a side effect or a main effect will vary according to the perspective applied; mental disorientation might be an unwanted side effect to a physician but a desired main effect for an illicit drug user.

This begins a process of reinterpretation of these ostensibly neutral medical terms, identifying them not as natural facts but as aspects of the overall result of taking the drug that specific people involved in the transaction identify as desirable or not.

The interaction between what a drug's takers want and expect to happen and what they perceive as actually happening produces the possibility that some effects may either go completely unnoticed or may be attributed to some other cause than having taken the drug.

Users get their interpretive knowledge from other people they stand in a particular relation to (fellow users, perhaps, or authoritative experts, among other possibilities). We can think of this knowledge as part of a culture, someone's culture, and ask who shares what kinds of cultural knowledge about this drug and its effects. And we have to remember that experts don't always know everything, so that their teaching may lead to effects unexpected by them or the users they instruct.

Drug users' knowledge, if adequate, lets them identify unwanted side effects and deal with them in a satisfactory way. Users concentrating on a desired main effect (relief from a headache) may not observe an unpleasant side effect (gastric irritation) or may not connect it with the use of aspirin. They interpret their experience most adequately if those who prepare them for the drug's main effects likewise teach them the likely side effects and how to deal with them. Illicit drug users typically teach novices what side effects to look out for, give reassurance about their seriousness, and suggest ways of avoiding or overcoming them; this mechanism probably prevents a great deal of potential pathology, though it can only operate for drug users adequately connected to networks through which the information passes. Many LSD users knew enough to become expert at "talking down" people experiencing "bad trips," and marijuana users routinely teach novices what to do if they get "too high." Physicians probably vary in the degree to which they teach patients the potential side effects of the drugs they prescribe. Patients physicians prescribe drugs for seldom share a user culture. Since the prescribed medication may produce potent side effects, they can experience profound effects without knowing that their prescribed drug caused them, should the physician fail to pass that information on. Physicians themselves may not know about the side effects; the drug may have become available before the effects had been discovered, as seems to have happened when oral contraceptives were introduced and many women experienced edema, depression, vascular difficulties, and other undesired effects that no one, at the time, attributed to contraceptive pills (Seaman 1969).

RESEARCH AND COMMUNICATION. Knowledge and the social channels through which it flows affect the interpretations and responses of a drug user to the experience the drug produces. Where does that knowledge come from? We can call its production "research," using the term in the extended way I have been speaking of knowledge. Research, so conceived, consists of the accumulation of ideas tested more or less systematically against experience of the empirical world. Researchers may use elaborate techniques and equipment or rely on simpler and cruder devices and modes of analysis. At one extreme, research pharmacologists systematically test the effects of a drug on a wide variety of organ systems; at the other, casual experimenters with a drug they think will get them high take it over a period of weeks, noting their own reactions and possibly comparing them with those of other experimenters with the same drug.

Having identified knowledge as variable and as variably dispensed by people of different kinds—different professional status, different in rank, different especially in presumed expertise—we can ask where the knowledge people are dispens-

ing comes from. Who creates knowledge about drugs, and how does it differ depending on who's asking the questions? What do people of different kinds want to know, and how do they find it out so that they can apply it to their own experience and pass what they learn on to other users?

Knowing these things, we can collapse all this work, no matter who does it or what methods they use, into the general category of "research" and look to see how people doing research, broadly defined that way, actually do it.

Research, especially research concerning the subjective experiences produced by drugs, done by no matter who, relies heavily on conventionally accepted rules of logic, inference, and common sense and/or scientific reasoning. Those rules help people decide when they have "experienced" something and what produced the experience. Even when they identify a variation from the ordinary that might be due to ingestion of a drug, drug users often have to decide whether it is an ordinarily uncommon event or something special that might be due to the drug. Marijuana users, for instance, often experience considerable hunger and have to decide whether it is "ordinary" hunger or drug-induced. In deciding these questions, users make use of such commonsense notions as that antecedents produce consequences, lay versions of scientific procedures like Mill's method of difference.

This leads to the often-raised question of whether drug effects are entirely mental constructs or whether they are in some way constrained by physiological events in the body. To what degree can people, as research on placebo effects suggests, have drug experiences that have no physiological base? Experimental work (Schacter and Singer 1962) suggests that there must be some physiological basis for the experience. Without arguing the matter, I think there must be some physiological event to be interpreted, but that it needn't be drug-caused. Human beings experience a variety of physiological events all the time; for people who have been alerted to the possibility, those ordinary events can be interpreted as drug-caused, as can events that really result directly from ingesting a drug.

In any event, people who want to demonstrate to themselves and others that they are experiencing a "drug effect" have to take account of the rules of common sense and folk or professional science. They can't convince themselves of the validity of their experiences unless they can manipulate some actual sense data according to those rules to produce an acceptable conclusion. (To the degree that other systems of producing knowledge are employed—divination, for instance—users appeal to those systems' rules for validation.)

The kind of research done on a drug depends on the facilities, technical skills, and motivations available to those who do it. Since I describe the varieties of social structures producing research later, I won't go into that here. Similarly, whatever knowledge has been accumulated may or may not be available to the ultimate user of the drug, depending on the constraints on communication in the organizations the drug use occurs in.

The entire argument rests on a comparison of the structures isolated when you ask who controls the conditions under which people ingest drugs, identify effects, and pass judgment on those effects. Isolating three major cases on this axis gives me a way to organize the search for interesting processes and other results.

Drug use occurs in three varieties of social structures, distinguished by the degree of control the ultimate users exercise over their own drug-taking and over the production and distribution of drug-relevant knowledge. In one variety users retain control for themselves; the major empirical case is illicit drug use for pleasure, though the use of patent medicines provides another interesting possibility. In a second variety, users delegate control to an agent presumed to act on their behalf; the major empirical case is modern medical practice. Finally, in some cases, most prominently chemical warfare, users have no control over their ingestion of the drug or over the production and distribution of knowledge associated with its use.

User Control

The preceding groundwork starts to pay off here. The principle involved says that if something happens in one place, it ought to happen in all similar places. And likewise insists that we not allow ourselves to be fooled by external appearances. Things that are alike in important ways may not look the same on the surface, so we have to look for underlying similarities that indicate similar processes at work. And we also have to look for situations that embody that kind of variation. The comparison of illicit drug use for pleasure with medically prescribed drug use provided a perfect pair of cases to illuminate the underlying processes in drug use by seeing what fundamental similarities lay underneath the surface differences in these two, seemingly quite different, situations. Both situations share one important thing: something happens when people put drugs into their bodies.

In a situation of user control, like the illicit use of drugs for pleasure, users take as much as they want on whatever schedule they want; they initiate and regulate their dosage themselves. They rely on knowledge generated in user groups to organize their drug-taking activities and interpret their drug experiences. They may feel substantial pressure to use from drug-using associates, but their use is voluntary and under their control—no one has issued anything as authoritative as a medical order and no one has forced the drug on them over their objections, as occurs in chemical warfare and forced medication.

Users generate knowledge about drugs that interest them largely by their own research, though that may include consulting such scientific and medical sources as pharmacology texts or the *Physicians' Desk Reference*, available in libraries or online. They use the lay research techniques available to them, largely self-experimentation and introspective observation, methods particularly appropriate when the effects to be investigated consist largely of subjective experiences difficult to tap in other ways. Such methods, unreliable in individual cases, are less likely to be influenced by idiosyncratic errors when a large number of users pool their observations and produce generalizations consonant with their collective experience. The reliability of generalizations so constructed depends on the efficiency of the communication channels through which information moves and the adequacy of the mechanisms for collating it.

Ordinarily, information about an illicitly used drug accumulates slowly, often over many years, in the pooled experience of users, who compare notes on their own experiences and those of others they have heard about. When users maintain social connections over a long time, even though very indirectly and even though they are connected only through tenuous links, a large number of experiences circulate through the system and produce what can be called a "drug culture"—not the mélange of political and cultural attitudes the term is often applied to, but rather a set of shared understandings about the drug, its characteristics, and the way it can best be used. The development of knowledge about marijuana probably best approximates this model. Many years of extensive marijuana use in the United States created a large and multiply connected network of users, who collectively produced a vast body of lore, which reaches most people who ingest the drug, and which does not vary much by region or social group.

Other methods of cumulating and collating knowledge occasionally occur. The drug known as STP underwent a hip equivalent of the mass testing of polio vaccines when someone threw thousands of pills containing it from the stage at a Be-In in San Jose, California. No one there knew what the pills were, but many took them. Within a few days most interested people had heard something about their effects. Information accumulated at the Haight-Ashbury Free Medical Clinic and other places where people suffering adverse reactions turned up. In a short time, information about the major effects, appropriate dosages, likely side effects, and effective antidotes had circulated widely.

The simple description of user-generated knowledge (informed, of course, by the comparison that I later make with medically prescribed use) generates several categories of considerable analytic value. What methods do people use to create knowledge? Who uses those methods and what knowledge do they produce? What advantages and deficiencies does each method have? What size samples do they use? How do they collect the data and what data do they collect? What methods do they use to collate their results? In general, the idea is to use any criterion or variable of interest in one case across the board, in all the other cases you know about.

Knowledge produced this way has certain defects. It cannot discover anything not capable of being discovered by the simple techniques known to a mass population of users. If, as was alleged, LSD damaged chromosomes and thus produced birth defects in offspring even after drug use ceased, typical styles of user research could not discover it. That kind of knowledge requires more sophisticated equipment and techniques of analysis than users have available. Further, user research will probably miss any unwanted effect whose onset is delayed, since it relies on simple and immediate cause-effect relations; if the effect occurs a year after use begins, the user population may not discover the connection. (If, however, the user population includes well-trained scientists, as was always the case with LSD and is increasingly true with respect to all psychedelic drugs, this problem can be overcome.) Finally, the effectiveness of the research is limited by the connectedness of the user network. The operation depends on redundancy for the reliability of the knowledge produced, and poorly connected networks may gather insufficient shared data to overcome the unreliability of the individual datum. Underground news media might help with this difficulty; insofar as they are widely read, they can provide an otherwise nonexistent link between isolated users or user groups.

This is a perfect example of using the same criteria for every case. If user-created knowledge has defects, we know that we should look for how medical researchers solve those problems, since we automatically suppose that they have those problems too; that is, we don't give them a pass on possible problems that seem characteristic of methods with a less good reputation (e.g., not done by trained professionals). And, similarly, we take the virtues of good research, whatever they are taken to be in one case, as something to look for in the other cases we have isolated for study.

But knowledge produced by user research has the great virtue of being directed precisely to the questions users want answered. If they want to know whether the drug will make them high, the available research, conducted by people who share that interest, provides an answer. In this it differs from research done for medical or conventional "scientific" purposes, which is typically directed to questions raised by scientists or physicians, not by ultimate users of the drug, who only want to know if the drug in question will cure what ails them.

Users thus have available, supposing optimal conditions of knowledge production, relatively reliable and accurate answers to their questions about the drugs they use. They use this knowledge to maximize the benefits they're hoping for, whatever those benefits might be, and to minimize side effects. Often, because they participate in user groups, when a question arises whose answer they don't know, someone who does know is readily available. This is particularly important in dealing with potentially dangerous or disturbing side effects. Naturally, users don't often take drugs under optimal circumstances; when they have to make do with incomplete, inaccurate, or unavailable knowledge, users often have predictable troubles. This is particularly obvious when a drug first appears and relevant knowledge hasn't yet been produced and disseminated.

As noted, a criterion produces useful knowledge when you apply it across the board. So, for instance, using what we have learned from the analysis of "bad trips" produced by a new drug like LSD, we can guess that drugs newly introduced by the medical profession and pharmaceutical manufacturers will produce troubles traceable to their failure to fully understand the possible other ("side") effects (besides the one they were hoping for); or prescribers and manufacturers may know about those effects but not pass that knowledge on to the ultimate user.

Another instance of user control—the use of patent medicines—shows the importance of the character of user networks. If my informal observations and speculations are correct, people produce knowledge about patent-medicine effects either on their own or in small family groups. Consider laxatives. Most people probably do not discuss their problems of constipation with others suffering from the same complaint. Users can't easily identify one another as fellow sufferers and thus as potential sources of information. Parents may share the results of their own experiments with their children, as may spouses with each other, but the knowledge produced by individual experimentation probably doesn't move much beyond that. Specialized groups (e.g., residents in a nursing home) might share such information, but, in general, knowledge probably doesn't cumulate outside of families (perhaps descending, like toilet words, in the female line); each new user or small group has to rediscover it. My speculations may be incorrect, but they highlight the importance of communication channels in understanding the experiences of users who control their own drug use.

The case of laxatives shows us another kind of variation in where and how people investigate drugs more or less on their own, and to whom and in what circumstances they pass what they have learned from their own experiments on to other interested people. This case tells us that our "accounting scheme" (see the discussion in Kornhauser and Lazarsfeld 1955) for understanding drug effects should take account, in every situation we know about or can imagine, of the variety of impediments to easy and full communication of experiences, the way the nature of the user's social circles impedes or furthers communication about private experiences, and so on.

When you put all these things in, the accounting scheme gets quite complicated. Think of the complications as a listing of the parts of the machine, at work inside the black box, in which ingestion of a substance produces an experience the user recognizes as due to taking the drug.

Control by the User's Agent

When users delegate control to an agent, interesting variations occur in the production and distribution of knowledge, with equally interesting differences in the kinds of experiences users have. The major empirical case is that of physicians prescribing medications for their patients (another possibility occurs in the religious use of drugs, exemplified in the relation between Don Juan and his pupil Carlos Castaneda [1968]). A patient takes the drug the doctor prescribes, in the amounts and on the schedule the doctor recommends. The doctor's prescription reflects what the doctor wants to accomplish, rather than what the patient wants; their desires may coincide but needn't and often enough don't.

Now the comparison begins to pay off, where what we learn from the more unconventional case suggests categories and possibilities that our ordinary view of more conventional activities ignores or writes off as uncommon, the result of individual idiosyncrasy, and other nonsystematic causes. Thinking about what a Canadian Royal Commission (Le Dain et al. 1972) delicately called the "nonmedical use of drugs" provides us with categories we can apply to other situations of drug-taking.

The case of medically prescribed drugs embodies a conventional notion of how and under what auspices people can legitimately take a drug. When we ask when it's all right for someone to take a drug, most people will probably say, "When a doctor has to prescribe it for you." The doctor's prescription embodies a complex idea: that using the drug for this purpose exemplifies and puts into practice the results of scientifically verifiable research, as that has been judged by the editors of medical journals and other scientific organizations. Any other use of drugs has to make a case for itself, demonstrating its efficacy or its harmlessness, or both. The first exclusion includes over-the-counter drugs and patent medicines. The second includes alcohol and tobacco (even though the evidence against such conclusions is widely known and accepted).

So, when we think about user control of the process, we might better say, just because "everyone knows" it, that no one can take drugs without someone authoritative giving permission. We know that because, in the case of marijuana, LSD, and other banned drugs, people have been subject to legal penalties when they used those drugs without permission. But then we should ask: who gives permission? And how do those people have the right to give permission? That leads us to doctors and pharmaceutical laboratories and manufacturers and their interconnections. Having isolated the element that distinguishes these two cases, we can find out something about what goes on in the black box that produces "drug effects" by seeing what common processes receive different inputs in the two cases and then comparing the results. The comparison shows us the workings of a process that ordinarily goes unremarked.

We can now use the comparison to see how features of information production and communication vary between the two situations, how that variation produces variation in what users know, and how the latter variation in turn produces different kinds of drug experiences.

Looking at users taking drugs without medical and legal sanction, we notice that they do have information about drugs, dosages, effects (main and side), ways of dealing with unwanted side effects, and similar matters, even though these ideas don't come from conventional sources. We have to redefine what elements constitute research, verification of research results, communication of those results to interested parties, and all the other things involved in the production and distribution of knowledge. We note that the focus of research interest changes when users do the research, away from "bad," unwanted effects to effects that may be disapproved by the law but which users define as good, as effects they want to experience. We discover ways of doing research to produce that desired knowledge that don't involve conventional laboratories, and we find ways of communicating and making the results available for use and for further testing that don't involve publication in refereed journals, judgment by professional peer groups, and so on.

This isn't the whole explanation of what goes on in the black box that produces drug experiences, but it gives a greater range and variety of variables than, say, conventional studies that describe correlations between variables like race, age, gender, socioeconomic status, and so on. Given that experience varies with available knowledge, we know that understanding these experiences and events requires knowledge on a greater variety of variables and their interconnections. Exploring these elements of the black-box machinery gives us more analytic power.

Doctors use at least two criteria to evaluate drugs. They want to alleviate some dangerous or unpleasant condition the patient suffers from, in a way that both parties can clearly see. The drug effect that most interests doctors is one that produces demonstrable (in the best case, visible to the patient's naked eye) improvement. But doctors also use a second criterion: they don't want the drug to interfere with their control over the patient. The rationale for that desire is well known: since (the rationale goes) the doctor knows what will help patients better than the patients know themselves, patients must surrender their right to control their own drug-taking to the physician if they want to get maximum results; patients who reject the physician's advice may experience impaired health. I don't believe that rationale is factually correct, but it's unnecessary to demonstrate that to recognize that doctors think they have a legitimate interest in maintaining what Freidson (1961, 1970a, 1970b) usefully called "professional dominance."

The first part of the machinery consists of the system of evaluation doctors use to judge drug effects. What do they want? Simple enough. They want patients to get better, however they define that, so that everyone knows (including, importantly, themselves) that they did something that produced the kind of result that people with their powers are supposed to produce. So we know that we will want to know, when we look at other cases comparatively, what the people administering the drugs want to get as a result of their intervention.

Knowing that what patients experience will depend on what the prescribing doctor tells them, we can ask if doctors tell patients everything they know, or if they hold some knowledge back. Once we learn that they do sometimes hold some information back, we will want to know why, what they expect to achieve by withholding it. And we will often see that their effort rests on a desire to keep control, to keep those who will actually have the experience from having any voice in choosing what it will be.

Patients usually rely on physicians for their knowledge about dosage, main effects, and side effects of the drugs prescribed for them. But physicians may withhold some of the knowledge they have from patients, information patients might use as a basis for disobeying medical orders (Lennard et al. 1972). Henry Lennard gave me a telling example. Certain tranquilizing drugs occasionally produced an unusual effect on male sexual functioning; a man who took them might experience orgasm without any ejaculation occurring. This understandably caused those who had the experience some anxiety. Since physicians prescribe these drugs to relieve anxiety, Lennard asked psychiatrists why they didn't avoid that result by telling patients that this might occur. "If I did that," ran the typical answer, "the patient might not take the drug and, *in my judgment,* he should run the risk of that anxiety in order to protect himself from his basic anxieties." That is, patients went without information relevant to their condition because the doctor who had the information made that choice for them.

Physicians also withhold information about side effects because suggestible patients might experience effects they have been told about, even when there is no physiological basis for the experience. They believe this risk outweighs the risk of morbidity associated with lack of information, but I don't think that result has ever been demonstrated.

Sometimes physicians don't give patients adequate information about the experience the drug will produce because they don't have the knowledge themselves. Research on drugs for medical use is organized quite differently from user research, and its organization creates substantial barriers to a free flow of information. A highly specialized discipline like drug research has its own journals, professional societies, and scientific worlds, which practicing physicians usually don't belong to. They don't follow the latest developments in pharmacology, read its journals, or attend meetings of its scientific organizations. They depend for their knowledge of drug effects on such general medical literature as they keep up with, on their immediate colleagues, and on the information provided by pharmaceutical companies through their literature and salespeople. Most physicians' knowledge, especially of new drugs, probably comes from the last two of these sources (Coleman et al. 1966). Some physicians, especially those in specialized practices who see many cases of the same disease, may engage in casual experimentation similar to that done by illicit drug users, trying different dosages and treatments on different patients. They may then pool their observations with like-minded specialists and generate knowledge similar to that available in drug-user cultures, with the same advantages and drawbacks.

We learn things about the medical business by raising these comparative questions. When pharmaceutical companies do research on drugs, they work on the things that will enhance their interests. How can we make sure we meet government standards that insist that the drug actually do something for the patient's disease, that the drug doesn't do more harm than good, that the dosages recommended be the "right" ones, and so forth. Physicians, of course, may not be interested in furthering the companies' financial goals, but they do want to take advantage of the "latest" discoveries without having to spend a lot of scarce time doing it. So they rely on the source closest to hand, the salesperson the company sends out to spread the word about its new products. Since this knowledge dispenser has an interest that isn't the same as the doctor's or the patient's (whether these coincide is a researchable question whose answer we shouldn't prejudge), physicians end up with a partial view of what the result of taking the drug may be, which they can then pass on to their patient, editing the information in a way that assists them in maximizing their own interests.

They also often rely on other doctors for information. Research has shown (Coleman et al. 1966) that some doctors, more adventurous than their colleagues, lead the way in trying out new drugs, and their more timid colleagues learn from them.

Another serious barrier that keeps practicing physicians from learning more about the drugs they prescribe arises from the organization of pharmaceutical research and manufacturing. While pharmaceutical companies, the scientists who work for them, and the physicians who participate in their drug-testing programs may want to produce medically valuable drugs that will help combat disease, they are also interested, as many congressional investigations and investigative reporters have shown, in profits (Harris 1964). They design their research to produce marketable products that they can sell, profitably, via physicians' prescriptions, to the public, and which will also pass government tests of purity, efficacy, and lack of dangerous side effects. They look primarily for drugs that produce (or seem to produce) effects of the kind physicians want, or can be persuaded to want to produce, on diseased patients. They appear to investigate possible side effects only so far as required by prudence and the law. (There is now a large literature on the organization of pharmaceutical research laboratories, their characteristic patterns of investigation, the structure of incentives for researchers, and the relations between the two. See, for instance, Fisher 2009).

Pharmaceutical research, so organized, produces the knowledge about a drug's main effect that a doctor might need to treat a patient, and the companies' advertising communicates that knowledge to physicians. If the physicians who get the information look carefully, they can find material on side effects and contraindications, but it isn't pressed on them. In general, companies don't emphasize information that would make the physician less likely to prescribe the drug, and thus decrease the profitability of a drug they believe has good commercial possibilities.

While some gaps in what gets from the researchers and their employers to the practicing physician arise from these kinds of venal concerns, others arise because of the division of medical labor, with one specialist not knowing much (or anything at all) about what another specialist is doing and what effects those interventions might have (Freidson 1975). We can now add to our inquiry into the workings of the black box of drug experiences, questions about the incentives that instigate action on the part of all the potential participants in this knowledge game, motivating some people to look for X and others to look for Y, and similarly for who would have reason to tell someone about this symptom and not that one.

So physicians may not know that the drug has some of the effects it has, or may decide not to tell the patient what they do know. When, for either reason, patients who have had the drug prescribed for them don't know what effects it can have, they run two risks. They may have pronounced, extremely unpleasant, and even dangerous experiences but not realize that those effects result from the medication. As a consequence, they may continue to take the drug that produces the unwanted side effect. For instance, certain commonly prescribed antihistamines occasionally produce urethral stricture; allergic patients who take large quantities may experience this but never report it to the allergist because it doesn't seem to be in his department. If the condition becomes severe, they may consult a urologist, who might discover they are taking large doses of antihistamine and cure the difficulty by recommending one that doesn't have this side effect. But not all physicians know about this connection, and the patient's failure to report or the physician's to make the connection can lead to serious difficulty.

Some researchers don't know about possible side effects because those effects take a long time to appear, or appear in such a way that well-meaning workers may not suspect what's going on. And the people who do know—the patients— may not communicate in such a way as to tell one another their own observations about what they're taking and how it seems to affect them. Of course, they can only report what they're capable of observing with such "equipment" as they have available, in most cases probably no more than a conscientious recording of their own experiences and symptoms and how those seem to relate to the drugs they're taking. Whatever difficulties the researchers have, lay people have more, because they lack the knowledge, money, and facilities to gather the data that might help them understand what they observe in their own bodies and minds.

Nor do they have the resource that users of recreational drugs often have, the access through informal networks to data from large numbers of people who have used the same drug and reported the results to friends who pass the information on to their friends, who then pass it on . . . though that sometimes happens, as I noted earlier, among people suffering from the same disease who meet in clinics that specialize in what they have, for example, diabetes or epilepsy.

Patients may also experience symptoms that have an insidious and gradual onset and never recognize that any change in their condition requires explanation. This was apparently what happened to many women who took birth control pills (Seaman 1969). They suffered serious and continuing depression, but it appeared gradually and seemed nothing out of the ordinary, so they didn't realize anything had occurred that might be attributable to the hormone. Such gradually appearing reactions occur especially with drugs taken for medical purposes; the mood changes they produce can appear so slowly as not to be noticed; or users attribute them to psychological difficulties, changes in social relationships, or other causes unrelated to the medication. Thus, the physician may treat the patient who begins to experience mood changes as neurotic, and the difficulty, when the user does become aware of it, will be not only undiagnosed but misdiagnosed. This must have happened frequently among early users of oral contraceptives, especially unmarried women, who physicians often consider especially prone to neurotic symptoms (Seaman 1969).

In either case, the drug experience is amplified and the chance of serious pathology increases because doctors either don't know enough about the drug's effects to warn patients or choose not to warn them. Patients, not knowing what's likely to happen, can't recognize the event when it occurs and so don't respond adequately themselves or present their problem to an expert who knows enough to respond adequately.

We've seen that knowledge accumulates in illicit-drug-using groups when users are in touch with one another and communicate the results of their personal research to one another freely. Though it seems that the organization of the medical and scientific professions ought to promote full communication of adverse drug reactions to practicing physicians, an important study showed that that often doesn't happen (Koch-Weser et al. 1969). Hospital physicians were asked to report all adverse drug reactions, and simultaneously, clinical pharmacologists made independent checks on the same hospitalized patients. The physicians didn't report from two-thirds to three-quarters of the adverse reactions to prescribed drugs verified by the pharmacologists. Physicians tended to report those adverse reactions in which morbidity and danger were high, and in which the connection between the drug and the reaction was already well known. This means that the system works poorly to accumulate new information, although it is relatively efficient in reconfirming what is already known. Add to this the probability that patients are less likely than illicit drug users to compare experiences on a large scale. That combination of circumstances creates a substantial risk that adverse information will never be accumulated so that it can be passed on to the drug's ultimate users, so that they can use it in interpreting reactions after they take the drug. (That this happened in one major study means that researchers should look for it in every case, following the principle that what has happened once can happen again.)

This is a useful research tactic. Once you have your questions out in the open, you can often find relevant data others have gathered, for their own reasons, that will help answer some of your questions about things you probably won't investigate yourself.

Many of the difficulties users have in interpreting their experience will result from the stage of development of knowledge about the drug. I have argued elsewhere that adverse reactions to illicitly used drugs decline as their use increases and a fund of knowledge grows among communicating users, allowing them to use that accumulated wisdom to regulate dosage and deal with adverse effects (Becker 1967). I think, for instance, that research would show that as the incidence of LSD use increased, the number of diagnoses of LSD-related pathology (bad trips, psychosis, etc.) decreased substantially, which I have always taken to demonstrate this connection.

The idea of a "natural history" comes out of a long-lived sociological tradition, which says that once you have located a generic social form, it's likely that you

*will find associated with it standard sequences of events that produce it. Some-
times you can think of these as "careers," in rough analogy to the series of steps
that might constitute an individual's career in an organization. More generally,
it's a series of steps that takes place in more or less the same way, for much the same
reasons, in a number of similar settings. It's not a "theory" that tells you a career
or natural history must take this or that form, but rather a suggestion to look for
something like that and, if you find such a series in your case that looks more or less
like others that exist elsewhere—more or less, not identical—then you can begin to
look for the black box and its insides that produce the more-or-less-same results,
These sequential models, or stories, serve as raw material for comparative analysis
just like any other collection of things that seem similar but are not exactly alike.*

*That's a general comparative strategy. When you compare two things, don't be
disappointed that they aren't alike. The differences give you a toehold from which
to start the comparative examination, trying to unearth the mechanism that
could account for the similarities—the common features—and the differences
in the inputs that produce the varying outcomes. That's the heart of any exercise
in comparative reasoning: to find something whose variations produce different
varieties of the same underlying kind of event.*

A natural history like the one associated with LSD may occur with the
use of drugs in medical practice. Doctors want drugs that will make a decisive and noticeable improvement in a patient's condition. Pharmaceutical companies and researchers attempt to produce such drugs. Because
everyone involved wants the drug to produce a noticeable improvement,
company recommendations, insufficient research, and physician inclina-
tions combine to produce a tendency to prescribe dosages larger than required for the desired medical effect, large enough to occasionally produce serious side effects. Because the research done prior to use of the
drug on patients didn't look thoroughly into possible side effects, no one
connects these occurrences with the new medication. For a potentially
profitable drug, as in the case of antibiotics, adrenocortical steroids, or
oral contraceptives, its use will be heavily promoted and widely publi-
cized, and physicians will sometimes, maybe even often, feel pressure
both from patients and from the example of their more innovative peers
to begin prescribing the new drug. Massive use, combined with a tendency
to overdose, will produce so many adverse reactions that someone will investigate and establish the connection. More such reactions will occur
before the information filters through the barriers I've already discussed,
but eventually the manufacturers will lower the recommended dosages,
and the incidence of adverse reactions will decline. Furthermore, when
such reactions do occur, physicians will recognize them and treat them
more effectively. Eventually, presumably, the number of adverse reactions
will reach a minimum based on the number of physicians who don't know

about them or don't communicate their knowledge to patients so that the reactions can be recognized, reported, and treated.

The introduction of oral contraceptives apparently reproduced some version of the steps of this natural history. When they were first introduced, both manufacturers and prescribing physicians were determined to use sufficiently large doses that they wouldn't have to face the wrath of a pregnant woman who they had assured that that wouldn't happen to her. The large doses produced serious side effects in a variety of organ systems, as well as occasional severe psychological depression. As more and more people, both lay and professional, learned about these effects, many physicians (and others) didn't want to publicize them, because women who knew about them might refuse to take the pills. Eventually, doctors discovered that one-tenth of the conventional dose ensured effective contraception, with many fewer adverse reactions. Both physicians and users, alerted by massive publicity, reported adverse reactions and dealt with them more quickly.

To what degree does the process I've described occur because the investigation and production of medically prescribed drugs is carried on by profit-making corporations in a capitalist economy? Obviously, those elements of the process that reflect marketing strategies designed to maximize profit—focusing research on products likely to produce high sales at low costs, a relative neglect of potential side effects, and downplaying information about dangerous effects—might well not occur in a noncapitalist economy. On the other hand, most of the other elements, reflecting as they do the interests of an organized medical profession as distinct from the interests of patients, would presumably occur in any developed society containing such a group. Physicians' desire to achieve discernible results and to maintain control over patients would probably continue to influence the dissemination of knowledge from researchers to physicians to patients and, consequently, the kinds of experiences medical patients have as a result of using prescribed drugs.

How large an entity do we want to incorporate into an analytic black box and its associated processes, like the one I'm constructing here? Do we always have to incorporate an entire economic structure? Probably not. But it's always a possible avenue to explore.

We should recognize that black boxes get all kinds of inputs: not just the specific characteristics of, in this case, individual takers of drugs, or prescribers of drugs, or specific instances of the production and distribution of knowledge, but also of such environing conditions as the economic system these events of individual drug use take place in, or the political system that governs the distribution and availability of drugs (which comes up shortly, when we see yet another variety of control over drug ingestion).

Carlos Castaneda's not exactly trustworthy, but nevertheless informative, account (1968) of his instruction by Don Juan in the use of psychedelic substances to promote extreme religious experiences describes the delegation of control over drug-taking to a religious, rather than a medical, agent. The relationship between the two, and its effect on Castaneda's drug experiences, looks very much like the medical model. Don Juan often gave Castaneda insufficient information to interpret what he experienced and avoid unpleasantness, because he felt Castaneda's inexperience (read "lack of professional training") would make it impossible for him to understand; because he wished to retain control over his student's progress; and because he wanted his pedagogy to produce the result he sought, even though the experience might be unpleasant or frightening for Castaneda in the short run and might ultimately result in failure. The disparity between teacher and student interests and goals parallels the disparity between physician and patient interests and goals, and some of the resulting experiences of the user who has delegated control seem very similar.

Control by External Agents

The black box contains the machinery that creates the experiences people have when they take a drug. That gave me a new and important key to what goes on inside that box: many of the separate elements vary according to the type of situation they are working in, as differentiated by the "variable" of who controls the drug-taking. Once I understood that the locus of control of drug use varied from one situation to another, from user-controlled use (people who take drugs to get high because they enjoy that state) to control by the user's agent (people who take drugs because an agent whose authority they accept tells them to, as a doctor tells a patient to take this pill twice a day), I was ready to look for other kinds of control, and it wasn't hard to recognize that there were many places where people got drugs through no doing of their own, that there was a third (maybe more, but I only found three of interest) form, embodied in chemical warfare. I already had the clues about what to look for in the black box. Now I only had to find out what form they took in this new and different case.

People sometimes find themselves forced to ingest drugs against their will, the whole process being under the control of independent agents who administer the drugs for their own purposes. The external agent's purposes sometimes conflict directly with those of the user, as when people find themselves the victims of chemical warfare (Hersh 1968) in the form of a poison-gas attack or a contaminated water supply. In other cases, external agents administer the drug because they believe the best interests of the community require them to, as when people with tuberculosis or leprosy are medicated to prevent them from infecting others (Roth 1963). In such cases, and in such similar instances as the forced medication of mental hospital inmates and the administration of amphetamines to allegedly hyperkinetic schoolchildren, those administering the drug frequently insist, and probably believe, that the medication serves the ultimate interest of those who take it as well, however much the "patients" may wish to avoid it. In both chemical warfare and forced medication, the characteristic features of a serious disagreement about the legitimacy of the drug's administration and the consequent necessity of coercion to effect that administration appear. The crucial feature of the social structure in which the drugs are used, then, consists of an imbalance in power between those administering the drug and those it's administered to: drugs are forced on unwilling users.

I first wanted to know, obviously, why people were taking these drugs they don't want to take. The answer was obvious: they do it because they can't do otherwise. Relations of power (and, sometimes, stealthy actions) saw to it that the drugs got into them. I also saw immediately that the people administering the drugs did it in the service of their own interests, whatever those might be, and that identifying those interests and the people who pursued them would explain the kinds of experiences users had under such circumstances. I'd get the categories, the things to look for, from what I'd discovered in the other two cases.

The people who administer drugs coercively usually have goals quite divorced from anything the user might desire. Although physicians in ordinary medical practice often have goals somewhat divergent from those of their patients, they must nevertheless take realistic account of the possibility that patients will cease coming to them unless the treatment proves satisfactory. When those administering the drug have sufficient control that users cannot escape, they can safely ignore the target's interests altogether and act in ways solely designed to serve their own interests, personal or organizational. The situation in which medical personnel force drugs on patients doesn't go that far, just far enough to deny that patients have any right to an opinion about how much of the drug they should take and when they should take it.

The emphasis on the interests of those administering the drug shows up in the calculation of dosage. In contrast to the more-or-less careful self-regulation characteristic of user-controlled drugs; and the attempt to prescribe a dose that will produce a result satisfactory to the user who one is acting as agent for, characteristic of agent control; external agents who have no countervailing motive (as is true in the case of chemical warfare) usually try to administer a maximum dose, one that will not fail to produce the result they're hoping for. Chemical warriors seek to kill or incapacitate their targets, so they aim for dosages in the range of the

LD50 (the technical term for the dose at which 50% of those dosed will die). When the people administering the drug have more complex motives, as in the mass administration of tranquilizers to hospitalized mental patients, they look for a dose that will let patients continue to take care of themselves but prevent them from being violent and totally suppress any psychotic symptoms that interfere with hospital routine. In general, external agents give people doses higher than those taken in medically prescribed or self-regulated use, because they mean in the one case to kill or disable and, in the other, to control the target population rather than cure their diseases or give them pleasure.

The processes that go on in the black box affect each other. If you want to give people massive doses of a drug they don't want to take, you have to coerce or trick them into actually ingesting it and keep close watch over any part of the process of ingestion that can't be so coerced. You don't have to force people to breathe, in order to get the lethal dose of poison gas into them. But you have to make sure they swallow, if you want to give them a drug orally.

Since those who administer the drug set the goals unilaterally, they have to use coercive measures to ensure that the desired dose gets to its target. As the divergence in goals between the two parties increases, the difficulty of administration increases proportionally. Physicians often worry that patients, suspecting that a prescription is not good for them, will not take their medicine in the amount the physician thinks necessary. Where the divergence in goals and desired doses is relatively great and obvious, as in tuberculosis and mental hospitals, hospital personnel usually supervise patients' ingestion of medication very closely, watching to make sure that they actually swallow the pills; even so, inmates often discover ingenious ways of evading forced medication.

In chemical warfare, where the parties' interests are diametrically opposed, the problem of an "effective delivery system" becomes extremely important, thus highlighting the degree to which other forms of drug ingestion rely on users' voluntary cooperation. Chemical warfare agencies concern themselves with foolproof means of dosing entire populations, and so work on such devices as aerosols, which guarantee ingestion by saturating the air everyone has to breathe, or methods of contaminating urban water supplies. In their zeal to dose all members of the target population, they create a problem for themselves that doesn't bother those who administer drugs in more selective ways that require user cooperation. Police officers attempting to subdue political demonstrators with a pepper spray or tear gas, if they fail to allow for a wind blowing toward them, may get a face full of their own medicine.

In any of these cases, the people doing the administering seldom give the people taking the drugs any specific or intelligible information about what they will feel once the drug is in them, and their goals may in fact include making sure that their targets don't know what the effects will likely be or even that they have had any drug given to them at all. Making sure that the drug is adequately and success- fully delivered can constitute an important goal of what researchers look to maxi- mize when they develop one of these drugs.

Those who administer drugs to involuntary users either don't care about providing them with any knowledge about it or actively attempt to prevent them from getting that knowledge. Hospital personnel seldom inform inmates receiving forced medication about main or side effects or how to interpret them. They may suggest, "This pill will make you feel better" or "The doctor thinks this will make you feel better" or "The doctor thinks this will help your condition," but they seldom give more detailed information. The difficulties created by the lack of knowledge I discussed earlier can thus arise, though they may be counteracted by the develop- ment of a users' culture, similar to the ones created by people who use recreational drugs or who suffer from similar diseases, among people con- fined in total institutions and subject to the same drug regimen.

Where the people or organizations administering the drugs aim at destruction or incapacitation of the target population, they may try to prevent any knowledge that the drug is being administered, or what its effects are, from reaching the people who ingest it. They want to prevent their targets from taking countermeasures and, by preventing the users from reaching an understanding of what is happening, create (in addition to the drug's specific physiological effects) panic at the onslaught of the unknown. Like military chemical warriors, members of the psychedelic left hoped to exploit just this phenomenon in the 1960s by putting LSD into urban water supplies. Not only, they hoped, would the drug interfere with people's normal functioning by causing them to misperceive events and hallucinate; in addition, not knowing that they had been given a drug that was causing these difficulties, the public would be frightened as well. (In fact, Chicago's Mayor Richard J. Daley need not have worried about Yippies putting LSD into the Chicago water supply during the 1968 Demo- cratic Convention. As Army Chemical and Biological Warfare investiga- tors had already discovered, LSD breaks down rapidly in the presence of chlorine, and the Chicago water supply routinely contained so much chlo- rine that you could easily taste it. This defect in LSD as a chemical warfare agent led the army to an attempt to produce a water-soluble version of THC [tetrahydracannabinol, one of the active agents in marijuana], which otherwise is most easily ingested in smoke.)

CONCLUSION

If drug experiences somehow reflect or are related to social settings, we have to specify the settings in which drugs are taken and the specific effect of those settings in order to explain the experiences of participants in them. So it's useful to investigate the role of power and knowledge in those settings; knowledge on the part of the user of how to take the drugs and what to expect when one does; and power over distribution of the drug, knowledge about it, and the decision to take or not take it. These vary greatly, depending on the character of the organization within which the drugs are used. In illicit drug use, the effects of the drug experience depend on the social links and cultural understandings that grow up among those who use the drug. In the use of medically prescribed drugs, the effects reflect the profit orientation of pharmaceutical manufacturers and the characteristic professional dominance exercised by physicians. Where drugs are forced on people, the results reflect the unilateral exercise of power in the interest of the stronger party.

Analyzing the contents of the black box that produces drug experiences gives us tools for more extensive investigations into other things that may not, on the surface, seem to have much to do with drugs. Moving beyond the specific case of these drugs to the extension and generalization of the ideas the case provokes produces more general ideas that a researcher can apply to more (and different) cases. (That's usually what authors talk about in the last part of an academic paper.)

Naturally, these are pure types, and many situations in contemporary society are mixtures of them. Some people, for instance, originally begin taking a drug because a physician has prescribed it for them, but then they continue to get supplies of it in illicit or semilicit ways; their use probably contains features of both user control and control by the user's agent. Folk medicine probably consists of a similar mixture, since folk curers may not have professional interests that diverge from those of their patients to the same degree that those of modern physicians do; then again, maybe they do. That's a researchable question.

Empirical cases usually don't fall neatly into one or another of these categories. Rather, the pure categories I have discussed show most clearly how knowledge and power can influence the experience of a drug user. I'd like to know more about the pure types I have described (my analyses may well be one-sided and incomplete) and also about the numerous marginal types that certainly exist. The progress of a field of inquiry consists in just that kind of elaboration of the contents of the black box and their workings; perhaps better said, progress comes from moving those mechanisms out of the black box and into the open where we can investigate them more fully.

When you bring these processes to light, you almost immediately see more cases to apply them to, cases that in turn produce a better understanding of still other processes still hidden inside the black box and invisible to us. You can always find more black boxes to open, more mechanisms to describe and explore. For me, that's the way serious investigation develops and knowledge grows.

Working that way, whole new fields of investigation and scientific endeavor open up for us.

Opening the black box, examining the mechanisms hidden in there by earlier discussions, made me conscious of the ambiguity of the very idea of a "drug." Much of what I have said about use enforced by a powerful external agent could be applied with very little change to our daily ingestion of the pollutants in air, water, and food. Is smog a drug? It certainly is a combination of drugs being administered to us via an aerosol, just like a poison gas. Shouldn't we call it a drug? Or at least think of it in similar terms? Why don't we?

Some people consider the fluoridation of city water supplies an instance of chemical warfare against them, sometimes going so far as to attribute the action to a foreign enemy. Are fluorides drugs? We apparently label as "drugs" an arbitrary selection of the materials we routinely ingest. We might usefully look at the entire commonsense classification of ingested substances—a classification that, it now seems to me, we unthinkingly borrow from in scientific investigations—to see how we decide to call some things foods, others drugs, still others pollutants and whatever other categories people commonly use. We could then ask what the consequences of such differential labeling are. We take different kinds of regulatory actions with respect to foods, drugs, and pollutants. What are the differences? How do they affect the distribution of knowledge and power with respect to ingestion of these materials and, therefore, the distribution of various kinds of experiences among those ingesting them? By extending this analysis of drugs, we might gain greater understanding of such diverse phenomena as smog poisoning, malnutrition, and indigestion.

We could similarly extend our investigations in another direction, by comparing chemically induced physical and psychological experiences to those produced by diseases of various kinds. We could investigate, for example, how information about the effects of diseases is generated. What kind of research supports the stories we read in newspapers and the articles published in medical journals? Who does that research? With what ends in mind? And how do they communicate their results? In what social channels? With what barriers to overcome? Knowing these things, we can then see how the resulting distribution of knowledge affects people's responses to their symptoms. (Of course, a lot of people write about these matters already. I don't suggest that no one has thought of these things; I'm just proposing a general way of combining what are now disparate fields of inquiry that often don't talk to one another and are unaware of one another's results.)

Beyond that, and of more general import, we can investigate the sociology of normal physiological functioning. Consider that medical symptoms exhibit themselves as departure from normal function: breath that is "shorter" than normal, appetite that is "less" than normal, pain that is beyond normal expectation, bowel movements that are "unusual," and so on. What is the folk wisdom with respect to "normal functioning"? How is it taught and learned? How does it vary from group to group? Many disciplines, from medical anthropology to public health, touch on these matters.

5 *Complicating and Combining Black Boxes: Where Is the Value in Art?*

For most of my life as a sociologist, and for more of it before and alongside that life, I've been interested in the social worlds where art gets defined, made, distributed, enjoyed, stored, and all the other things that happen to it. In *Art Worlds* (1982), I began the job of putting some of that knowledge together in a coherent picture. Individual case studies took up a lot of my time, both before and after the book. They all described one part or another of what I kept realizing was still, and remains, more complicated than I thought it was in 1970 (when I started working on the question) or 1982, when I published the book.

This long experience of discovery shaped, in some large part, the way I now understand the sociological research enterprise, what it consists of, and what it produces: black boxes, opened up and described, nested one in another, connected to each other, accepting inputs from and providing outputs for each other—and no end of boxes and processes in sight. That gave me a good way to describe the world of drug experiences, as I did in chapter 4. And now, as l reread some of the specific fruits of my work on the arts, it seems like a good way to think about those worlds and their activities.

Art Worlds didn't end my work on art. It began it.

Since then, I have, for various purposes and occasions, written about some other aspects of such worlds, defined for working purposes the way I did in 1982: "Art worlds consist of all the people whose activities are necessary to the production of the characteristic works which that world, and perhaps others as well, define as art. Members of art worlds coordinate the activities by which work is produced by referring to a body of conventional understandings embodied in common practice and in frequently used artifacts" (Becker 1982, 34).

One large part of the research activity in sociology and other disciplines concerned with art deals with how artworks gain and lose value. It's not the only interesting question, but it's surely interesting enough to focus this chapter on. I've approached the question, naturally, by seeing the creation and use of value as one of the important activities that participants in art worlds involve themselves in, and artistic value as one of the important outputs of the machine I've called an art world.

Working with this basic framework, I collected a lot of smaller case studies, by myself and others, specific instances of things that happened in, and so made up the substance of, the abstraction I was calling an art world, all of them centering on who does what to make art valuable. I've used these instances here to show how you can complicate a black-box machine, starting with a simple premise and allowing the cases you collect to tell you what you have to add to your original picture.

Each of the three cases examined in this chapter opens for inspection one of the black boxes involved in the workings of art worlds and details some of its inputs, outputs, and intermediary processes. I wrote these case studies for scholars interested in the substance of artistic activity, but I treat them here as examples of the way you can exploit the particularities of a case to enrich understanding of that kind of black box in the worlds of art and, simultaneously, create new boxes that can enrich future studies.

AESTHETIC AND FINANCIAL VALUE: THE CASE OF CONTEMPORARY ART

Raymonde Moulin's *Le marché de la peinture en France* (1967) described the complex of social relations and shared conventions that characterized the markets in which paintings and other works of visual arts changed hands in mid-twentieth-century Paris. The book gave me an understanding of the basic machinery that created value in the visual arts, a way to think about a big piece of that puzzle. Earlier students of this area of social life more or less took that value as either a simple result of economic forces acting in a classical market, the value indexed by the prices of works sold at auction and elsewhere; or the equally direct expression of aesthetic values, themselves justified by philosophical reasoning and discoverable by the trained sensibilities of connoisseurs and art historians. In either case, these results came from the workings of a more-or-less uninspected machine, its operations considered so obvious as not to require inquiry into how they worked. I thought that there was more to it than that, something that a sociologist could study.

Raymonde Moulin's book about the French art market in the post–World War II period gave my inquiry a good start and some important analytic tools. Discussing the French art market of the 1950s and '60s, she observed that well-developed art markets invariably and necessarily make it difficult, perhaps impossible, for their members to distinguish economic from aesthetic value. In a characteristic statement, summarizing the operation of the basic processes of art markets, she says: "The speculator [in contemporary art] makes two bets, closely connected in the short run, one on the aesthetic value, the other on the economic value of the works he buys, each of the values guaranteeing the other. To win this double bet is to confirm oneself as at once an economic actor and a cultural actor" (Moulin 1967, 219).

With these remarks, she complicated the explanation of artistic value by suggesting that it wasn't a single thing but resulted from the interaction of two different systems of value. That opened the way for a far more interesting kind of analysis: understanding artistic value as a black box of social arrangements, in which economic and aesthetic motives, acting as inputs to acts of artistic consumption, are so mingled as to be hardly distinguishable from each other. That gives us some new questions to investigate, which in turn produce some outputs we hadn't thought about before.

Shared Economic Values

Shared economic values form the basis of the economic activity that underlies, one way or another, all societies. Every society constructs ways of exchanging goods and services and, usually, some sort of standard for determining what constitutes a "fair" exchange. The most common solution to this problem, the one that pervades all modern societies (though it's never the only one, even there) is to create a money system. Using its standard unit, we can evaluate all objects and services, which makes the complicated economic activities that underlie our daily lives possible: the purchases and sales, the borrowings and lendings, and all the rest of it.

Art markets operate, in some large part, on the basis of just such systems of economic value. As markets, they are arenas in which objects are bought and sold on the basis of value expressed in universal, neutral monetary units: dollars, francs, pounds, yen. The exchanges take place in institutions organized for the purpose: stores (art stores are usually called galleries) and, most usefully for Moulin's work because their activities and prices are public, auctions (see Smith 1989). These institutions operate on the basis of rules mutually agreed on, or at least accepted, and understood by all participants, and in them the prices of works index their value.

Shared Aesthetic Values

People create aesthetic value by collectively recognizing some works of art as having it. It's the beauty I recognize, and simultaneously know that you and other knowledgeable people recognize, that matters in an art world. You can imagine a purely private, totally unshared aesthetic standard. In fact, we don't have to imagine it. We all have such standards and preferences. We like things that others don't, and they prize things that we don't. These aesthetic likes and dislikes may stem from personal experiences not commonly shared, so that we are fond, like Roland Barthes (1980) as he contemplated the image of his mother, of a photograph of a beloved relative or friend because it reminds us of that person. Objects have all sorts of private meanings that give them great emotional and, we might say, aesthetic value—but to us alone, not to others, who think they are just peculiar tchotchkes. (See the investigations of Csikszentmihalyi and Rochberg-Halton [1981] on the meanings of household objects).

Shared aesthetic standards matter more than private and idiosyncratic ones because, like other shared beliefs, like the economic rules just discussed, they create the basis for collective action. If we agree on standards, we can agree more easily on what to do in situations in which we've agreed to be governed by those standards.

We can act quickly, relying on others to react to what we do in ways we anticipate just because they share our aesthetic judgments. If we all agree on the criteria that identify a "good painting," then we can admire each other's judgment as exhibited in a collection, agree to help finance work of a certain kind, and engage in all the other forms of collective action that make up the routine doings of an art world. If we operate solely with privatized and unshared aesthetic standards, we can't act in that coherent or coordinated way with others. We are, in the most literal sense, "in business for ourselves."

Aesthetic rules operate in institutions that define themselves as "artistic," as organizations whose activities encourage art or make art possible. In organizations like that, aesthetic judgments are paramount and override other considerations. Or, at least, that's the story their participants tell about themselves. Museums say that they use aesthetic standards— what is the most beautiful or the most expressive—when they choose what to acquire and exhibit. Or, another criterion Moulin points out, what most displays the trend of art's history, what has been important to that history, what is important to it now, what will be important in the future: "The artistic choices made by dealers are based on the selection already made by history" (Moulin 1967, 100; see also 430–31).

Blurred Values

To repeat Moulin's key finding: in a well-developed art market, none of the actors involved can accurately and consistently distinguish aesthetic from financial value when they judge works of art. I don't mean by this, and Moulin didn't mean, that the two systems of value conflict with each other. It's more confused than that.

Sociologists say that value conflict occurs when one set of values recommends behavior that another set of values, held by the same people, condemns. In the classic textbook example, the businessman goes to church on Sunday, where he learns the value of charity, and returns to work on Monday to practice the value of acquisition, forgetting all about charity. But that also exemplifies the way temporal or spatial segregation can solve a problem of value conflict. If you keep the two injunctions in separate situations, you never have to obey both of them at the same time, and the conflict stays only hypothetical. The trouble starts when they operate in the same place at the same time with respect to the same actions.

Moulin meant something more complex than having to serve two masters, hoping not to get caught with both of them in the room at the same time. She emphasized two further results of this chronic confusion of aesthetic and financial value. The two values may not conflict at all. In pursuing one you may simultaneously, and without difficulty, pursue the other. Which seems like a fine thing. But suppose that one set of values has a low reputation. People don't want anyone to think they are pursuing that particular ("bad") goal and would rather everyone thought they were pursuing the other goal, the "good" one. Although they'd like to appear to be pursuing just the one, they can't do that. You might even, and in many worlds certainly would, prefer to think about yourself that way, not just create the appearance. Because people are jealous of their self-regard.

That's what happens in the market for paintings. If the relevant audience thinks a painting aesthetically worthwhile, it's because people in a position to know—connoisseurs—think it more beautiful, more expressive, more whatever their aesthetic system prizes, than most other works. Not only that; they also think it's a unique expression. No other painting will ever be just like it. So it's rare in the nth degree: there's only one. And it's one of a relatively small number of works that have this quality of unique expression, so it's rare, too, by belonging to a class of objects with very few members. Even if another object is just as good, so that there are many with this sort of unique quality and substitutability is thus possible, the class of possible substitutions is very small and, in practice, substitutions seldom occur (Moulin 1978; 1992, 15–18).

If something is rare or unique in this way and people want it, it's almost certain, in a market economy, that the ownership will be settled by purchase and, if it's highly valued, by competition among buyers, which will raise the price, auctions being the most visible example of this process.

Thus, aesthetic value—the process repeats itself at less rarefied levels, as Moulin explains in the discussion of "lesser" markets, which I'll discuss shortly (1978; 1992, 34–43)—is mirrored in market value. If an object is beautiful, and standards of beauty are shared (as they must be if there's going to be an art world at all), then price will accurately reflect aesthetic worth. (Heinich 1991, 149–167, adds considerably to the complexity of this relationship in her discussion of the enormous prices paid for Van Gogh's works in the late twentieth century.)

Turn this equation around. If an artwork is very valuable, it must be because knowledgeable actors in the art world think it very beautiful (or whatever they value, letting "beauty" stand for whatever the relevant actors take to be the aesthetic sine qua non). The object *must be* beautiful, because it's axiomatic in this world that monetary value accurately reflects aesthetic value. It's often observed that a valuable object has a kind of aura that comes from being worth so much. Looking at a painting that's just been sold for millions of dollars inevitably produces, in people who accept the values of the world the transaction occurred in, an awareness of a special "something." It's like looking at the money itself, as if those hundred dollar bills lay before you. Not exactly, because the object isn't really the banknotes; it's that rare something worth all those notes.

In other words, Moulin has identified a process by which art-world activities turn inputs of aesthetic value into financial value, and financial value into aesthetic value; she has turned what would otherwise be a simple correlation whose meaning is obvious into a process to study.

So actors in the art world in which these transactions occur become and remain fundamentally and irremediably confused. They don't, and can't, know with certainty whether the objects their world is organized around are beautiful *or* valuable. Why should they worry? If the two coincide, so much the better. Right? Unfortunately, no, because the financial motive has a bad reputation in the art world. No one wants others to think they are acting from economic motives alone.

And with good reason. If I'm in a position to profit from my judgment, I might be tempted to make the judgment that profits me rather than the one toward which the standards "we" all subscribe to impel me.

The Personal Problem

If I'm an individual member of an art world, I might worry that this possibility will show itself in my own actions. Suppose I'm a critic. I try to find, before others do (thus demonstrating my superior connoisseurship), artists who already have produced, or soon will produce, rare works of artistic genius. Suppose further that I'm successful in this; I find a few such people other knowledgeable members of that world have overlooked. At the moment, these artists, unknown and without reputation, can't sell their work for much. No one wants it. But *I* recognize the beauty and expressivity of their work and see how it sits precisely on what will eventually be the main line of the history of painting. I enjoy it for just those qualities. I love these paintings for what I regard as their intrinsic artistic value.

Furthermore, since these painters can't sell their work, when I buy paintings from them, I help them financially. They can use the money I exchange for their paintings to pay the rent, buy food and clothing, and buy more canvas and paints so they can make more paintings. Even further, if I (as a well-known critic) buy their work, this vouches for its value to other, more timid buyers. Seeing the work in my collection, they will more willingly take a chance and buy these artists' work too.

Just at this point, if I'm a conscientious member of this world, I can easily begin to have moral qualms. If this happens—if others buy work whose artistic value I've recognized ahead of the mob—then the value of the paintings I bought for a few dollars will go up. By expressing my critical judgment in the act of buying, I've lined my own pocket. I can't do the good things I would like to do—own beautiful works, help struggling artists—without running the risk that others will think I've done them for low financial motives, and having to deal with my own feeling that maybe I actually *have*.

The Organizational Problem

That's the personal problem. Every personal problem, as sociologists as various as C. Wright Mills and Everett C. Hughes have noted, has an organizational counterpart. If, Mills (1959) says, I'm depressed because I don't have a job, my personal problem is the individual version of the whole society's problem of not being able to provide employment for all willing workers. If, Hughes says, society has created criteria for a social status that lead to a contradiction—if we expect doctors to be male and white and then allow women or blacks to become doctors—the women and blacks who become doctors will experience this as a personal dilemma, as will the patients they come in contact with. And the hospitals and other medical organizations they work in will have an organizational contradiction on their hands (Hughes 1971, 141–50).

The organizational problem that corresponds to the personal problem of not being sure if I'm acting from good or bad motives when I acquire works of art is a problem of trust. If, as members of the art world, we conventionally assign responsibility for judgments of aesthetic worth to experts, we expect those experts to act in a disinterested way when they apply the standards we all share. We expect them to decide that this work is good and that one not so good because the accumulated weight of their knowledge, experience, and sensibility lead them to that judgment. We particularly want to know that they haven't made those judgments because they, or the institutions they represent, will profit from them.

That's most glaringly a problem with respect to the question of attribution (Moulin 1992, 18–21). We often have trouble knowing with certainty who painted a particular work, and the decision about who did affects the work's price. A painting by Rembrandt himself is much more valuable than one from the studio or school of Rembrandt painted by one of his associates (Alpers 1988). The great critic-connoisseurs of the nineteenth and early twentieth centuries made their reputations by delivering authoritative pronouncements on such questions, relying in part on their scholarly studies of the details of an artist's style and partly on a less describable sensibility, an indefinable ability to "know" that this painting was a "real" Titian as opposed to an apparently similar one that only looked like the real thing. But such connoisseurs often worked closely with dealers, especially dealers selling to gullible American millionaires, and present-day scholars find good reason to think that the prospect of a sale that would bring those critic-connoisseurs a large commission sometimes affected their critical judgment about an attribution. No one has to prove that such things actually happened. It's unnerving enough to know that they *could* happen for the problem to become an organizational one.

In the speculative market for contemporary art (as opposed to the blue-chip market in established Old and Modern Masters, to use Moulin's important distinction) the problem of attribution doesn't seem relevant. But the problem of aesthetic value is. Did this curator recommend this exhibit to his superiors and his governing board because it would enhance the value of his own holdings in the work of that artist or group? Did the curator collaborate with a dealer in assembling this exhibit, knowing that by enriching the dealer in that way he'd be arranging for the return of a similar favor another day? Museum staff and gallery owners so often collaborate in organizing exhibits that no one automatically frowns on the practice. But it raises these questions, to which, because of the way these values converge and blend (as Moulin described), no one knows the answers.

This chronic and perplexing problem takes many forms. The inputs to the process take varying forms, and participants often find novel solutions, not easily predictable in advance but following a social logic that we can reconstruct after the fact. Each new case can give us access to more versions of the process and its results. Thus, the story of Dennis Adrian, a well known critic and adviser to a group of affluent Chicagoans with advanced artistic tastes, expands our understanding of the potential out-comes this kind of value confusion can produce. And it shows the nuts and bolts of opening up black boxes and investigating their contents: how you do it and how the results produce more parts to look into and reckon with.

THE ADRIAN GIFT

Dennis Adrian early recognized the artistic gifts of a group of Chicago artists who came to be known first as "The Hairy Who" and later, more respectably, as the Chicago Imagists. The artists involved included Roger Brown, Jim Nutt, Ed Paschke, and others. As a result of Adrian's champi-oning of their work, and of the concurrent activities of the art critic of a major Chicago newspaper (Franz Schulze of the *Chicago Sun-Times*), a local gallery owner (Phyliss Kind), and a number of Chicago collectors (some of them active in creating the then-new Museum of Contemporary Art in Chicago) who Adrian advised on their art acquisitions, the work of this group was widely exhibited and collected and consequently rose substan-tially in value.

Adrian himself didn't have much money: "I have had to form a collec-tion with what are, not to put too fine a point on it, rather less than aver-age means" (Adrian 1982, 7). He lived simply, had no steady employment ("trying to exist as a critic and teacher of art history"), and didn't deal in pictures privately, as so many such critics and advisers do. But he had a large collection of these now valuable paintings, bought at the begin-nings of the artists' careers for relatively little. Some people might have thought, and in fact some people in some circles in Chicago's art commu-nity apparently did think, that his championing of the Chicago Imagists was a clever way of providing for his old age. No one used language that blunt, although the critic of the rival newspaper in Chicago, Alan Artner (1982) of the *Chicago Tribune*, came close in a review published when the collection was first exhibited. And, because these realities don't always wear their appropriate sociological labels on their sleeves, we have to read between the lines and interpret the innuendo and metaphor to under-stand the mechanisms at work. I'll provide some marginal commentary to make the meanings clearer:

Artner's Review	*Becker's Comments and Elucidation*
When [Adrian] began collecting them [the Chicago Imagists] more than a	This was written in 1982.

(continued)

Artner's Review	*Becker's Comments and Elucidation*

decade ago, the term ["maverick"] seemed appropriate; they were not yet marked by an accepted style. But in short order many of the young strays were rounded into herds and branded. Then began the campaign aimed at turning homegrown stock into international champions.

Artner uses a ranching metaphor to describe a plot to increase the value of the work of these local artists.

Adrian not only befriended and collected these so-called Imagists, but wrote on their behalf. Scarcely a week went by without a mention in his columns for the *Chicago Daily News* [another Chicago newspaper]. A book by a colleague [i.e., Schulze] had given them a corporate name and outlined their milieu. Adrian's effort was to provide a distinguished lineage.

Here are some of the deeds constituting the alleged conspiracy Artner is hinting at: publicity, the invention of a name and a "school," and the creation of an artistic lineage that legitimates the value placed on their work.

Everything from folk art to works of the Old Masters was invoked. It was not unusual to find Phil Hanson [an Imagist] compared to Paul Klee or Karl Wirsum [another Imagist] to Paul Klee. The game was merit by association and it characterized several catalogue essays written for the Museum of Contemporary Art.

The conspirators, Artner suggests, collude to place the paintings in the history of art by reference to accepted modern masters in the essays they prepare for museum exhibits.

But that was not enough. Just as some of the artists had been recommended to certain dealers, specific works were brought to the attention of collectors. So great was this advocacy that now, nearly 15 years later, one can trace the Adrian influence in collections from Hyde Park to East Lake Shore Drive to Glencoe. Of course, he had help; the critic is only one link in the nexus that leads to a "school" of art. But few others on the scene were in a position to give counsel on works-in-progress, urge that they be exhibited, issue written superlatives *and* provide personal advice for purchase.

As adviser, Adrian can influence collectors whose own actions are highly influential.

He alludes here to wealthy areas of Chicago where some of the collectors lived, allusions that "everyone" who participated in this local art world understood to refer to specific people.

Participants in such morality plays often use this kind of coded language, clear enough to the people involved but needing translation to make its connection to the moral meaning of what they're doing visible.

The process had as one of its outputs the variety of interpretations that participants made of each other's activities, which in turn became inputs in the further activities of everyone involved.

Adrian, then, is the artists' friend. If their work gave rise to hesitations or doubts, these were never expressed publicly. He maintained a level of enthusiasm that set his writing apart.

Since Adrian never criticizes the work of these artists, his judgments are suspect.

Helpful as it assuredly was for the artists, there nevertheless was a catch. An MCA [Museum of Contemporary Art] staff member, who has tended the collection, estimates that one-quarter of its artworks were presented to the critic as gifts. They bore witness to close association and were tokens anyone with reciprocal feeling would have prized. But a critic is not just anyone. To borrow a famous phrase, the position requires "the punctilio of an honor most exact." It dictates an allegiance to principles that friendships, however welcome, cannot help but test. It prescribes the apparent paradox of getting close to the art while remaining distant from the artist. Adrian has preferred to work with proximity all around.

Artner suggests Adrian's reasons for not being critical.

Here is the moral imperative: to be interested only in aesthetic values, ignoring other motives for appreciating and praising works. By being so close to the artists and others involved, Artner says, Adrian has rendered his motives suspect.

His collection includes few pieces by artists he doesn't know and none by artists he hasn't in some way encouraged. (To have gained the support of so keen-eyed a collector is encouragement in and of itself.) But one must never forget that Adrian is also a tastemaker, a role he has relished, occasionally to his detriment. So if any artist here has escaped the attention of other Chicago collectors, one may rest assured it will not be for long.

Finally, a prediction that Adrian's untoward behavior will continue in the future.

As the rest of the story shows, the underlying mechanisms, with so many possible inputs, can produce surprising results.

Adrian, perhaps stung by such talk, then made a great quixotic gesture. Though he needed the money and could ill afford the gesture, he bequeathed his entire collection, which had by then become quite valuable, to the Museum of Contemporary Art. By making this bequest, he assured himself but also, more importantly, the art world, that his judgment really was disinterested. Because he would not (unless he changed his will, always a possibility) profit from these works, his acquisition of them became solely an expression of his recognition of their artistic worth.

This bequest didn't satisfy Artner, who commented, "The museumization of the Adrian collection is, for some, the ultimate confirmation of his judgment." That's one possible interpretation: that the conspirators put the finishing touches on their work by having it all legitimated by an exhibition in a major museum. Alternatively, someone more charitably inclined could say, with equal justification, that Adrian, recognizing that both good and bad motives could be read into the same actions—his collecting and promoting of the work of these artists—chose to do the one thing that would prove he hadn't profited from his acquisitions and thus that he couldn't have acted from financial motives, only from aesthetic ones: he gave the works away. (Pierre-Michel Menger suggested to me that even such a grand gesture has overtones of self-aggrandizement: "The collector who prefers to keep his canvases rather than sell them to pay his medical bills perhaps makes a 'symbolic' bet on their future value since he will emerge more mature personally and known for having made an aesthetic choice that paid off.")

These events occurred so publicly that we can't expect to find straightforward statements by any of those involved, indicating what they intended by what they did. We have to interpret what they said in the light of our knowledge of the workings of art worlds. This gives the interpretation I'm about to make a circular character: the events I'm going to interpret constitute part of the knowledge we need to create the larger understanding of the art world that makes it possible to interpret and understand specific events such as Adrian's gift. That is, of course, methodologically unsound, but nevertheless necessary. The alternative is hopeless naïveté.

Adrian signaled his intentions not by anything he said about the major gift to the Museum of Contemporary Art, but by what he said in the catalog about an earlier event. He began his career as a collector, he said, with twentieth-century prints and drawings: Max Beckmann, Louis Corinth, Otto Dix, Joan Miró, Pablo Picasso. He also developed an interest in younger contemporary artists, especially those he had met in Chicago:

The increasing prices (and values) of works by modern masters pre-
cipitated a kind of unusual crisis for me. It happened that some serious
and extremely expensive medical problems left me frighteningly short
of money: the things on my walls started to swim in a haze of dollar
signs and quite a number of colleagues and friends said "Why don't you
just sell a few of these things and solve the problem?" It was somehow
impossible to explain to them that to sell a lot of things would seem
like a terrible defeat and loss. I had worked very hard to get them and
I wished them to remain works of art, not turn into "assets." For this
reason, after parting with two things which alleviated the immediate critical pressure, I decided to give my collection of 19th- and 20th-
century prints and drawings to the Art Institute of Chicago, to which
I had made an earlier gift at the request of the curator of that department. It was a step I have never regretted; these 40 or so things remain
works of art—not assets—and they remain accessible to me and others
interested in them. (Adrian 1982, 6)

Adrian here makes the point I have been making more impersonally.
He doesn't talk about his motives, only about the nature of the objects.
By giving his collection to a museum—thus, as Moulin has noted, taking
them out of the market more or less permanently—Adrian assured that
they would never be "assets," that they would not, *could* not, be understood as objects of economic acquisition. (Not having a large income,
Adrian didn't have the economic incentives created by American tax
laws, which give substantial tax reductions to donors of valuable objects
to public museums.) By giving them away, he had forgone the value critics might accuse him of having created for his own benefit by manipulating his position as a critic and adviser. Clearly, what was true of a small
collection of minor works by well-known artists is even more true of a
major collection of artists who now, as I write this in 2013, are established
masters (but perhaps not forever, since nothing guarantees that Adrian's
judgment will continue to be honored in the future).

That only such dramatic and drastic measures can provide the necessary assurance shows just how deeply and irremediably embedded in the
operations of art worlds and markets the confusion of values I'm discussing is, the degree to which it constitutes a mechanism (a black box) that
inputs acts of acquisition and outputs evaluations of artistic worth and
personal morality, which then operate as feedback to the actors involved
in their further judgments and purchases.

THE BLACK BOX OF ART WORLD JUDGMENTS:
MOULIN'S EXPLORATIONS OF OTHER ART MARKETS

That's the beginning, not the end, of the ramifications of Moulin's original insight into how artistic value comes into being. She complicated the story of that black box further by seeing how the system she isolated there worked in other art markets, in which some of the major inputs and outputs she'd described took different values.

Is that a surprise? Should we expect to find the things she found in the market for high art in these other markets? Will they display the same tendency to blur the line between aesthetic and economic motives and actions? Will the same kinds of ethical dilemmas and complications arise for actors in them?

This is where investigating mechanisms, rather than correlations, becomes particularly valuable. A lot of researchers hope to find stable correlations between more general and more easily measured causes and effects, between easily available socioeconomic variables like income, education, and class, and artistic tastes, showing what kinds of art people of various classes prefer, or display on the walls of their homes. (David Halle's [1993] critical assessment of this kind of work, based on his own research, shows that these correlations are neither as stable nor easily interpreted as has been claimed.)

The results of Moulin's comparison of a variety of art markets, instead, identify another phenomenon of interest, another element that takes different values and produces different results in the same basic mechanism. Moulin's early research didn't look for generalizations about what kinds of people made what kinds of adjustments to this situation. Instead, she looked for the kinds of conflict the confounding of the values she'd described produced. And she identified the crucial mechanisms involved as conventional practices that produced patterns of scarcity, shaping both economic and aesthetic values.

When I wanted to know why someone would be so "irrational" as to give away valuable artworks that he could have traded for money he needed badly, I could find useful leads, clues to what to look for and where to look for it, in the confusion of values Moulin had identified as present in the markets contemporary art is traded in. Using that particular conflict as an input to specific processes in the art market made sense of what otherwise seemed an inexplicable output, Dennis Adrian's surprising donation of his collection to a museum. Her analysis of these processes turned Adrian's action into a researchable problem and told me where to look for the solution.

In a later paper (1978) called "The Genesis of Artistic Rarety," Moulin

exploited her own findings about the market in contemporary art to identify and solve an entire family of art-market problems, using as tools the
contents of the black box whose workings she had dissected for the market in contemporary art. She looked for, and found, other worlds, whose
players exchanged other kinds of artworks, and she traced variations in
the kinds of value attributed to those works, the processes that led the
players to the judgments they made of them, and the widely varying market forms and activities that resulted. None of her findings suggested that
these connections were logically or historically "necessary," or that they
would continue to exist.

They did something much more interesting, identifying scarcity as a
variable, rather than an unvarying element of art markets. Investigating
several kinds of markets related to the one in paintings showed the possibilities of variation in the numbers and varieties of possible art objects, in
the value actors found in them, and in the markets that arose to trade in
them. She expected that the tools she had already created would explain,
as well, forms the world hadn't produced yet, or might never produce, in
addition to the great variety of already existing markets. Armed with the
possibilities her study alerts us to, we can understand a fuller range of
market organizations and of associated motivations and judgments. The
black box producing artistic value got more, rather than less, complicated
as a result of her analysis.

Her 1978 article first describes the "classical" art market that she analyzed in her earlier book, in which collectors, dealers, museum curators,
auctioneers, art historians, and others cooperate to collectively, each
group in its way, validate the worth of the works they buy and sell. History
had led to the juncture she studied, in which market participants identified as an instance of art an object that was neither artisanal—the work
of skilled craftsmen collaborating to turn out the works people and institutions (the king and the Church, for instance) had hired them to make,
which required great skill but did not display the unique individual mark
of the artist of genius who had made it—nor an industrial product, one of
a potentially infinite series coming off some version of a factory assembly
line. Participants in this market required the work to be the unique product of an identifiable individual's artistic sensibility and, further, insisted
that it not be useful in any way other than as an artistic object. The whole
apparatus guaranteed these attributes. The provenances reputable dealers
provided proved that the work came from the hand of a recognized master; historians of art testified that the work indeed exhibited the uniquely
identifiable marks of the master's hand; museum officials accepted these
guarantees and proudly displayed the work in their buildings; critics de-

bated such works' meaning; and collectors bought them as objects of display and enjoyment. Because the artists who had produced the works had died, or soon would, the supply of works accepted as artistic was strictly limited; and because they had been carefully made of durable materials, they would last for a long time. So, "The work of art is the ideal type of a rare [economic] good in strictly limited supply whose value is therefore determined by demand" (Moulin 1978, 242). The holder of such a good has a monopoly and commands a monopoly price. Moulin considers a number of variables that affect the relative artistic worth of individual works, which I won't go into here.

Then she describes four other markets, in which the variables that shape the market for Old and Modern Masters—quality, reputation, scarcity, and so on—play varying roles, producing differently organized mixtures of economic and aesthetic activities, all aiming to create the same kind of valuable scarcity. The world had performed an experiment for her, and for us, producing these variations on the mechanism she'd found, in which different inputs into the processes she'd identified let her (and us) see what differences in markets resulted from these variations. The historical "experiments" she took up included traditional popular culture, ethnographic art, contemporary art made to frustrate the standard art-market operations that produce scarcity and monopoly, and photography. She uses each as an analyzable variation on the processes that shape a market (the inner workings of the black box). The analysis identifies the variables, the range of their variation, and the things affecting each variation, all of these becoming part of the analytic apparatus now available to us.

TRADITIONAL POPULAR CULTURE. Ordinary members of older societies (not, for instance, kings and queens or very rich people) used their typical household objects every day for the most ordinary uses (cooking pots to cook with, washing and drying apparatus to deal with dirty clothes, etc.). Never valued as works of art but now replaced by industrially produced objects, these objects have lost their utility and, over time, have been thrown away because they wore out. They're rare not because there were so few of them but because so few survived. Their value comes from being typical members of their now almost extinct class of objects and, as such, worth more because of this historically produced scarcity (rather than for any aesthetic reason). All sorts of people—"local scholars, members of local learned societies, passionate regionalists, volunteers at local folklore museums" (Moulin 1978, 245)—collaborate to find new value in these formerly ordinary objects, seeing them as priceless relics of a past long gone. National museums, organized to collect and celebrate them (the Musée des Arts et Traditions Populaires opened in Paris in its own building in 1969), also serve to warrant them as valuable and collectible, and to distinguish the more valuable from the less valuable, providing a sort of scholarly apparatus to sustain the activities of dealers in secondhand goods and antiques. (I'll discuss a more personal and eccentric American museum specializing in such objects in chapter 7.) But the machinery supporting this market is haphazardly organized and not well regulated, making the calculation of value less sure than in the models it's based on.

ETHNOGRAPHIC OBJECTS. Ethnographic objects have many of the same characteristics: used for everyday purposes in the societies they originated in, destroyed when no longer useful for those purposes. For European and American painters and sculptors, who have for more than a century turned to works of "primitive art" for inspiration, these objects, unlike those of popular culture, have a de facto claim to artistic interest. Individuals in a few scholarly disciplines—primarily anthropologists and museum curators—attest to ethnographic objects' value as objects of both scientific interest and artistic merit; they make the crucial distinctions of quality that create a "residual scarcity" enabling interested parties to sell the chosen objects for appreciable amounts. (Debary and Roustan [2012] discuss the Quai Branly Museum in Paris as an example of this kind of collection and the problems it produces.)

As in the case of ordinary household objects from our own society's past, people operating in these art worlds use the limited number of objects actually conserved and their specialist-verified artistic quality to decrease the number available as objects worth collecting, thus increasing their potential price.

CONTEMPORARY ART. Some contemporary artists, and the dealers who handle their work, take advantage of the constant change in ideas and standards of excellence in art to manipulate the scarcity of what would otherwise be ordinary objects of no special value. These artists use their de facto monopoly on their own work, which takes on great importance in an art world that values priority, being the first to do something (tackle a new subject, use a new technique, try out a new way of manipulating ideas), as an asset. They give their work to a dealer, who becomes the temporary monopolist. Often skilled in manipulating appearances and events to this end, the dealer creates a demand among collectors and museum personnel. In this world, control of information creates a restriction of the supply in the short run (no one knows what will happen with this artist or work in the long run) that leads to short-term competition and a run-up in prices. At least, that's what the artists and dealers hope for.

They try to manipulate the existing system by producing either *nothing* or *multiples*, both of which attack the idea of uniqueness at the heart of the gallery system and thus try to discredit scarcity. Some artists make multiples, using industrial processes to abolish the unique work by making many identical copies, multiplying it rather than destroying it. In the end, of course, they always do limit the number of copies and create scarcity that way. But Marcel Duchamp's transformations of ordinary mass-produced objects into art by signing snow shovels and porcelain urinals made that move to control supply not fully workable. In its most fully realized form, this form of art makes the artist's thought the main thing, devaluing the physical object, which becomes just one possible embodiment of that idea, as a commodity. This is an art of "nothing," of ideas sometimes embodied in actions undertaken in accord with them.

But, as Moulin says, "the art of 'no matter what' is not the work of 'no matter who'" (Moulin 1978, 242). These fateful actions produce value only if the maker is someone everyone already recognizes as an artist. And these artists can and do turn their ideas into salable commodities by putting them on paper, documenting them in photographs or films, and otherwise creating objects that bear the unique mark of their maker, through a signature or in some other way. "In the moments when the effective scarcity of the work and its autonomy disappear simultaneously, artistic scarcity is socially recreated in order to be given economic value" (249).

PHOTOGRAPHY. Since its invention in the nineteenth century (the "officially" recognized date is 1839), photography has created controversy because of its ambiguous relationship to the ordinarily accepted criteria of what it takes to be a work of art. Early critics argued that such a mechanical process could never reveal the all-important unique hand and sensibility of the artist at work, thus could never be unique in the way the conventional art market required "real" artworks to be. Others, however, accepted photographs as sufficiently artistic to be part of the world of fine art exhibitions, and galleries opened selling fine art photographs alongside paintings and sculptures whose claim to be art couldn't be argued with. It proved relatively easy to justify photography as revealing the unique vision of the photographer, thus satisfying the first requirement necessary in constructing an art market.

Daguerreotypes, the first photographs, existed as unique objects that couldn't be reproduced but were soon replaced by less cumbersome negative-based processes, which could be. So it was harder to control the supply of prints, since there was no way to limit the potentially limitless number of prints you could make from a single negative. There was also no way to guarantee that negatives couldn't be copied indiscriminately. Organizers of markets in photographic art have never dealt with this problem completely successfully. But they've found substitutes for a guaranteed limited supply. An image printed by the photographer who made the negative it was printed from has, by the conventions of this market, more value than one made by someone else. But in the case of some important photographers who didn't habitually make their own prints, dealers successfully substituted the requirement that the print had been made "under the supervision" of the photographer, which allowed eminences like Henri Cartier-Bresson (who never did his own printing) and Dorothea Lange to sign prints so made and then limit the number of signed prints.

In another direction, "vintage prints," made by the photographer at the time the negative was made, could be differentiated from later ones made by the photographer or others and could thus be limited. The death of the photographer put an absolute limit on how many such authentic prints, revealing the artist's hand and/or intention at work, could exist, and created the condition under which a monopoly price could be asked.

Moulin's general summary of the situation in these other markets is that scarcity is a necessary condition for artworks to have economic value but, as she says, it's not enough: "It is not the same as the pure scarcity found in the market for postage stamps" (1978, 254). Other conditions, suggested by the several cases she examines and compares, complicate our understanding of possible inputs to and outputs from the black box in which art markets create artistic value. Moulin describes the multiple ways the scarcity necessary to the operation of a profitable market can come about. The limitation in the number of objects identifiably different can be created by the operation of historical processes of the destruction of things once thought useless that later come for some reason to be seen as valuable; or by the recognition of a new criterion, such as the artist's signature, that can give the necessary unique value to any object at all; or by the importation of criteria from other realms of art. Photography dealers tried for a while to create scarcity the way dealers in other kinds of works on paper had, by "canceling" (defacing) the original negative from which copies could be made. That had always worked for etchings and lithographs, but the possibility that an identical negative might have been made created the possibility that more prints could still be made. Dealers in ethnographic artifacts had to contend with artisans from the ethnic groups involved who were happy to make as many copies of household objects as tourists wanted to buy, and as a result dealers invented the criterion of "having been used for its intended purpose," so that a grease-stained, worn sculpture of a sacred figure that had been used in an indigenous household could be sold for far more than a brand new spotless version.

So Moulin's investigation of further cases created more categories, more ways of getting the same work done, more kinds of people participating in setting whatever standards came to apply in the markets in which these objects were traded. The result of her work wasn't just new knowledge about organizations, knowledge that hadn't been available before, but also descriptions of new mechanisms that affected the workings and results of any market in which people bought and sold art.

ADDING HISTORY AND CLASS

More things vary in the art market than even Moulin's comprehensive analysis suggested. I used some events in the world of contemporary art in New York circa 1980 to add still other possibilities to the mechanisms in the black box governing the operation and outcomes of art markets. This case adds, as an analytic dimension, the kinds of information that market participants have about the artworks people were trading and the social categories of people engaged in that trading, which, though not unexplored in Moulin's thinking, could take many more values than the ones she had assigned to them. Her cases focused on the accuracy of information about the authenticity of paintings: were they really works by the artists supposed to have painted them? Or were they copies and fakes, made by others who wanted to pass them off as done by artists with great names? Were they the work of "the master" himself, or had they been done by an assistant? In some of Moulin's cases, authenticity was more complicated. Yes, the artist employed assistants who did some of the work, but they did it under the artist's direction; once established, that fact validated the worth of the work.

The case I'm going to consider now added still another dimension and mechanism to the workings of the black box that produces artistic value: the consequences of variation in the ways information about opinions about value circulated.

The way dealers and others publicize artworks affects how artists make those works and how others understand and appreciate them. The incident that inspired me to complicate the developing model of the black box producing artistic value occurred in the 1980s in New York. People interested in contemporary art—collectors, dealers, curators, and critics, not to mention artists themselves—began to take that idea seriously in the 1980s as they worried about what an alleged mammoth increase in the amount of "hype" and merchandising associated with contemporary visual art was doing to that art and the artists who made it.

My new "case," the flurry of interest and controversy about "hype," highlights the workings of class and prestige and of "old" and "new" money in the making and unmaking of art organizations and reputations, as well as the element of timeliness of information and its effects on investment strategies. I'm adding those dimensions to the explanatory system Moulin described. The events I'm going to discuss now revolve around a simple question: who knows what when? The variation provided by the range of possible answers to questions like that exposed more processes and elements to be included in any understanding of events in art worlds centered on collecting valuable objects, and that variation tied the internal workings of art worlds to systems of class, power, and prestige in ways far more complicated than those suggested by simple questions of social-class differences in taste.

THE AMERICAN ART MARKET IN 1983. Writing in the *New Yorker*, Calvin Tompkins noted that a painting by Julian Schnabel had been sold at auction for ninety-three thousand dollars and remarked,

> For a number of people, the Schnabel sale neatly epitomized the 1982–83 art season, which has been dominated by the attention paid to non-expressionist painting and by complaints that this attention was the product of publicity, "hype," and rampant commercialism. (1983, 80)

Roberta Smith said, in the *Village Voice* (1982), after suggesting that Schnabel deserved a lot of credit for his accomplishments:

> At the same time, Schnabel has brought a circus-like atmosphere to his art and his career which has clouded the view. In his public persona, his preposterous titles, and the scaled-up emptiness of his worst work, he has acted out the Romantic old-fashioned idea of what it means to be an artist in such larger than life, often hilarious terms that he has turned himself and his work—for the time being quite hopelessly merged—into a cliché, making a mockery of the very things he has dignified: himself, his art, and painting in general.

John Bernard Myers voiced the same worry this way in the *New York Review of Books*:

But how then to account for the enthusiastic reception now being given a wholly new batch of painters, around New York for only a few years, all of them in their early thirties or late twenties? [New, that is, compared to such aging stars as Willem DeKooning, Sam Francis, Roy Lichtenstein, and Frank Stella, among others, who dominated the market for contemporary art at the time.] Variously called New Realists or NeoExpressionists, they have "arrived," from Germany, Italy, and the provinces of America. The new painters, for all their brashness and ineptitude, have attracted a lively market which admires big, splashy, noisy, turbulent canvases, filled with soft-porn and hard-core banality. The new collectors are willing to pay handsomely in the tens of thousands, and do. (1983,)

Complicating the workings of the input-output system helps us understand and interpret these complaints.

DISTRIBUTION SYSTEMS. Fully developed art worlds have elaborate distribution systems that get the artist's work to people who might be interested in it, usually (but not necessarily) trying in the process to make some money for the artist and others so that the work can continue to be produced. In earlier parts of this chapter I've more or less taken the existence of those systems for granted. Tompkins and Smith and Myers were now complaining about changes in the distribution system that, presumably, they had until that point considered OK. (Some of these changes affected the "Hairy Who"/Dennis Adrian case considered earlier.)

Whose cooperation do visual artists need to distribute their work? A number of professional groups usually operate simultaneously, and their cooperation can take many different forms. Each has to do the jobs Haskell (1963) outlined in his analysis of one such form, patronage: provide financial support and give artists an adequate place to display their work and a knowledgeable audience whose members understand what they are up to. At one extreme, private patronage, while less common in the twentieth century and beyond, still occasionally happens (Marcel Duchamp was a classic twentieth-century example). Public patronage exists as fellowships and commissions, but it provides no one with a steady, dependable income. Public sale for the mass market occurs for kitsch only, sold in the rows of galleries along San Francisco's Fisherman's Wharf, parts of Chicago's Michigan Avenue, and in the lobbies of Hilton hotels.

Painters want their work distributed, in some large part, so that it can be completed by being viewed and evaluated by relevant actors. No one knows work that isn't distributed; no one thinks well of it or thinks it has historical importance. It has no reputation and, as a result, no market value. In this circular process, no one distributes what doesn't have a good reputation. What distribution systems, with all their built-in professional biases, do affects judgments about what constitutes great or important art.

The concern about "hype" arose from the workings of the latest wrinkle, at the time, in distribution. The gallery-dealer-auction system, which assumed its present form in nineteenth-century France and has been the standard pretty much since then, was changing. As it now operates, and has operated for the past century, the system had the effect Moulin described, totally confounding artistic/aesthetic and financial worth.

As Moulin explained, remember, the market in old and contemporary masters is relatively stable. Works once thought very important seldom become completely unimportant. If nothing else, they continue to be valuable, whatever their artistic merit, because of their historical importance. Of course, their actual market value fluctuates, as does the value of all collectibles, in line with the ups and downs of the financial markets. In particular, during recessions and depressions, people who need cash sell art and prices drop precipitously. This has little to do with aesthetics, resulting from changes in the investment policies of people who might otherwise be buying art.

The market in contemporary art, according to Moulin, is more speculative. Players in that market have more trouble answering the big questions: "Is it good?" and "What is it worth?" We can best understand what goes on not so much by referring to questions of art and aesthetics but by comparison to the phenomenon of new issues in the stock market. In both cases, information, and especially inside information that others don't yet have, plays a crucial role. (Marvin Scott [1968] describes an interesting parallel in the way experts in horse racing gather and use information that others don't have or, more accurately, haven't bothered to get, to win their bets.) You make money and enhance your reputation for fine aesthetic perceptions by making judgments about artists and works that others will only later accept as authoritative. New artists and new stock issues have yet to prove their worth. They prove it by becoming attractive to knowledgeable people. The way this happens isn't new, and it has always involved the manipulation of information.

Artists, dealers, critics, curators, and collectors all collaborate, as we've seen, in well-known ways to make new works valuable. Critics influence others by writing about, praising, and buying for their own collections the work of artists hitherto not well known. Some people who find the critic's judgments valuable will be collectors with reputations for knowing a good thing, whose purchases in themselves make the work more "important" and valuable. The collectors' purchases embolden a dealer, and together these influence others to buy the artist's work. If this circular process continues, after it has gone on for a while, a museum's curators may decide the artist deserves an exhibition, and the work, with the cachet of having been exhibited in such a place, becomes even more valuable.

John Bernard Myers found it difficult to understand who was the prime mover in this process:

> The question, however, of who creates the "market" for high-priced contemporary painting is not so simple as it would at first seem. Perhaps the most widespread view is that the market is the result of favorable reviews. Critics give people certainty of taste and knowledge. If enough writers say an artist is superior, then no doubt he is taken to be. Thus, there are those who maintain that the prestige and fortune of the Abstract Expressionists, among them Pollock, Rothko, Gottlieb, and Still, were created by Clement Greenberg. . . . [But Greenberg] has liked a wide variety of painters and sculptors, many of whom did not become famous or make money. (1983)

Myers goes on to make the same point about the alleged influence of reviews in the *New York Times*: some artists who its critic Hilton Kramer praised became very successful; others didn't.

Myers's problem in fact had a simple solution. It doesn't matter who starts the process. But it only works if whoever starts it persuades the other participants in the value-creating process to cooperate. What leads to that cooperation is often a bandwagon effect, in which (to put it in the best light) others come to see what the prescient early entrants into that particular market saw. In a worse light, we could say that now that everyone seems to agree on the worth of this new work, no one wants to be left out in the cold, perhaps financially but certainly in the matter of taste and the ability to see what everyone else sees and values. (Ashley Mears [2011, 156] described the same process in the way a young woman who didn't look very different from the hundreds of others working as fashion models suddenly became "the model of the year" in New York one season, purely as the result of one agent booking her for a large number of appearances at one time. This sudden spurt in her bookings convinced other agents that she was "hot," so they booked her too, and then she was hot, on her way to being "the model of the year.")

This kind of activity calls into question the equation of artistic and financial worth. People buy "hot" young artists hoping to have bought something that will simultaneously appreciate substantially in financial value *and* come to have a permanent reputation as a sterling example of the way the history of art is going. Reputations are so volatile that, as in any speculative market, no one knows whether they reflect "true worth" or "mere hype."

The minute the automatic connection between aesthetic and financial value comes into question, it opens up other questions. Especially questions of corruption. Are critics (like Dennis Adrian) who invest in work they find wonderful only feathering their own nests? Are collectors who sit on the boards of museums doing the same by recommending exhibits that will enhance the value of their speculative purchases? As we've seen, the mixture of values is so complete that pursuing one estimable objective, wanting to own and support fine art, is to pursue the other, trying to make a killing. (You can see that earlier models of the black box still come in handy.)

Artists, of course, know all this very well. So some, perhaps most, of them can begin to create their work with an eye to how it will fit into the distribution system. Dickens, after all, wrote his narratives so that they reached dramatic climaxes in rhythms that coincided with the length of the serial publications in which they appeared. (Sutherland 1976, 21–24). Composers write pieces of a specified length and instrumentation because that's what the systems that distribute their music—the symphony orchestra and concert hall or the avant-garde and the universities and music schools—can handle. In fact, artists almost invariably create their work with an eye to how it will be distributed.

The reason all this is a problem is that no one can be sure whether the system and the people involved in it are corrupt or not. Everyone wants to know something that hasn't happened yet: the development of an artistic career and a body of work, the development of a corresponding reputation. No one can predict either of these things with any reasonable assurance of being right. The artist's development can't be manipulated, although people can try to influence it through criticism, suggestion, coercion, or temptation. The techniques of reputation-influencing are somewhat better understood, although not as well as practitioners of public relations like to insist.

The key variable, as in the stock market or at the race track, is information (a new variable this case gives us to incorporate into our black box model). Some people, of course, may have better judgment than others. But others, whatever the quality of their judgment, may have better information. And, as the Adrian case showed, it may be more important to know who's buying, or interested in buying, a certain artist's work than to know whether the work is "really" any good or not. Nor is that a matter of corruption because, after all, we usually rely on the judgment of people more informed than we are. The suspicion of corruption arises when the information isn't public. In the stock market that's called "insider knowledge," and you can go to jail for trying to profit from it.

The language of the contemporary art world has this speculative ring to it. No one wants to wait for the judgment of history, to take that risk. That will mean missing out. You won't be able to have the beautiful painting you would love to live with if you don't buy it now, because others will see how good it is and its price will go sky-high. You won't be able to make a killing waiting for the judgment of history, either; it will be old news and worth nothing.

This explains the complaints about "hype." The mechanisms of publicity can be used to create a surge of "mass behavior," a collective feeling that the boat is pulling out and we're not on it. I'm using "mass behavior" as a technical term for the process by which large numbers of people individually decide that some particular course of action seems a good one and all those individual choices converge on the same line of activity: they all buy Toyotas that year or decide to wear blue jeans to work or cut their hair in a new way or grow beards. No group gets together and decides to do any of that. It "just happens." Decisions of that kind are especially open to influence by advertising, publicity, and other communications aimed at people as individuals, as opposed to people as members and functionaries of communities and organizations. (The best discussions of this process are Blumer 1951, 185–89; 1969; and Lieberson 2000.)

This points to what might be a historically unique feature of the contemporary art world (though I doubt it). The art world has, historically, been a community of taste. Its members knew each other, met at parties and clubs, knew each other's tastes and possessions. They competed with each other, to be sure, for priority: to know first what others would eventually know, to esteem and collect a new kind of work marginally ahead of others, and so on. But they competed in a game they all knew with people they knew. They knew what "everyone" thought, because they knew "everyone" and couldn't be led to think something was valuable unless the other members of their community agreed. They never had to worry about being surprised by news of something that had happened in the world of art without their knowing about it. Hype can't occur in a community like that.

Hype can occur, however, when an arena of social activity is not a community but rather is populated by a mass, in the technical sense I used above: people who don't know each other but whose behavior nevertheless converges on the same ideas and activities. Without a community of taste to dominate the activity of the art world, people can use the techniques of commercialized publicity to reach isolated individuals (or small coteries, much the same thing) and make them feel that something important is going on that they know nothing about. Then reputations can be created that may be based on no more than talk and rumor. So the situation decried by these critics is one in which the art market and world have grown to the point where the community isn't so exclusive and closed as to make that impossible.

John Bernard Myers described the situation that so appalled him this way (and he probably spoke for many others):

> What a gaggle of go-getters these turned out to be—all over town. The most nauseating group was the young married women with time on their hands specializing in "art for offices"—sometimes whole suites of offices where masses of brightly colored prints, drawings, and gouaches decorated the walls of jerry-built high-rises. Some specialized in cheering up doctors' and dentists' waiting rooms or placing kinetic light-ups and movables opposite operating chairs. Other entrepreneurs concentrated on the big corporate patrons. They engaged themselves in filling the lobbies, courtyards, plazas, and terraces of the new glass and steel edifices rising along Madison, Park, and Third Avenues. Invariably this was done with tangles of bent cable, slabs of Corten steel, high-buffed stainless, or massive hunks of granite, both round and square.
>
> Another group specialized in tapestries to lighten the grimness of vestibules and stairwells. Somewhere, in Ecuador perhaps, natives were hooking away at big zigzags, arcs, circles, rectangles, or polka dots of eye-filling intensity to soften the impact of elevator banks. New business was pouring into foundries in Long Island, upper New York State, or New Jersey to "fabricate" jumbo-sized constructions by artists famous, near-famous, or quite unknown, who prepared mole-sized maquettes for elephantine productions. These celebrations could be found on the lawns of benign industrial plants, secure amid the expensive landscape engineering, visible proof of business supporting art and improving the community. (1983)

This angry tone and bitter language have occurred often enough in social history, every time an old elite loses its privileged position in some world. It's the way WASP citizens of New York and Philadelphia reacted to finding the streets of their cities filled with peasant immigrants bawling at each other in strange languages. It's the way the old French elite of Quebec felt and talked when their towns filled up with the English managers and technicians who ran the new factories, people who had never heard of the old family names, which, after all, meant nothing to them. It's the way the elites of rural California felt when the managers of the large corporations that had bought their lettuce ranches showed no interest in preserving the old systems of deference that characterized their towns. (And why should the heads of those corporations have worried about such things? Their children wouldn't go to school with the children of braceros.)

This is the language of a displaced elite. W. I. Thomas once remarked that social disorganization is a stage between two stages of organization. The upheaval created by people like those Myers observed would eventually be replaced by a new kind of organization of the art world, in which a new sort (or maybe new sorts) of community would dominate taste, collecting, and all the associated activities, perhaps along the lines Myers so feelingly described.

And so we can add still another element to the black box of the art market: the element of changes in social class structure and organization, the variations in the uniformity of acceptance of hierarchies of taste, prestige, and power that include, as one of their side effects, influencing the markets of art and the associated reputations of artists, artworks, collectors, and all the other kinds of people involved.

This is how we can apply the description of an input-output system to a situation it hasn't been applied to before, producing new dimensions (in this case, the timeliness of information and the relative homogeneity and cohesiveness of a collecting class) that from then on become part of the "normal" apparatus for the analysis of the next case(s) someone applies them to. We don't finish the analytic process by demonstrating a conclusion the system predicts. We continue the never-finished analytic process by looking for new cases in which information might vary both in obvious ways (how timely? shared among how many people?) and in ways this case didn't alert us to. The variety of ways people have organized these situations will always be greater than our imaginations can invent.

6 *Imagining Cases*

So far, I've been discussing reasoning from real cases, cases based on solid research (or at least personal acquaintance) that we can extrapolate from to make good guesses about what we will find elsewhere. But we can often make good use of cases not so well verified, not verified at all, or even clearly imaginary and hypothetical.

Everett C. Hughes, who I learned to do sociology from, loved reasoning from cases. He often started a class with a story he read in the morning paper, telling us about an event that had happened far from our homes in Chicago and then asking a lot of questions about it. One morning he read us an account of a race riot in Durban, South Africa, in which crowds of black South Africans attacked the East Indian quarter of the city, filled with small merchants who ran the groceries and other convenience stores where these black inhabitants bought their necessities. Why, he wanted to know, had they attacked the Indians? Weren't their real oppressors the white Afrikaners who controlled the government, which vastly curtailed their civil liberties and put them at risk of their lives much of the time? Why didn't they attack them?

Of course, we didn't know the answer to that. We had the proper sentiments: the Afrikaners, bad people doing bad things, deserved any punishment that came their way. But most of us hadn't even known that any East Indians lived in South Africa, although a very famous person, Mohandas Gandhi, had once fit that description. So we couldn't imagine why the black population was attacking the Indians. Then Hughes raised another interesting question: the news reported that the rioting mobs had burned down the stores and homes of the East Indians. What kind of houses did these people live in, that could be burned down so easily? We couldn't answer that question either.

Hughes, with the vast array of cases he had piled up over many years of random reading, could. He told us a fascinating story about the role of the middleman in highly stratified societies like South Africa. The people in the top level of societies with such caste systems don't want to dirty themselves (the "dirtiness" will be a ritual uncleanness, but contaminating and degrading just the same) performing services for people in the lower level. But someone has to provide food and other goods and services for them or they won't be able to exist. A third group, belonging to neither the top or the bottom, does this dirty work. In many societies around the world, Chinese immigrants played this role. In others, Jews did that work. As one consequence of such an arrangement, members of that middle stratum appear as the immediate oppressors of the lowest group. The black population didn't see white Afrikaners oppressing them. They saw the Indian landlords who charged them rents they couldn't afford, who sold them food and other necessities at prices their meager wages barely covered. So when something ignited a riot, the Indians lived close by and were the people they could attack. And did.

The question about the buildings burning as they did produced another story about the kinds of houses built in such areas and why they took the form and used the materials they did. I don't remember the details of that lesson, just that there was one and Hughes taught it to us.

We students learned at least two things from this. Any story, any event, anywhere, at any time, arrived at by any method, could become the object of a fruitful sociological analysis. And, just as important, if you wanted to make interesting sociology out of the morning newspaper, you'd better know a lot about what was going on all over the world, because the richest sociological possibilities lay in the smallest details of those stories.

Another class session taught us another interesting lesson. Hughes was expounding his ideas about some event in a central European country—again, I don't remember the details—and in the middle of his analysis, a student held up his hand and said, "I'm sorry to tell you, Professor Hughes, but I've just been in that country for a year and the facts are quite different from what you're telling us." Some of our professors would have taken serious offense if anyone had talked to them like that. But Hughes just said, somewhat grumpily, "It isn't like that? Well, what is it like?" And the knowledgeable student gave him, and us, the details as he had seen them. To which Hughes said, "Well, that's interesting," and went on with a new and different analysis that took this newer and presumably more accurate description into account and led to a different explanation,

We learned an equally important lesson from that. The truth of the observation that led to the analysis didn't matter. Didn't matter? No— not at this stage of the game. The utility of such observations came from the possibilities they evoked, not from the facts they might be taken to have proved. How could that be true? Isn't science supposed to produce true findings and general propositions based on and supported by such findings? Apparently not, because after the alleged facts had been demolished, the ideas remained—not as proven fact, but as possibilities suggesting dimensions and elements that, in some form and at some value, seemed likely to be part of whatever was going on in the black box that produced the events you were interested in: a riot in Durban, unrest in a central European country, or any of the other phenomena that came up for discussion in that exciting class.

Hughes recommended, too, that we look to fiction as a source of possibilities we could explore to see what dimensions and elements might be present in something that interested us. He didn't mean that in the way many other sociologists did, which was to say that novels were a sort of second-rate sociology, a sociology without the emphasis on coherent theory and rigorous testing of ideas but nevertheless often presenting interesting interpretations of social issues that more rigorous scientific work could make epistemologically respectable. He meant that they could be as useful as a set of rigorously obtained facts for the specific task of generating some researchable ideas or, better yet, some clues to what was going on in some process that interested you. The facts might be all wrong, but that didn't matter for this specific purpose.

We can think of the processes that interest us—the things going on in the black box, as it works with the inputs it gets and produces the outputs we want to understand—as a huge tree of branching possibilities, a chart of all the possible ways something might go. Starting at A, it could go to B or C, and each of those might produce a few branches (B going to D and E, C going to F and G)—all of these possibilities for what the result might be—and each of those might branch the same way. It's easy to see that in a short while the number of possibilities is, practically speaking, endless. If you think, as Hughes did and I do, that we can't, realistically speaking, predict what will come out of such a welter of possibilities, but that we can talk about where the branches appear and what form they take and what the processes in the black box seem to be as they work with these quite varying inputs to produce the varying outputs they do produce—if you think that way, then more-or-less fictional accounts can help you find clues as well as fact can. So can, to push the point to the extreme, total fiction: imaginary cases.

I've written about this before. *Telling about Society* (Becker 2007, 151–66) describes a class of reports on society that needn't be true to be interesting and scientifically useful. That class includes mathematical models and ideal types, both familiar tools of social science thinking, but also what I called there "parables," a category I'd like to broaden here by just calling them "stories," that is, fictions. An imaginary or fictional report doesn't give an accurate account of anything real, the kind we expect from scientific investigations. Instead, it tells you how something real would work *if* it worked the way the mathematical model or ideal type or what the story describes does. The report isn't true, but it's useful in pointing to the kind of things your research should look for and focus on.

The rest of this chapter calls attention to some imagined stories like this, fictions of one kind or another, to make the way they work and the ways we can use them clearer. The discussion of the problem of organizational stability that follows uses an imagined case to make a theoretical point about why social arrangements don't change all the time, as it seems from some reasonable points of view they might. I invented the case of the flute player it contains, but its imaginary character doesn't interfere with its usefulness. The discussion of the relations between social scientists and the people they study that follows, relying on a less peaceful example, shows how a fiction can clarify the dimensions of one of social science's big research problems.

THE POWER OF INERTIA

Stability poses a perennial problem in the study of social organization. I'll begin with the world of so-called "classical" music. One of the remarkable things about that world is how stable it has been for a long time. Things have changed, but not much. Orchestras of about the same size have been playing the same repertoire, with occasional additions, for almost a hundred years, on instruments not very different from those players used almost a hundred years ago. The personnel change, but the new ones look and sound much like the old ones. The United States still imports conductors, mostly from Europe, though it doesn't import orchestral players as much as it used to. The public hasn't changed much. Rich people pick up most of the tab, and some members of the upper-middle class attend regularly. More people hear music in the twenty-first century than did, say, in the 1930s, because of the ubiquity of radio, television, and recordings. Fewer people make music in their own homes, perhaps for the same reason. So the classical music world and its ways of doing things are, all in all, quite stable.

Stability poses a theoretical problem for sociology. Any activity—making music is the example here—can be done in many different ways. I like the John Cage position, according to which (I heard him say this once in a public performance but have never found it in print) "Music is the moral evaluation of noise." That is, any sound or combination of sounds can be music, can be thought of as music—any sound made any way, with the help of any object as an instrument, with or without the intention of the maker. It's music if you listen to it in a way that makes it music, paying close attention, and in the mood Samuel Johnson described as "willing to be pleased." Our conventional ways of making and listening to music—the orchestras and concerts and recordings and all the rest of it—represent the choice of a very few from among all the possible ways of doing those things. The theoretical problem is to understand the narrowness of our choices of how to make music when there are so many possibilities. (The extensive literature on the sociology of music is reviewed critically in Hennion 1993, 11–18, and elsewhere.)

Sociologists differ on how to solve this problem. One variety of sociological thinking takes the stability of social organizations as natural, the ordinary state of things (sometimes called the equilibrium point). Institutions, on this view, represent a Best Way to do things. Once people find that best way, they stick to it because it is, after all, the best way, the one that meets certain needs or ensures that certain functions necessary to the continued existence of the organization or society will be performed. Once such a "functional equilibrium" has been found, things just naturally go on that way. If anything interferes, the world tries to reestablish the Best Way. The stability of the music world is not a problem for such a theory. Once you have identified the functions the organization serves, you have done all the analysis that's necessary. (See the trenchant criticism of this view in Hughes 1971, 53.)

Another variety of sociological thinking, to me more realistic and useful, thinks all that is a fairy tale. On this view, social organizations are generally flying apart; they stay organized no more than is necessary for people to get done whatever they have for the moment decided they want to do together. People get together, or find themselves together, and work out how they'll do what they're going to do and then try to do it, in circumstances that are never quite what they imagined, with problems and hindrances popping up that they never anticipated. For this point of view, the stability of the music world creates a substantial theoretical problem. How can things possibly go on just as they have been?

In fact, music doesn't stay the same; it's always changing. Look at all the innovations music has incorporated in the past century: everything from serial methods of composition to minimalism, all sorts of alternative music systems from around the world (the musics of India, Japan, and China, for instance), electric and then electronic instruments, a variety of tonal and harmonic systems.

The music of Harry Partch provides a good example of such changes (Alex Ross [2008, 522–24] gives a brief account of his life and work). Partch, a somewhat eccentric composer, composed for a forty-two-tone scale (conventional Western music uses a twelve-tone scale). Since no instruments existed for forty-two-tone music, he had to invent and construct them himself, which he did (since he didn't have much money) mostly out of scavenged materials (for instance, discarded laboratory glassware he found in the trash of university laboratories). After he made the instruments, no one knew how to play them, and so he had to teach a generation of Partch instrumentalists. He not only had to teach them to play the instruments but also, because no forty-two-tone notation existed, he had to invent a notation and teach them to read that as well. Since no musical literature, no compositions, existed for a music based on forty-two tones, he had to write that too (which, of course, was why he had gone to all this trouble in the first place).

Partch's music was, just like more conventional concert music, performed by instrumentalists who rehearsed a work they then played from a notated score composed by a composer. They typically performed, as we say, "in concert," in a hall, for an audience who had come especially to listen to that music. They recorded the music, which was issued on discs and sold through more or less the same distribution channels as other recorded music. For all the unconventionality of the works, a lot of the conventional practice of music-making stayed the same.

Now consider a possibility that differs much more from the way we conventionally make music. I've based this possibility on a story I heard about a man who lived in a place where bamboo grew. Whenever he felt like making music, he picked a piece of bamboo and made a flute from it. He made holes in the bamboo tube, using the *I Ching* as a randomizing procedure to determine where to put them. In that way, each flute he made gave him a different scale to work with. He then spent the day experimenting with the new flute, seeing what melodic and harmonic possibilities the scale gave him, composing whatever seemed appropriate to those resources and the day and his mood, and then—this is the crucial difference between what this experiment accomplished and what you might get from an electronic synthesizer—at the end of the day he burned the flute. That day's music was that day's music; when the day was over, its music went with it. (Did this ever really happen? It's not important to the use I'm going to make of the story.)

These three ways of making music—conventional concert practice, Harry Partch's innovative compositional practice, and the randomly constructed bamboo flute—suggest the analytic dimension I think is responsible for the stability of conventional music making: inertia. (We could also call it, with somewhat more of a political twist, hegemony.)

In conventional music-making, nothing goes away at the end of the day. We don't invent a new scale every day. In fact, we hardly ever do, unless we are as eccentric and individualistic as Partch, or like to experiment mathematically as Easley Blackwood (1986) did when he systematically explored the possibilities of scales made by dividing the octave, electronically, into increasingly fine units. Instead, we use one of the several scales in common use. We don't really invent new melodies every day, either, even those of us who improvise. Paul Berliner's research on jazz improvisation (Berliner 1994) shows that even the most inventive jazz players work with a small library of short phrases, which they vary and combine endlessly, starting on different degrees of the scale and at different places in the bar, to make enormous numbers of distinct, and distinctive, variations. He shows further that the people playing those phrases typically haven't invented them but instead have taken them from a vocabulary of such phrases that goes back to the beginnings of jazz playing. Thus the phrases he finds in the improvisations of trumpeter Booker Little (born 1938) can also be found, in slightly variant forms, all the way back to the beginnings of jazz trumpet playing, in the recorded solos (which Little surely knew) of Dizzy Gillespie (1917), Roy Eldridge (1911) and Louis Armstrong (1901), and even in the early piano solos of Earl Hines (1903).

Similarly, we don't burn our instruments when the sun goes down. They cost too much. We're used to them. We know how to play them. We don't have to explore their possibilities. We've done that, and the possibilities remain in our fingers, built into our bodies the way David Sudnow described his own learning of jazz piano practices being built into his hands (Sudnow 1978). So, instead of burning our instruments, we take good care of them, have them repaired when they need it, and buy insurance so that we can replace them if anything happens.

Those decisions aren't unconnected. We use the instruments because they have built into them a selection of tones that isn't new and different, a selection we're used to and can work with. We use those scales because they're built into the instruments we have and know.

In short, a way of making music is what sociologists of science have come to speak of, not very originally but certainly intelligibly, as a *package*. Each piece in the package presupposes the existence of all the others. They're all connected in such a way that, when you choose any one of them (an instrument, for example), you find it enormously easy to take everything in that package, everything that comes with that choice (the kinds of notes it can produce and the kind of music written for such notes), and an enormous amount of trouble to make any substitutions. The package exerts the hegemony. The package contains the inertial force, if I can attribute agency to such a conceptual creation.

Think about Partch. When he spent a year at the University of Illinois as composer in residence, he worked for months with students there building instruments (some of his very large and very fragile instruments were troublesome and expensive to transport), teaching them to play on what they built, teaching them his invented notation, and working on particular pieces, all in order to prepare (between September and May, let's say) a two-hour concert. A major orchestra playing around that time spent no more than nine hours, and more likely six, preparing a similar amount of music. You might describe the difference between nine months and nine hours as a rough measure of the inertial power of a conventional musical package.

The package contains more than such musical considerations as scales and instruments. It also contains the social situations in which music gets made and those in which the players and everyone else involved gets trained. Symphony concerts don't take the form they do just because the instruments already exist and someone has written the music in an already established notation. They are what they are, also, because concert music is a business. The people who make that kind of music get paid for it, not as well as they might like, but well enough that raising the money to pay them is a serious problem. That means that the orchestras who hire them must also hire people to make sure that the money is there: fundraisers, marketing specialists, ticket sellers.

All that money requires tending, so orchestras also need bookkeepers, accountants, and lawyers. The players usually belong to a union, so there are labor relations to take care of; the inability of players and management to agree on a contract has killed off a few orchestras and endangered more. The economics of the symphony business make it necessary for players to have certain skills, for example, the ability to perform a difficult piece of music creditably or excellently with only a few hours' rehearsal (because the rehearsal must be paid for at union rates). After all, it isn't a necessary feature of making good music that you be able to learn to perform a particular piece quickly; that's a business-driven requirement, as Samuel Gilmore's (1987) explorations of such alternate musical organizations as university-based ensembles, which often rehearse a lot longer, make clear.

Part of the concert-music package is an associated set of educational organizations. Professional training schools produce players who can do everything the other parts of the package require: quick studies with virtuoso skills who can adapt to a variety of conductors. Elementary and secondary schools teach some rudiments of music (Hennion 1988 describes the way French schoolchildren are taught sight-singing [*solfeggio*], something less possible in the United States, where penny-pinching state and city governments have often made such instruction impossible) and take children to "children's concerts" to give them a kind of minimal exposure to music, which might make them into potential customers for the concert business, if not for live concerts then perhaps for television and recordings. We can add to the package such frills as critics, theorists, and scholars. I'll leave their relations to what I've described as an exercise for readers to do at home.

Every part of this package could be done some other way. Music could be supported in some other way than by raising money from rich people and selling tickets. It could be an amateur activity, as so many other kinds of music are. Children could learn to play instruments proficiently in school instead of learning to be consumers, the way some of them learn to be proficient enough players of rock outside of school (Stith Bennett [1980] describes this in detail).

That's the package that creates the inertia that keeps things the way they are. Notice that its existence doesn't in any way require anyone to do anything in the conventional way, or prevent innovation or unconventionality. You want forty-two-tone music? Go ahead and write it. But you'll have a lot of trouble getting it played, because no one will have the instruments to play it on or know how to play them, and, for that matter, no one will know how to listen to it either, since it isn't one of the kinds of music they learned to hear in school or from records. You want to pick pieces of bamboo and invent whole new musical systems from the ground up every day? Be my guest. But keep it to yourself and don't expect anyone to cooperate with you. You want to do it on a computer? Fine, but then you'll spend time you might have devoted to composing to learning more about computers than you ever wanted to know, like Michael Joyce, who wanted to write interactive fiction and thought a computer would be the way to do it. It was, but it took him three years, collaborating with Jay Bolter, to develop Storyspace, the software that made it possible, before he could write the first story (Joyce 1990).

You can do anything as differently as you like, but it costs a lot. The more you depart from the standard package, the more you find that everything else connected with making music has gotten more complicated and difficult. You have to recruit and train people who otherwise would have been ready to go, you have to learn new ways of doing things, you have to construct machinery or adapt it to your purposes instead of being able to use off-the-shelf products. All of that will eat into the time and resources you might have devoted to making art, which is what you set out to do.

So, no surprise, most people, confronted with that kind of choice, decide to do things as they've been done and as most other people still do them. At every turn, you have to choose between an easy way to go and a hard way, and people who have some art they want to make are likely to choose the easy way. Not because they're lazy, but because they want to get on with the work they set out to do. That may not look like the exercise of power, but it is, in its most insidious form: the structuring of choices so as to make one choice "obvious."

On the other hand, this isn't such an extreme of power as to prevent people from innovating. There are always enough people around to keep things moving a little, enough people with new ideas and the energy to give them a try. The question about change isn't whether such people exist (they do) but whether their ideas will be incorporated into the workings of the rest of the package, whether the changes will be institutionalized so as to gain the advantage of having all the apparatus already in place. Alternatively, can innovators create for themselves a new apparatus, which will do all those things the regular system does for older kinds of work? You could say that rock music did that, creating a network of performance sites and training institutions independent of what had been there before. Rock music didn't take over jazz venues or recruit the audience of jazz; it found new venues (San Francisco's famed Fillmore Auditorium replaced an "Over Thirties Ballroom" whose clientele had gotten too old to dance) and created a new audience.

To show what it takes to make an enormous change, we can look at Pierre-Michel Menger's study of the classical compositional scene in France (Menger 1983). When composer-conductor-theorist Pierre Boulez came to control about 80 percent of all government money available for classical music (the kind of thing that can happen in so centralized a society), he declared a shift of emphasis from composition to "research in sonorities," concerned less with producing works to be played in concert and more with investigating the new possibilities introduced by digital music. That, as Menger tells the story, produced a paradox: governmentally supported music that was radically avant-garde, neither conservative nor popular, but instead esoteric in the extreme.

That suggests one last aspect of the power of inertia, implicit in what I've already said. Boulez could do this because he could, by virtue of the centralized government-supported apparatus he controlled, control the definition of what constituted music. That control of definition exists in all professionalized music worlds. I began by referring to John Cage's wide-ranging and democratic notions about what constituted music. But then I pretty much proceeded, as most sensible scholars would, to ignore those ideas, by accepting the notion that music is what is conventionally thought of as music, which is to say professionalized music that someone makes a living from. Within that enormous restriction on what I defined as music, I mostly concentrated on conventional concert music. By doing that, I accepted the most insidious exercise of power: I let the people whose business it is define what that business includes, which versions of it are serious and important, and which versions don't matter much.

Now I'll repair that error. Take an unbiased look at music-making, as Ruth Finnegan did in her study of the new English town of Milton Keynes (Finnegan 1989). Look and listen as she did, using a more inclusive Cagean definition, and find all the places in such a city (with a population of about two hundred thousand) where people are making music. You find all the rock bands, church choirs, and amateur orchestras. You find the large number of organizations that make specialized ethnic music: the Milton Keynes Irish Society, the Bletchley Edelweiss club (devoted to Austrian, Swiss, and German music), the Hindu Youth organization, and the less organized but still musical Italian, Vietnamese, Chinese, Sikh, and Bangladeshi communities. The schools, of course, had musical organizations and programs. So did the clubs and pubs. And the garages were filled with young people playing rock and hoping to become the next British band to make it big.

I'm not making a sentimental anthropological plea that we remember and honor all these wonderful people, or even the Cagean aesthetic plea to enjoy ourselves by listening to all the wonderful sounds we can hear if we just pay attention. It's an analytic point: when we talk about music and power, we have to recognize that people are actively making music in all these ways but that the power of professional definition prevents us (us scholars, anyway) from taking them seriously.

What does it mean for a kind of music-making not to be taken seriously? At the most material level, it means that all the standard, already-in-place, ways of paying for music-making (not just salaries, but the provision of instruments, places to play, and so forth) will not be available to you: no grants from the National Endowment for the Arts, no fellowships, no commissions from players and groups. More generally, all the apparatus I described above, all the available stuff that makes it so easy to make music, is available only to people who make what the people in charge of that stuff recognize and define as "music." Which does not include the full panoply of music-making that Cage wanted us to recognize and Finnegan found in Milton Keynes.

Hermano Vianna's study of the world of funk in Rio de Janeiro (Vianna 1988) gives us a striking example of what it means not to be part of the world defined by the professionals. Based on intensive observation of funk musical events in Rio, Vianna estimated that between one thousand and two thousand clubs in the metropolitan area (whose population is around 5 million) drew as many as a thousand people a night for two or three nights each weekend to listen and dance to funk music imported from the United States. One striking finding of his research is that, until he wrote about it, "no one" in Rio, which is to say no intellectual or journalist or opinion maker or social scientist, knew that this was going on. It was something poor, mostly black, people did in their own neighborhoods, neighborhoods to which experts on popular culture never went. So, from a certain point of view, Rio's funk scene "didn't exist."

Another surprising finding: this wasn't a case of cultural imperialism, culture from the metropole forced on a helpless population in a dependent country through the devices of modern mass marketing. The companies producing these records in the United States—typically small, struggling enterprises—couldn't afford the price of cultural imperialism. Nor were the records the Brazilian funk fans liked popular or even well known in the United States. The only way the disk jockeys who ran these parties could get the records their fans liked was to fly to New York, spend the day scouring stores for possible music, and then take the fruits of their search back to Rio for the next evening's performance. This is a long way from the stereotypical picture of greedy multinationals exploiting the "natives" of a poor country.

The poor funk lovers of Rio made their own world (although, to be sure, using all the devices of contemporary society like sound systems and flights to New York) and so could overcome the inertia that might be imposed by the existing packages of the music world. In that way, their activities show us what's possible, as do Partch and the bamboo flute maker, all showing what you could do if you really wanted to and what the price would be. And all of that reveals how organizations stay stable (by raising the price of innovation) and how they change (through the activity of people who, for whatever reason, don't find that price prohibitive).

Some people may think that invented stories—fairy tales—have no place in social science. My invented story of the bamboo flute maker sits here among several other stories provided by scholars who didn't invent what they told us but based their accounts on knowledge earned the hard way, by intensive empirical study. But we can reason from imaginary cases in a useful way. The invented story provides an extreme case I'd never found in my wanderings around musical worlds, a useful endpoint that defines an analytic dimension along which the real cases, based on serious empirical work, can be arranged to answer a serious theoretical question. In this case, the dimension was stability change, and the story of the bamboo flutes anchored the extreme case of constant change that helps us understand the causes of the relative stability that the empirical world shows us.

A DYSTOPIAN CASE: "THE LAST SEMINAR"

Invented cases give us a way to work out the possible consequences of a situation we're interested in. Just such a story performs that useful function for thinking about a question that bothers and perplexes many social scientists, especially those who do fieldwork, who work closely and for a relatively long time with the people they eventually write about. They worry about their obligations to those people. They wonder whether they are harming them in some way instead of doing the good they'd like to be doing. Stan Cohen, a gifted student of deviance and many other subjects, wrote a story, a kind of dystopian fable, that uses an invented case to confront his colleagues with one possible result of their work.

Cohen's grim fable, "The Last Seminar" (Cohen 1988, 297–310), tells an upsetting story of an ordinary professor in an (unnamed) ordinary British university, someone just like, we can suppose, most of the people who read it when it first appeared. The professor teaches in an unspecified department, probably sociology but maybe social work or criminology; he teaches courses in penology, among other subjects. In the story, people of the kind his courses and those of his colleagues deal with—criminals, prisoners, people who are mentally ill, poor people—begin to appear, unexpectedly, in classrooms and elsewhere on the university grounds, first sitting quietly listening to the professor lecture, and eventually taking the university over by, it seems, force of arms and other violence, including arson. It ends with the campus in flaming ruins.

Cohen's story provided a graphic and forbidding extension of a larger process that has continued to go on in universities in Great Britain, as well as in the United States: the increasing presence in university buildings and on university campuses of people who have no obvious connection with a university's educational activities. He tells the story of the subjects of sociological research making their presence known, and he uses that fictional, imagined event to discuss some serious problems of research ethics. But, by talking about people who really had "no business" being in the university proper but who show up there anyway, the story reminds us that people besides students and scholars do play a role in our university lives; it invites us to think about the whole range of possibilities that brings to mind. Cohen didn't pursue this extension of his tale, but I will.

One kind of visitation to the university by nonacademic people occurs when students get unruly and thus provide the occasion for police personnel of one kind or another to enter the premises. Just such an event occurred at Essex, where Cohen taught, some years before he wrote "The Last Seminar." A student strike had shut down the entire university for an extended period. Then, one day, a contingent of police invaded the campus, clubbing some students and effectively clearing the blockade that had deprived the university of needed supplies for weeks.

Many, perhaps most, of the university people who witnessed or heard about the events had probably never thought much about who had a "right" to be on university grounds. But the arrival of the police on that day seemed to many university people to raise that question and, by extension, the more general question of just who had a right to be involved in university affairs broadly understood.

All this had a connection to a very specific question people like me, and the sociologists at Essex (Cohen was one of them), had been thinking about, though the connection was indirect and requires some explaining. The theme of "The Last Seminar" was much on people's minds. The relation of people like us—researchers in the social sciences—to the people we gathered data on and wrote about had begun to worry us all. We'd left behind the innocence of being happy when we used the tricks of interviewing and participant observation we'd been taught, and continued to teach to our students, to "get access" and "gain rapport." We rejoiced at our good fortune when people agreed to share their experiences and secrets with us, things they might have preferred that the whole world not know about. We were proud of our ability to be "one of the boys" (or girls).

By the 1970s we all knew this relation wasn't as innocent as we liked to think. What were the terms of this one-sided giving of information? Did we give anything back in return for the information we got, so useful for writing our theses or articles or books? Was the exchange as unequal as it seemed to be when we took a hard, conscience-prompted look? Were we exploiting our superior educations and class positions to take advantage of innocent people, poorer and more powerless than us? The answers weren't obvious, although many of our colleagues published accusatory articles on the topic. Some people said that we gave, in return for data, our undivided attention and our caring acceptance of their lives, however unsavory those might seem to middle-class people who hadn't achieved our level of "insider" understanding. Others thought our research could lead us and others, perhaps people in positions of power who could undertake effective interventions, to an understanding that might improve the lives of the people who gave us our data, and so allow us to pay back their acceptance and even trust.

Still others derided these perhaps self-serving analyses, pointing out that our "respondents" or "subjects"—what to call these people, what name won't be condescending, continues to be a problem—would almost surely continue to be poor, deprived of opportunity, and in no way better off for their kindness to us. The people in power who already had the good things of life, these critics thought, wouldn't use our research findings to improve things, but rather to oppress the already oppressed even further (in the not-very-likely event that our research produced anything they didn't already know that would be useful for that purpose). We, on the other hand, even if we shared the privations of the people we studied during our research—ate unhealthy food, slept in unwholesome places, suffered in the cold, ran risks vis-à-vis the law—would waltz off with our precious "data" and turn it into articles and books from which we would profit by building privileged academic careers that supported a far cushier way of life than our informants enjoyed.

That's the crudest version of the opposing positions on this difficult question, to which Stan Cohen applied himself often.

"The Last Seminar," embodying the problem dramatically as a specific question about the right to be present on university grounds, and especially in university classrooms, presents a stark analysis of one way the relationship might play out. Fictional, of course. Imaginary and "over-drawn," unlikely actually ever to happen just like that. But in another way quite realistic, exposing in a raw and undisguised form the tensions that might exist in these relations. The fable's irony stems from the un-comfortable feeling many researchers had, and often still have, that they really don't know, in the most literal sense, what they're talking about when they describe the lives of the people they've studied, that they therefore perhaps shouldn't be writing about such things at all. Gilberto Velho, the distinguished Brazilian urban anthropologist (see, for instance, Velho 2002), once suggested to his departmental colleagues, who often discussed the situation of Brazilian peasants, just as often disagreeing about what peasants thought about this or that question, that they hire a peasant to stand in the hall outside their meeting room so that when they disagreed about some matter of fact or interpretation with respect to "what peasants thought" or "what peasants did," as often happened, they could summon the peasant from the hall to give an insider's opinion. It was a barbed joke they didn't appreciate.

Cohen's imaginary case raises, in fictional form, questions about our research practice and experience and forces us to reconsider (perhaps not always in the direction its author intended) some general problems of social research. Focused on rendering the specific case in upsetting detail, it didn't try to investigate the possible variations in such relationships. That's what I'll do now.

OUR PEOPLE AND US. Analyses of conceptual problems meant to be general usually reflect the specific examples the analyst has in mind, though those cases may never be named. "The Last Seminar" takes as given that our relations with the people we study are unequal, the way they would certainly be between, say, prisoners and researchers, or delinquents or (less successful) criminals and researchers. Most discussions of this problem assume that we will be studying people poorer than us, less educated, and more at risk for disease and early death, arrest and imprisonment, unemployment and suffering at the hands of unfeeling bureaucrats who administer welfare schemes, and a host of other bad things.

In another direction, discussion of these problems often assumes that we're likely to harm those we study, presumably inadvertently, by (in the phrase often invoked) "serving the interests of the powerful." The question of the harm we do or might do to the people we study deserves more attention than this ideological and typically not empirically based charge, as do the assumptions implicit in the creation of offices designed to ensure the protection of people who become the subjects of social research.

My own research experiences put me in situations where the people I interviewed or observed, or both, differed in many ways from the research subjects who invaded university classrooms in "The Last Seminar."

In some of my projects, I studied people who were, in general, just like me. In my first field research (Becker 1963, 79–119), done for my master's thesis, I studied musicians of just the kind I was: people who played in bars and clubs or for private parties of various kinds, for not very much money, but (some of us) intent on becoming good jazz players or, at least, competent professionals. I did not and could not take advantage of the people I studied because I had no more power over the conditions of my life than they had over theirs.

The same was true of the very similar group of musicians Marc Perrenoud (2007) studied in southern France.

You might object that, true as that might have been, the other musicians, the ones I was studying, were stuck with being that and no more, while I, a privileged kid of the middle class, a student at a major university, would eventually leave this life and become the professor/professional my class status made it possible for me to be. Middle-class people who studied factory workers might be (and sometimes were) criticized this way. I certainly had the possibility of entering academia and eventually took advantage of it. But so did many of the people who figured in my study. The kind of music I played was almost entirely a part-time job. With few exceptions, people who did this work had "day jobs" as well, often quite good ones, though just as often not such good ones. But "everyone knew" that it was only prudent to have a day job. I differed no more from them than they did from one another. And, within the world of music, we shared and acted on the understanding that the only status differences that mattered had to do with how you played. The power differentials we considered important were those that put us at the mercy of club owners (often enough small-time hoodlums capable of violence, though it was seldom directed at us), audience members, and others who prevented us from playing what we wanted to play. That privation doesn't compare with going hungry or being arrested, but, in our world, we all suffered that privation equally.

The only thing all marijuana smokers (another group I studied; see Becker 1963, 41–78) had in common was that they smoked marijuana. And when I studied them, I was just like the people I interviewed in that defining characteristic too. Otherwise, we were as various in class origins and positions as we could have been. Some were poor, some were from well-to-do families; some were black, some were white; most were young, but some were older, most were men but some were women. Insofar as we were oppressed because we smoked dope, we were all oppressed in just the same way, by being subject to arrest and imprisonment for our indulgence. It's true that some of us were better prepared, because of our class position, to deal with that possibility (our families might have "connections" that would enable them to influence the outcome of some escapade of ours), but it was equally true that the possibility of being caught was remote and that a user who took the simplest precautions had nothing to worry about. (Which isn't to say that everyone took those simple precautions; many of us were young and not very thoughtful.)

In neither case did I hide what I was doing from the people I was writing my field notes about. They typically responded to my requests for information or interviews by trying to be helpful, often because they thought bringing what they regarded as the truth about their activities to public attention would be a helpful thing, or with indifference. I don't remember anyone ever suggesting that I was taking advantage of them. However, an old friend, when I started asking a lot of questions about his experience with marijuana without telling him it was an interview (I ordinarily did tell people that, but our casual conversation had drifted into the area of my professional interest), got angry and shouted, "You son of a bitch, you're interviewing me!" He was angry because he thought I was taking advantage of our friendship, which, certainly, I had unthinkingly done. That's quite different from taking advantage of a powerless person.

In other cases, the people I studied were at least as privileged as I was and potentially much more so. The medical students I spent three years hanging around with to gather data for *Boys in White* (Becker et al. 1961) were on their way, for the most part, to lucrative careers and secure upper-middle-class status (despite the commitment they had all made, because they knew it was something that would help them get admitted to the University of Kansas Medical School, to a life of practicing general medicine in a small town in the rural western part of the state, a commitment few of them honored when the time came). They thought what I was doing—sociological research—was "interesting" but not the most profitable way you could spend your time. Some of them questioned me about how much I earned doing this work and how much I could expect to make at the peak of my career. When they heard the numbers, they nodded sympathetically and soothingly and made it clear that they felt sorry for me. My only superiority to them (and to the undergraduate college students my colleagues and I wrote about in *Making the Grade* [Becker et al. 1968]) was in age, and that didn't count for much.

Physicians and hospital administrators typically treated medical sociologists (a numerous subspecialty at the time) as a lesser breed, better than nurses perhaps but not a lot, as was evidenced in the constant jockeying of sociologists in that specialty for a "better" position vis-à-vis their "subjects."

Students of white-collar crime similarly often have an inferior position to those about whom and from whom they get data. When Baker and Faulkner (2003, 2004) interviewed investors in a fraudulent oil drilling scheme in southern California, they were certainly interviewing people who were dumber than they were, since Baker and Faulkner knew better than to invest in such a scam. But they were almost as certainly interviewing people who had more money and, probably, a higher class position than they did, people who had the money to lose in such a speculation. And when Edwin Sutherland interviewed Broadway Jones (a.k.a. "Chic Conwell," the author of *The Professional Thief* [Conwell and Sutherland 1937]), though Jones was later reduced to lecturing to college classes to make some extra change, he had lived very high in his time, and it's not at all clear that he thought (or should have thought) the modest life of even so successful a college professor as Sutherland preferable to the one he had led, even though he was at least theoretically subject to oppression by the police of a kind Sutherland never risked.

Sociologists of science (e.g., the field study by Bruno Latour reported in Latour and Woolgar 1979) study people who resemble us in many ways, often university teachers and researchers themselves, mostly in fields in the natural sciences with more prestige than social science, scientists who often enough don't think social science is "real science," though they often charitably cooperate with our (sometimes intrusive) data gathering.

So we aren't always better off than the people we study. Sometimes we are more or less equal to them, sometimes we are superior to them, and sometimes we are inferior to them. In other words, our relations to the people we study vary considerably along a scale of superiority-inferiority. At every point on that scale, the problems of relations between us and them will be different. To revert to language I introduced earlier, the black box that produces the results of research for the researched has the possibility of such variation built into it as a possibility.

Which immediately raises the question of what scale we're using to calculate these comparative ranks. "The Last Seminar" seems to use a very conventional scale: money and social rank and legitimacy, as sociologists usually measure the latter, when they talk about "deviance," "oppression," and the like. But it's well attested in the research literature that people use a multitude of different scales to measure rank. In many situations, skill at a particular task outweighs any other consideration. (See the discussion of contradictory status systems in Hughes 1945.) In general, the people we work with and get our data from use a variety of scales, according to the situation and their interests in it, which can't simply be deduced from what we think those interests might be, or ought to be. We have to find out what scales they use and verify those conclusions.

How does the researcher-researched relation differ when the statuses of the parties differ in these ways? Here are some guesses, informed by my own experiences and reading and by experiences others have told me about.

People who feel superior to us—in class, professional status, or otherwise—often patronize us and, feeling sorry for us, help us out by giving us the data we want from them. That's the motivation Robert Park told students to rely on when they went out to do the fieldwork he assigned them. "Tell them you're a poor student and your teacher wants you to do it; they'll feel sorry for you," and often they did. Sometimes they feel that it's a sort of civic duty to help science out that way. The schoolteachers I interviewed for my PhD dissertation treated me as a sort of junior teacher who was working on a degree as they once had or might have done. We can take advantage of such generous motives to get what we want, and that might be a little devious, but it certainly doesn't amount to anything as despicable as taking advantage of powerless people.

We can use the knowledge we get in ways people more powerful than us don't like: to take one possibility, we can generate publicity that they might feel harms their interests. If they think we've injured them in some way, they can and will do something about it, or try. The dean of the medical school we studied was very angry when he read the first version of *Boys in White*, and he demanded to see our "superior." He meant Everett Hughes, who he mistakenly thought would see things his way. When Hughes didn't agree with him, he threatened to sue us if we didn't change some things in the book. We didn't, and he didn't, but the threat was real and more than a little scary. The negotiations that followed, masterfully handled by Hughes, were negotiations between two parties of more or less equal power, this being a surprise to the dean, who was used to being un-disputed boss in his own institution and in his relations with nonphysi-cians. He might have pursued the matter, but probably (I never discussed it with him afterward) decided that any kind of legal action would just generate more publicity and be even more harmful than our scholarly book, which was not likely to be widely read or known.

Other possibilities exist in relations with people in other kinds of status relations to us. Getting information from people is always a nego-tiation; Hughes described the result as "the research bargain" (Hughes 1984, 524–29). The people we study aren't necessarily so powerless in rela-tion to us, so defenseless against our attempts to get what we want from them. In fact, they often tell us they aren't interested and don't want to play our game and just walk away. That's why questions of "getting access" occupy so much space in our discussions and in students' nightmares. (And why problems of nonresponse plague survey researchers as much as they do.)

Dealing with our equals or peers is a quite different kind of situation. It's not easy for us to take advantage of equals by using a class differential in status or power, since in fact there isn't much differential between "us" and "them," as there wasn't between me and the musicians and marijuana users I wrote about. We can, of course, harm them by revealing things we learn, in an apparently confidential relationship, to others who might use the information maliciously, but they can usually do the same to us.

Let's return to "The Last Seminar." For all my quibbling about how my own experiences differ from those alluded to as the genesis of the events in the story, it evokes the problem it discusses powerfully and memorably. And it opens the way to more speculation of the kind I've just been doing.

Could we invent as interesting and compelling stories about a hypo-thetical future in which our peers or social and political superiors in-vaded the campuses we work in, and did—well, what would they do? I suppose they wouldn't come and sit in our classes and eye us suspiciously. Nor would they, probably, attack us personally or burn the buildings we worked and taught in. Do we have a story to tell as interesting as the one Stan Cohen told? A story that will alert us to something as ethically and morally important? Do we need a sociological imagination like his to create a narrative of middle- and upper-class invasion of the university world?

Fortunately, for few of us think as originally or write as well as he did, we don't have to invent those stories. We just have to record what's going on around us. I'll only mention what I know a little about—the situation in the United States—and won't speak about what I know almost nothing about, the situation elsewhere in the world.

Are our equals, our peers, present in the university already? Certainly. They're there as students and as the parents of students. They're there as journalists, who come to reveal the university's secrets to the world. My local newspaper, the *San Francisco Chronicle*, periodically "exposes" the (not really very hidden) outrageously large payments made to top administrators of the University of California in the guise of reimbursement for all sorts of expenses others in the university community have to pay for themselves (costs of moving for intimate friends, for example), payments that often egregiously violate the rules the university's governing Board of Regents has passed to prevent the regents themselves from doing just such things. And that has on occasion provoked some other visitors, mostly politicians, to investigate what was after all not such a big secret in the first place. I'm not sure that "peer" or "equal" is the appropriate descriptive term for these folks, though they aren't really so much more powerful than a university professor, or not for long, or not with respect to many of the things important to professors.

Have the rich and politically powerful invaded the campus? Of course they have. But "invasion" is hardly an appropriate way to talk about people who come bearing gifts. Often very substantial gifts, in the form of endowed university chairs, which some among us will be fortunate enough to occupy, or research centers in which we can work on our own projects instead of teaching large rooms full of undergraduates, or handsomely equipped libraries with all the obscure journals we might need in order to pursue our interests, or wonderful concert halls and theaters in which the world's greatest artists will entertain us, or lavish support for athletic teams we might not even be interested in, or. . . . What these invaders bring makes a long list.

The people and organizations who give these gifts may not appear there in person, but their names are everywhere in American universities. We can imagine that their influence is there in less open ways too. We needn't be conspiracy theorists, imagining that an administrator will lock us out of our offices and forbid us to enter the campus because we have written something a donor found offensive. But it isn't a possibility to dismiss out of hand. (Thorstein Veblen's *The Higher Education in America* [1918] discusses these possibilities at length.)

THE MORAL(S). "The Last Seminar," implicitly and not arguing the point, takes the particular cases of criminals, the mentally ill, and other conventionally despised groups and the people who have studied them as the general situation of researchers and researched. I said to myself, "That's a good idea, but the specifics don't fit my own research experiences. How would it be if the people I studied occupied the campuses I work at?"

That's the first moral: to apply general ideas and questions generated by the particular case we know well to the full range of cases encompassed by their definitions. In this case, fictional and imaginary though it is, to apply the concern about our relations with those we study to the full range of people sociologists have actually studied. Because sociologists have studied people up and down a variety of social scales, and their experiences with those people haven't always, and perhaps not even often, produced the acts of revenge the story describes. We can imagine people whose lives we have written about in ways they think disrespectful doing those things: ignoring conventional patterns of politeness and civility and disrupting settled professorial routines at first; and then the assaults and fires and all the rest of it, things we can imagine we might want to do if we had been so cavalierly mistreated by researchers.

In fact, no one I studied ever cared that much about what I wrote; they had far more important things to worry about. In the one case where my work created trouble, it wasn't the people I wrote about who complained. Medical students—the few who read what we wrote—didn't find fault with our descriptions. No. It was the school's administrators (our book presented a potential public-relations problem for them) who were worried, and they had plenty of weapons available, though in the end they seemed to have decided that any revenge would cost more than it was worth.

There's a second moral. Stan Cohen knew and always practiced the simple maxim that it's better, when we pursue our work of understanding and explaining society, to stick close to the nitty-gritty of life as we find it in specific cases than to develop our understanding of it by deduction from general principles. "The Last Seminar" seems to violate that maxim by indulging in a fiction. The lesson it teaches is that "nitty-gritty" is important as an aid even when it isn't "what actually happened." The fiction makes us think about a reality that, though it hasn't happened yet, is recognizably a reality that could happen. The details prompt our imaginations in a way abstract concepts seldom do. The story's details urge a serious reconsideration of our relations with people we study. It's a lesson.

And not only a lesson about our relations with the people we study. It's also a lesson about the usefulness of totally imagined cases, which can give us situations to think about that are unlikely to ever actually happen, which nevertheless uncover useful ideas and dimensions of things we think about. In this way they add to the tools we can use to construct better understandings of the social world.

7 *Where Do You Stop?*

Dianne and I had started spending three months every fall in Paris, another move in our efforts to improve our French, which we also pursued by watching TV5 Monde, the international French television channel. We saw a trimmed-down version of the eight o'clock news every day and so kept up with current events, including the great heat wave of 2003 that killed a number of people and exposed terrible flaws in the country's system for avoiding tragedy in such situations. (A similar event, the subject of Eric Klinenberg's *Heat Wave* [2002], had occurred several years earlier in Chicago.) When I was invited to give the Vilhelm Aubert Memorial Lecture at the University of Oslo, I thought I could best pay tribute to Aubert's quirky genius (see Aubert 1982) by exploring an offbeat topic I thought might have appealed to him: the black box that produced such disasters from time to time—not the disaster of the natural event itself but the troubles resulting from a community's failed response to it.

Thinking about one case in all its detail suggests places to look for more such cases, superficially different, in which the same black box and its processes, which we want to know more about, are at work. My casual investigation of the phenomenon of heat waves led me to snowstorms. Then, naturally for a San Franciscan, to earthquakes, and then. . . . My imagination kept finding new places to look for the variations that produced inputs to the black box I was investigating, which I now understood to be the one that shapes how people decide how much of anything is enough (as I'll explain shortly). Each successive instance provoked more tentative generalizations about further elements to incorporate into the increasingly complicated (and still provisional) model of the general process, whose variations produced the complexity I was calling my own attention to. (Looking for these instances embodies one of Robert Merton's favorite foci: the idea that is an example of itself. He used it especially in writing about self-fulfilling prophecies. Here the question of where you stop is one that was perfectly embodied in trying to decide when I should stop looking for further variations in the cases in which the phenomenon appears.)

HOW MUCH IS ENOUGH?

During the great heat waves of 1995 in Chicago and 2003 in Paris, many people, especially but not only elderly people living alone, died, and the news media in both cities were filled with discussions of what had happened, how and why it had happened, and especially whose fault it all was. The question was raised repeatedly, and continues to be raised: couldn't more have been done to prevent these deaths, by taking greater pains, by being better prepared, by having systems in place to monitor the conditions of life for older people living alone? Most simply and practically, couldn't air-conditioning units have been distributed to those who needed them? In Sweden, as French television viewers learned, social workers visit elderly people who live alone several times each day, checking on their well-being. Each social worker has something like four people to care for in this way. Why hadn't city governments in Chicago and Paris undertaken such simple protective measures?

In another direction, why had the news media covered the story as they did, laying the blame on a few city departments that failed to meet the challenges of old age in an urban setting? Later social science analyses also asked why the media so quickly blamed, for instance, the culture of various ethnic groups in Chicago. It had been said, for example, that black families didn't look out for old people the way Mexicans did. (Klinenberg 2002 gives a detailed account of the Chicago event.)

Heat waves and the pathologies that accompany them exemplify a larger problem: how much is enough? How much should people, organizations, cities, and nations prepare to deal with the physical, social, and human consequences of recurring (and therefore expectable) natural troubles? We can find clues to the dynamics of these situations by examining a wide variety of cases, whose variations add to our understanding of underlying dimensions and processes.

Consider snowstorms. Large cities in the appropriate weather zones can anticipate periodically being buried in snow, which then remains on the ground, possibly disrupting ordinary life for days, weeks, or longer. How well should a large city prepare for a major snowfall? Every city has some things on hand—snowplows, people trained to use them, emergency plans—to deal with an expectable level of snow trouble. That is, there's an amount of snow that has fallen often enough in the past to be considered "normal" ("normal trouble," in other words, a concept that pops up in a variety of ways in the analysis of disasters of all kinds, as for instance in Perrow 1984 and Vaughan 1996). Anything beyond that is an "abnormal" amount that occurs only once every five, ten, fifty, one hundred years (in other words, this is a variable). Of course, the preparations in place for the normal snowfall can't handle the abnormal amount. That's what happened to poor Michael Bilandic, who had succeeded the legendary Boss Richard J. Daley as mayor of Chicago, during the monumental storms of January 1979, for which the city was totally unprepared, didn't know what to do, didn't have the equipment that might have made something doable—all of which led to the city, its people, and its commerce being tied up for most of six weeks, and to Jane Byrne replacing Bilandic in the next election for mayor of the city. (This event is described in Granger and Granger 1980, 209–16; and Mergen 1997, 69–79, recounts other such combinations of meteorological and political problems.)

The normal amount of snow varies from place to place, from city to city. When I lived in Kansas City, where it snowed three or four times during the winter—but, as people said, "it never sticks"—a three-inch snowfall that stayed on the ground for three days was a major disaster. The city's substantial hills got slippery. Drivers not used to driving in snow easily lost control of their cars and had accidents. It wasn't very cold, so people didn't freeze to death as they might have in New York or Chicago. But a three-inch snowfall would not have been a major event in Chicago. After all, that's what happens in winter. It might take twelve or eighteen inches of snow in a few hours before Chicago has serious problems, doesn't have enough snowplows and trucks, and has its traffic and daily routines disrupted. I was once in Montreal when it started to snow heavily, and (Chicagoan that I was) I feared I would be stuck there for days before the airport could handle traffic again. Not at all. As soon as the snow began, fleets of plows appeared on the streets, removing the snow as fast as it fell. The eighteen inches that might have paralyzed Chicago were handled as a routine event. Of course, larger snowfalls than that occur every once in a while, and they paralyze Montreal.

The same is true of earthquake preparations. San Francisco is prepared for some level of seismic activity—call it X—but not for some larger level, 2X or 3X. A television program some years ago, called "The City That Is Waiting to Die," compared San Francisco's earthquake readiness to that of Tokyo, where quakes, small and large, are much more common. The program concluded that if the city didn't improve its readiness for a large tremor, as Tokyo had, a major disaster would eventually occur. The 1989 quake, some years later, caused a few highway overpasses to collapse, and several people died, but it was just a large quake, not the catastrophic Big One often predicted. As a result of that earthquake, one of the co-owners of the San Francisco apartment building we live in insisted that our building needed thirty thousand dollars worth of additional earthquake-proofing, although it stands on bedrock, which didn't move in the much larger 1906 tremor. Even though a major quake can be expected some day, possibly soon, knowledgeable architects told us that we would be wasting money. Any seismic event that could damage our building would destroy the entire city, so why save ours?

Disasters of human origin, such as the nuclear disasters at Chernobyl and Three-Mile Island, and similar events around the world, present the same problem. Diane Vaughan's classic examination of the Challenger space flight disaster (Vaughan 1996) and her description of her later involvement with the very similar Columbia accident (Vaughan 2004) add another dimension to the analysis. Here the disaster is possible but not inevitable. The responsible parties, aware of the possibility, could have taken steps to avoid it, but didn't. Vaughan explains this as the result of, among other things, the "normalization of deviance." The engineers working on the Challenger space craft knew the O-rings were unreliable in cold temperatures, but, since the rings hadn't failed in a number of earlier situations of cold weather, the responsible officials decided that was an "acceptable risk," a technically defined term that allowed them, in the interest of ever getting a flight off the ground, to violate some of their other rules and procedures. The same thing occurred in the Columbia accident, where persistent problems with insulation disintegrating and damaging the craft hadn't caused problems; so, again contrary to some of the team's own rules, they classified these as "acceptable risks" and routinely approved flights despite such damage. They normalized their own rule-breaking and so created the conditions for the expectable accident (Vaughan 1996, 119–52).

You can't avoid a heat wave or snowstorm, though you can prepare for it. But the trouble-making events in nuclear installations and in space flights are avoidable. You can follow the rules and have a better chance of avoiding an accident. But the two situations are only superficially different. Since the occurrence of natural disasters is foreseeable, though we can't say for sure when, a natural event—earthquake, heat wave, snowstorm—will eventually produce terrible damage and loss of life. Knowing this, we could prepare for these foreseeable troubles, just as the flight engineers and administrators could have more strictly followed the rules that would have prevented the accident.

To generalize from these cases: For every potential disaster, there's an expected range of dangerous outcomes, and there's another, less-expected range (statistically minded people might call it the second standard deviation) of much greater and much rarer troubles. It's in that context that cities and organizations have to decide what magnitude of disaster to prepare for. How big a heat wave? How high a temperature? Going down how far at night? Lasting for how many days? Do we need a special warning system for people, especially older people, who live alone? How much snow? What magnitude of tremor? How serious an accident?

But the extra preparations don't come free. Spend the money to prepare for this disaster, and you don't have it to spend on preparations for some other kind of disaster, or for the city's educational or health care needs. Spend the money to abort potentially risky space flights, and you have less available for other flights. So it's a familiar problem of trade-offs, somewhat disguised when people say "More could have been done." That's always true. But recognizing it doesn't solve the political problem: what would we give up for that extra cushion of safety in the heat wave? Similarly, engineers always know how to make their machine better and safer but also know that this could lead them never to certify it as "ready to go." (Compare Tracy Kidder's [1981] description of a computer that survived this process and "got out the door" with Latour's [1996] description of an advanced system of personal public transportation designed for the Paris Metro that didn't.)

We can think of this as an equation that models the relation between expenditure (E) and desired outcome (O). We want this level of O. It costs E. We don't have enough, doing things just as we do now, to pay for all values of O. So we adjust the equation by lowering O, what we want, or raising E, the amount we make available to get to this level of O. The inevitable political arguments are about how to do that. Occupational cultures that normalize deviance lower expectations. Momentary peaks of interest in "doing something" raise it.

Arguments over what to do very often treat the level of O, the desired outcome, as so obviously desirable as to be beyond argument. And who would have the nerve to argue that we must let some number of older people die in order to spend more on education or some other worthy project? When people put the argument this way, nothing is negotiable. But, in fact, both E and O in the equation are variable quantities, the final result of complicated calculations and negotiations. Here are some of the complications.

Money isn't the only scarce resource. Time, energy, interest, and enthusiasm are all scarce, as students of social movements have long emphasized. People and organizations have to be persuaded to care *more* about the heat wave, the snowstorm, the earthquake, or the rocket's safety, and to spend more of their time and energy and resources on it, giving it priority over competing demands.

If we think of resources as finite, the situation looks familiar: a zero-sum game. Putting rocket safety first may hinder making the launches that will persuade the government to continue paying for the project. That's misleading. Resources are finite, but not inflexibly so. People make extraordinary efforts in extraordinary circumstances. They find and use resources they didn't know they had or were even possible. Time is certainly finite; a day has only twenty-four hours. But the amount of available time is more flexible than it seems. Aubert and White (1965) identified sleep as a source of extra time: "If socially instituted sleep periods are longer than physiological needs require, it provides a constant supply of surplus time. The night contains a time-reservoir which can be drawn on both for emergency actions, ceremonies, and the completion of unfulfilled tasks" (193).

Some people, deciding that the twenty-four-hour day is inefficient, have tried to gain some extra time with a twenty-five- or twenty-six-hour day. But you can't ordinarily persuade anyone else to reckon time this way, so it's usually "impractical" and unworkable (Gleick 1988, 1–3).

Similar reservoirs exist for other resources. Families create different "pots of money," some set aside for emergencies or anticipated expenses associated with death (Zelizer 1994, 21–5, 109–11, 135–41; Lave 1988, 131–41). Organizations of all sizes routinely set aside "contingency funds" for similar reasons. University administrators have "discretionary funds" they can allocate for expenditures that might otherwise not be allowed. So inflexible financial limits are actually elastic. Every apparently irreducible necessary quantity of a resource is socially defined, especially how much of it is untouchable except in extreme situations. The amount available for E, the expenditure in our equation, is more variable than it often seems.

The amount O, the desirable level of preparation, also varies. An amount of preparation that seemed adequate for the improbable future disaster appears, when the rare but not impossible event finally occurs, nowhere near enough. The accuracy of predictions of disaster-producing natural processes depends on the time scale you use. Patterns of seismic activity invisible over a span of fifty years are obvious when you inspect the geological record over several hundred years. Extrapolating from recent experience misses larger patterns, which show up in disasters far greater than anything we expect when we calculate how much preparation would be enough. (Davis 1998, 14–39, summarizes studies of earthquakes in southern California.)

Short-term political considerations often weigh heavily in such calculations. American cities allow building in areas that repeatedly flood, or burn in devastating fires, because of the pressure exerted by real estate developers, builders, and others who get rich by ignoring those dangers; such pressure is often decisive in choosing the level of preparations considered "realistic." (See Davis 1998, chapters 2 and 3, on this process in Los Angeles.)

So physical realities don't dictate calculations of how much preparation is enough in any simple way, because there isn't any logical way to choose between methods of calculating O that produce different results. Our answer is given, instead, by our conventionally accepted ideas of what's likely, and we don't prepare for anything beyond that.

If we can call this first category of cases "disasters and accidents," a superficially very different one has a much less dramatic name: "collections." Museums and libraries collect stuff—books, artworks, anthropological and biological specimens, things considered valuable as part of a cultural patrimony or a database for research. Which things are worth collecting and saving? How many things are enough to make the collection useful? How long must we keep them? Because—it's one of the lessons of growing up—we can't keep all our favorite toys. If you never throw anything away, you soon run out of space.

If you can afford it (if E in your equation is very high but your financial resources easily cover the cost), you don't have to throw your toys away so soon. You can buy more and keep it all. Starting as a child, and continuing through her adult life, Margaret Woodbury Strong (daughter of a rich man and wife of a rich man) collected an enormous number of dolls and toys, but also all kinds of household machinery (kitchen stoves, washing machines, refrigerators, irons)—things most people would not think worth saving. And she didn't just buy one of each: she once bought all the bathtubs in a hotel about to be torn down and used them as planters around the perimeter of her home. She had no aesthetic or theoretical rationale for her choices. She just bought what she wanted. But she could afford to endow, build, and staff the Strong Museum (Ketchum 1982), now the National Museum of Play, in Rochester, New York, which contained some five hundred thousand such objects, some on public display and many more stored less publicly. (Of course, time, money, and energy limited what even she could do, so she just represents how much farther one might go than is conventional.)

More typically, organizations that throw nothing away eventually run up against the equation governing expenditure and outcome: spend more for exhibition and storage space (instead of on further acquisitions), or get rid of things. Nicholson Baker (2001) complained that many libraries, faced with this choice, had discarded irreplaceable collections of newspapers they no longer had room for, which they thought could, anyway, be replaced satisfactorily by microfilm (Baker thought otherwise). Museums of natural history partially solve this problem by displaying a few items publicly and keeping the rest in much more space-saving ways, but that's only a temporary expedient. Art museums, usually quite discreetly, "de-accession" (less euphemistically, sell) items they think no longer worth saving. Libraries place seldom-requested books in some form of compact accessible storage at a distant site, or work out cooperative arrangements with similar institutions.

No simple principle determining the value of things will tell us what's worth saving and what can safely be thrown away, another complication in evaluating the equation. Few people thought Mrs. Strong was collecting anything worth saving. But what seems easy to discard now is often not regarded that way later on. If we keep our collections to a "reason-able" size by getting rid of things not worth saving now, we will inevi-tably make what later generations will see as terrible mistakes. Some of what we discard now will be just what they prize, need, or want. That's why librarians collect and store material no one has any use for now. They suppose—and experience supports their assumption—that people (espe-cially scholars) will later find that stuff invaluable. Archeologists make great finds in the garbage dumps of the societies they study, the places where people discarded broken, useless things. Now our scholars use just that garbage to describe and analyze ways of life long gone. So scholars will use Mrs. Strong's collections of refrigerators and washing machines to study changes in household work in the nineteenth century, and the museum's extensive holdings of dolls and toys to study changes in the na-ture of childhood. Future scholars will surely find still other problems we haven't thought of yet for which these collections will provide ideal data.

The equation for disasters and accidents is relatively (only relatively) simple: how much is enough to prevent some foreseeable, if unlikely, ca-lamity? The collection problem is more complicated because we don't know the future value of something (what later generations will find it useful for) when we save or discard it now (will it be rejected as not having been worth saving after all?). That makes it impossible to calculate the tradeoffs involved. We don't know what will be gained or lost if we don't make this investment in conservation now.

Scholars and academics experience this problem personally: how many books are enough? Most scholars believe they need every book they own, without exception, and keep books against the barest possibility of dis-covering an as-yet-unsuspected future utility. But how many books do they really need to get their work done? My own working library for a spe-cific project is usually about twenty-five to thirty books, and I routinely sell surplus books. But sometimes I sell a book only to find that I need it after all. So I found, as I wrote this, that I once again needed Durkheim's *Suicide* (1951), my copy sold long ago when our move to a smaller apart-ment decreased the available space for books. Of course, I could and did borrow it from the local library. How do I calculate the tradeoff here? If I buy it—is that such a terrible cost? Compared to the peace of mind that came from cleaning out so many books I hadn't looked at in thirty years?

The rest of my environment complicates these calculations. I have easy access, in the United States, to free public libraries. But many European scholars assembled their collections exactly because, while libraries existed, and you could use them, you could never just browse. You had to ask the librarian for specific books and then wait for them to be delivered. Having your own library avoided that. But then you couldn't make the serendipitous finds that browsing in open library stacks gives American scholars who, even though they're better off, are never as perfectly supplied as they would like. The unknowable future need creates the urge for a library of your own.

These examples take the utility of what to save or buy as given. Of course we want to save lives, prevent the disruption of our cities and the crashes of our space craft, have access to books needed for important work. But the desire to maximize possessions varies among social groups, as became clear when I raised the topic at a dinner party in Paris. The women present (themselves scholars) immediately suggested a similar question based in their gender-specific experience: how many pairs of shoes are enough? And the hostess (an anthropologist) went around the table asking everyone, male and female, how many pairs they had. Men found the question puzzling and didn't always know the answer, but the women understood immediately and could give a precise answer.

The women knew, as the men didn't, that a more basic question was involved: what do you need different pairs of shoes for? Why isn't one pair (two or three at the most) enough, as is often true for men? The two groups made the calculation differently.

Clothing and appearance mean different things for men and women. You not only must not be naked, and be protected against the weather; you must be clothed appropriately for specific situations. Women have to prepare for more differentiated situations than men do. In Western and Westernized countries, men have perhaps three registers of clothing: formal (suit and tie), informal (no tie, perhaps chinos or jeans), and completely informal (or sloppy: sweats, shorts, clothes for dirty jobs around the house, etc.). Clothes vary meaningfully in price and style within categories, and some men, perhaps some categories of men, care more about this than others and monitor the subtle differences between brands and styles more carefully, just as some boys take the differences between brands of sports shoes more seriously than most adults do. But in general the number and variety of situations men must consider in choosing what they wear is small.

Women in contemporary Western societies, on the other hand, find themselves in a great variety of situations that require different kinds of clothing, each requiring appropriate accompanying shoes, which means you must have a larger supply of shoes than men do, to meet the more differentiated situational expectations for varying degrees of formality, sportiness, and being in style. Likewise, women's clothes and shoes can signify and hint at more things about age, cultural dispositions, sexuality, and attractiveness than men's do. And that means that how many shoes are enough will be more for women than for men. ("Required" here means that some other people, whoever they might be in an individual case, will expect you to respect these conventions and that you refuse to be the kind of person who doesn't honor them. I suppose this is why women so often feel they must wear a new dress to someone else's wedding.)

So we add to our equation that what we want (O, the outcome, in the equation), while variable, is also socially defined and socially constrained and thus more variable taken in the asocial abstract than in the concrete situations of everyday life.

Despite their obvious differences, catastrophes and collections have much in common. Heat waves (it has been demonstrated and much remarked on) don't kill people randomly. They select victims in specific race, class, and ethnic categories. You can think of these disasters, very generally, as part of a Darwinian process of natural selection whose survivors will constitute the world's collection of human beings, as the survivors of a similar selection by the proprietor creates the population of books in a library. So disasters make collections. This models a general process found in many disparate areas. I will describe just a few. Each provokes more complications in the rudimentary model I've been casually constructing (whose ramifications I'll leave as an exercise for readers, at least for now).

Biologists warn of the terrible consequences of reducing the planet's biological diversity. In the United States, major construction and harvesting projects have been halted by the discovery that the project would kill off a rare species. But which species to save? All the millions of kinds of beetles? A rare and beautiful species of deer on the verge of extinction? Animals generally considered "cute" or beautiful (but by who? using what criteria?) surely are more likely to be saved than beetles. Because there are so many more kinds of beetles but also because who, besides entomologists, likes bugs that much?

Further, the enormous number of interconnections between species make it impossible to know what else will be affected by our decision about this one species. And, further still, these consequences take one form in the next ten years and quite different forms a hundred, or a thousand, years from now.

We can't decide which species to save because, given these complexities, we can't construct a logically defensible common measure for the many disparate things we want to maximize. (I have taken these examples and arguments from Bowker 2004.) Every way of settling these questions runs into a similar impasse, which is why we solve them only by accepting some conventionalized solution, accepting it not because it's "right," but because (in a way that's perfectly circular) it's what everyone will accept.

Similar questions arise over the preservation of languages. There are many thousands of languages, but large numbers of them disappear every year. Keeping a language alive costs a lot: you have to preserve a population that speaks it and passes it on to its children via educational institutions, a method of writing it, a literature written in it, and a political basis for all that, because the political implications of keeping a language alive or destroying it are important. (See the discussions in Maffi 2001.)

The preservation of historic buildings embodies a similar process. Every building is historic in one way or another, but if they are all to be saved for their historical importance, then how will a city grow? Americans really don't have much of a problem with this, though they think they do, because their cities are so new. In contrast, a two-thousand-year-old city like Rome can only exist as a palimpsest, in which buildings contain the remnants of other buildings, in which every attempt to build something new uncovers something older, sometimes very much older, which these days has a prima facie claim to continued existence. (I'm influenced here by the many varieties of imaginary cities described in Calvino 1974 and discussed in Becker 2007, 270–84.)

Another version of the biological problem is more familiar and more intimate. How many children are enough for two people to have? The "correct answer" (that is, the conventionally acceptable answer) to this question has changed historically, and the criteria for arriving at the answer have changed as well. In earlier times, a couple had enough children to do all the work the family farm or business required for economic viability, taking into account the inevitable deaths (child mortality being much higher than it is now in Western countries) along the way. And parents wanted enough children to survive to support them in their old age. More recently, the appropriate number of children has been set in a more complicated way, involving questions about how many can be supported in the style the family, and their friends and relatives, think appropriate. Or, as Gilberto Velho suggested (1976, 272–74), how many children are required to achieve a "family project" of social mobility or preservation of class status?

A public version of the question asks how many children the society or nation needs or should have. So governments espouse family policies suggesting, or encouraging, or requiring so and so many children. We need more children to make more soldiers (France after 1870, Germany under Hitler). We need fewer children, to reduce the amount of poverty, pave the way for economic growth (China's campaign to reduce the number of children to one per couple), or keep the earth a livable planet.

Underlying all these specific problems is the basic question Emile Durkheim (1951, 246–58) raised. How do we know when we have enough—of anything? He argued that anomic suicide, the special kind that appeared in boom times as well as depressions, resulted from the feeling of insatiability people experienced when the norms governing ordinary consumption were no longer convincing and enforceable. Our wants and desires are ordinarily constrained by such norms, sometimes even by rules, governing what people like us should possess and be allowed to possess. Sumptuary laws once limited the clothing people of various social ranks could wear: nobility could wear suits made of the most expensive cloth, but tradesmen had to be satisfied with something less ostentatious. Expense similarly limits our clothing tastes and desires. We can't wear what we can't pay for. When people no longer feel or accept these constraints, as happens in a boom, they don't know when to stop (it's the "Emelda Marcos syndrome," accounting for her five hundred pairs of shoes).

Sociologists will not be surprised by Durkheim's general answer to all these questions about how much is enough: it's enough—preparations for disasters, books in a library, species in the biosphere, shoes in the closet—when everyone who has a voice in the matter agrees to accept it as enough. Since the answer results from compromise, it won't be logical and will be defensible only as what was possible, at that time, in those circumstances. It will work, like everything in social life, because it's what, at the moment, "everyone" (everyone who has an effective voice in the matter, at least) accepts as the way things are done.

Durkheim might have added, had he considered all these cases, all these permutations of the question, that it's no easy thing to get all the interested parties to agree—from the politicians and citizens trying to allocate revenues among competing worthy causes to the members of a couple trying to agree on how many children to have or, more difficult yet, on how many books the house can hold.

REASONING FROM MANY CASES

That's what I've been doing in all the above, laying out cases in which O, the outcome to be explained, resulted from an agreement to do what later on turned out to be a result no one wanted. My reasoning aimed to create a plausible idea of what went on in the black box that produced the levels of governmental investment that in turn produced the results in situations of extreme weather that occasionally shocked cities with results that could have been prepared for but hadn't been.

How can we understand these occasionally terrible surprises? I started with the case of heat waves. Occasional unexpectedly hot summers made people realize that they had taken for granted that weather would always vary within narrow limits, so that investments in precautions could be made "reasonably" or "sensibly." When a heat wave went beyond the expected, beyond what "usually happens," public officials and media began to recommend changing E, the level of investment, in order to lower the damage unforeseen events would produce (O). They ordinarily didn't have to do that and so had more money to spend on other equally desirable and seemingly more urgent projects. What went on in the black box seemed simple enough. The most recent, unexpectedly severe, O caused people to reconsider how they allocated limited resources, changing the value of E.

Then I added snowstorms. And earthquakes. Each new case looked a lot like the ones that had come before. People calculated the expected cost of avoiding a disaster's unwanted consequences and compared it to the cost of the potential loss they would incur if they didn't take the steps necessary to avoid the worst possibilities. That's what goes on in the black box. When events alter the way people calculate those probabilities, they change their allocations.

But earthquakes made me complicate the model in the black box. While heat and snow vary more or less regularly—every few years a season will go beyond the expected—earthquakes, which also vary more or less regularly, vary over a much longer period, which can occasionally extend into the hundreds of years. There will be a Big One, the experts assure us, but they can't tell what's going to happen in the near future or maybe even in the next hundred years. We have far more trouble evaluating the equation—figuring out what kinds of losses we're willing to gamble on—when the next occurrence will be beyond our lifetime, maybe beyond our grandchildren's lifetime. The uncertainty about when the Big One is going to happen affects calculations in a way we have to build into our model of the workings inside the black box, making us realize that something that seemed a more or less fixed quantity—how often the unwanted event is going to happen—is actually quite variable. That case complicates our model.

These are all disasters that, in some sense, the physical world creates for us (although weather scientists now tell us that hurricanes and catastrophic floods and tsunamis probably arise from human intervention after all). But the spaceship disasters, as Vaughan demonstrated, could have been avoided not just by preparing for their consequences but also by preventing them from happening in a way that isn't so immediately available to us with weather disturbances. Had the personnel of the Challenger mission accepted the cost of following their own advice, and not used the available bureaucratic resources to ease those restrictions and avoid having to take all the precautions that had already been decided were necessary, they might have avoided the disasters completely. Vaughan's research makes clear that some part of the E quantity, the expense necessary to avoid disaster, goes beyond just spending more money. It requires us to look to organizational elements, work cultures that systematically though unintentionally allow the underestimation of risk when nothing bad happens for a long time. We send the spacecraft up even when it's cold, even though we know the O-rings might not be able to withstand those temperatures, because, well, we'd done it before in cold weather without incident so probably nothing bad will happen this time either, because the bureaucracy's work rules allow for taking "acceptable risks," and, most important, because we all agree that's the thing to do. So "organizational culture," and the folk reasoning it contains, seems like an apt term for that part of E, that input to the ultimate event.

Which means that, inside the black box, more than simple frequencies of events affect people's calculations. All the things we know about work cultures make up another part of the apparatus in there, something we know we have to consider from now on for heat waves and snowstorms and all the other physical disasters in which E's and O's have to be evaluated in order to decide what to do. And, because these elements occurred in the space disasters in a way that became very public, we have to include all the political factors that Vaughan's analysis identified—for instance, keeping Congress in a mood to continue putting up the money for the space program. That includes the political forces behind the inevitable pushes for other things to spend all that money on: schools, health, and the rest.

"Realistic" political analyses generally treat the amount of support (most often in money but also in time, labor, and other scarce commodities) as given. After all, there are only twenty-four hours in the day, right? And only so much money. In fact, the amount of money, time, and other resources available for dealing with any of the problems the black box model poses varies enough that we have to include that variation and the processes that produce it in the model too.

The most surprising addition to my understanding of what goes on in the black box producing collective responses to problems came when I realized that collections posed the same kinds of problems of allocating resources as disasters do. To make this conceptual jump, I had to rethink E and O. If we understand E, in the case of disasters, as what it would cost to prevent something we don't want to happen, we have to see E, for collections, as the amount someone is prepared to spend (in time, money, and whatever else it takes) to get the things they want in their collection. And O as the sum of the good things we expect to get from having them there.

We may think Mrs. Strong's collecting frivolous or just plain goofy, but we shouldn't consider her choices that way, considering the analytic possibilities it opens up for us. Better to adopt the rigorous methods of economists, and treat her demand schedule, as they call it, as her business. Not for us to judge its wisdom. But the examples that followed her story can't be dismissed from serious consideration.

The consequences of mistaken allocations differ when the question concerns how much of something I should buy rather than how I can avoid getting killed in the next earthquake, but the problems posed have a family resemblance. My first case—Mrs. Strong's eccentric collection of dolls, toys, and household appliances and fixtures—made clear that when someone decides to collect something, the only real limit is how much money and time (and whatever else it takes to assemble the desired collectibles) they have to do it with. And that shows that the black box's operations require enough conceptual apparatus to deal with people who have, as some might say, "more money than sense," that is, put more neutrally, people who think some things are important that others think trivial.

The other cases I brought in, as I continued to add to this collection intended to help me elaborate my understanding of the processes going on in the black box that linked E and O (inputs and outputs, it should be clear now), wouldn't provoke charges of frivolity. Some people would immediately understand that a scholar's need for books (or a jazz fan's need for recordings) is serious. These cases add the point that O, the end to be achieved by the E we expend for books or shoes, is generally not just some idiosyncratic whim, but rather arises out of people's need to have a variety of, in these cases, books or clothing and shoes in order to do something necessary for the lives they live as scholars or as adequately attired members of whatever parts of their social milieu they participate in.

I didn't stop there. I added some matters of contemporary concern— the preservation of biological species, of languages spoken by relatively few people, of historic buildings—which complicated our model further by making us understand that choices like these don't necessarily involve individual collectors but, at the extreme, involve the whole social and physical world, considered as the entity making the choices by means of a kind of Darwinian selection mechanism, just like the one that produces beautiful butterflies and millions of beetles and all the rest of the contents of the world we live in. To make the affinity of this way of thinking to that sort of Darwinian model, I also brought in the question of how many children two people (or however many might be involved) ought to have and the further question of who gets to answer that question: the procreating pair, the extended family, the state?

By this time, I was adding cases indiscriminately, just to see how many variations I could think of. (I've been tempted to recommend that, seriously, as a methodological strategy.) I added, as a final word to my own scientific tribe, the connection of my energetic and undisciplined collection of cases to the fundamental questions a founder of sociology, Emile Durkheim, left us to ponder: how do we ever know when we have enough of anything, no matter what it is? I concluded, from the cases I collected in this hunt, that we know it's enough when everyone involved in the situation is willing to settle for the amounts of O and E, whatever units we measure them in, that this or that way of doing things will involve. Arriving at that answer involves all the elements of the processes going on in the black box, all the inputs and outputs we've talked about so far and all those yet to be discovered. (People interested in a more metaphysical analysis of the fundamental question posed by the title of this chapter might want to look at Eric Kraft's [1993] philosophical novel *Where Do You Stop?*)

HOW DO YOU END YOUR RESEARCH?

My investigation of these questions embodies the problem I'm investigating. Because it brings up this question: when do I stop working on a piece of research? How many varieties of situations—relating to the climate, organizations, disasters, or collections—did I need to conclude that I could stop looking for any more, that now I had "enough" cases to present my "theory" about how much is enough? Having learned a little about what goes on in the black box that produces decisions about the situations where the question arises, what can I say to myself and to my colleagues about possible solutions to a common and perplexing problem we all have to solve? As working scientists, we keep asking ourselves if our research is complete. Can I stop now? Should I stop now? If not now, when? (See the discussion in Small 2009. And for an approach to these questions in the arts, see the papers in Becker et al. 2006, especially Menger 2006 and Joyce 2006.)

Earlier in this chapter, I restated the general question in a sort of formula: how much are we willing to pay (E) to achieve an outcome we want (O): to avoid disaster of a certain size or to complete a collection of a certain kind? Put in those terms, the research problem is, How much time and effort (E) am I willing to expend to collect the cases that get me nearer to a general answer to that question (O)? Can I use this way of thinking to solve my own problems in finally finishing work I've begun?

Now I'm going to restate my version of Emile Durkheim's answer to the general question, one adapted to the specifics of my E and O and possibly good for cases of scientific and scholarly inquiry generally: you can stop looking for more cases, more evidence, when everyone who has a voice in the matter agrees to accept what you've done as enough. Not an answer justified by a logical argument, but as good an answer as we're likely to find.

That doesn't by any means answer all the questions. For instance: who do we include in the "everyone" who has a voice? In most research fields, you find the answer in the dominant working paradigm, the one accepted by the people you recognize as scientific colleagues at the moment you ask the question. That paradigm tells you what to do so that critics who might otherwise think you haven't "done enough" will have to shut up and accept your results. Thomas Kuhn (1970) said this in a variety of ways, not as an "ought," but as a factual statement about how working scientists solve the problem in the course of their daily work, and it's an answer found throughout the cases described and analyzed in Bruno Latour's *Science in Action* (1987).

To put it more technically: scientific communities generally have a list of precautions they expect their colleagues to take to avoid mistakes that would invalidate their conclusions in the eyes of their peers. Maybe these precautions really will do the trick, maybe they won't; probably they'll do the job pretty well most of the time. They won't give you the perfection of the idealized version of what constitutes sufficient proof found in "official" statements of proper method, but they embody the agreement of working scientists, who know they can seldom fully satisfy all those idealized criteria and know further that research that gets done will have to adapt to the realities the research situation imposes, taking what the NASA scientists involved in the disasters Vaughan studied would probably categorize as "acceptable risks."

The list of the "trials of strength" included in this consensus (Latour 1987, 78 and elsewhere; it's a key idea for him) changes all the time, as the specific scientific community confronts problems it hasn't seen before and, in particular, when it finds that some of its accepted methods no longer "work."

The O in this equation, the result wanted, never changes: to produce findings that colleagues will accept. But what E should be, what to pay in time, money, and effort for that acceptable result, has never been completely and finally settled. The classical example of a communally approved list of precautions whose observance guarantees acceptance is the laboratory experiment. The scientist creates two populations of specimens and applies the suspected "causal" factor to one of them and not to the other, making sure that the two populations don't differ in any other way.

If you do that, no reasonable colleague can quarrel with your conclusions. You know where to stop: when you've done what the experimental model says you have to do. Then the critics have to keep quiet. You paid E and you're entitled to O. All very well for physicists and chemists and others who work in laboratories where researchers can exercise complete control over all the possible influences, though Latour's description of laboratories (1987, 63–100; and 1988) makes me skeptical about how well the model works in practice. (I'm not the only skeptic. Interested readers can consult the sustained critical analysis made by Stanley Lieberson, the distinguished practitioner of quantitative sociology, in *Making it Count* [1985], noting especially the summaries on 3 and 171–73, but not failing to read the entire book.)

In practice, social scientists (including the psychologists, who depend so much on the experimental model, and the survey researchers, who try to import its powerful controls into the situations of normal social life that they study) can't exercise that complete control: they can't choose the people they study randomly (thus avoiding the errors created by biases in selecting participants); they can't measure whatever they like, because the "subjects" whose cooperation they need often refuse to do what's wanted (am I the only one who refuses to participate in telephone surveys?); and down a long list of social realities that prevent them from satisfying the criteria that would convince others the way a well-done laboratory experiment does.

So social scientists have to find other ways to agree on how much strictness their research protocols must exhibit to command that kind of assent from their colleagues. And, unfortunately, as Thomas Kuhn (1970, 160, 164) remarked, they have never succeeded in finding such simple bases of agreement about how much is enough as natural scientists have, though they keep trying. Here's one of the more innovative examples.

Donald Campbell and his colleagues (1963 and later revised editions), looking for a workable way to produce the agreement that certifies acceptable conclusions, made a pretty good try, and the story is instructive. Accepting the impossibility of doing true experiments, they decided to invent practical, workable standards that psychologists could use to convince others that they'd done the best that could be done, thus making it possible to get on with doing research. They developed, as an alternative to true experiments, "quasi-experimental" research designs. They listed potential "threats to the validity" of hypotheses (the list of threats, and the coauthors, have changed several times since the first version). These threats covered a lot of territory: historical events that affected your working conditions as they did the people who volunteered as experimental "subjects," variability in the backgrounds of those subjects, statistical artifacts, and so on. Over the years, zealous analysts added more and more possibilities to the list of ways you could go wrong.

Campbell and company tried to solve the problem of getting others to accept their conclusions by relaxing the definition of E (in this case, what you had to do to convince the colleagues whose opinions you cared about) in order to be able to have some O (interesting and useful results), not as much O as you'd like, but more than nothing. They saw that you had to give up some of the inexorable logic of the experimental approach to be able to do anything at all. But then you knew that your conclusion might not be fully justified: one or more of the threats you hadn't guarded against might invalidate the whole thing. Taking a practical approach to this dilemma, Campbell introduced a new criterion of how much was enough: control the *most likely* threats to validity, which might produce a doable result in situations where you didn't have the desirable full control. He devised a variety of alternative designs that relaxed one or another of the controls necessary for full experimental rigor, ranging from the one-shot case study (typically the implicit design of any serious qualitative field research) to increasingly elaborate approximations of the logically defensible full procedure. Each variation on the standard design guarded against a different combination of threats. None of them guarded against all the threats. Using this strategy, researchers have to make strategic choices, looking for the design that guards against the *most likely* threats to the hypothesis they want to test—not all the threats (that was impossible), but the likely ones (which is why he called these designs "quasi-experimental"). That produced the best approximation to the real thing in the circumstances of a given project.

That's a typical resolution—better thought through and better argued than most—of the "how much is enough" dilemma in everyday scientific activity. Guard against the most likely flaws and expect some failures and some criticism. It's the only real choice.

After you have gone down the generally accepted checklist of things required to adequately verify a conclusion for the kind of study you've done, and have finally done the research, you know whether your idea has been supported empirically or not. But neither our own simple observations of everyday life, nor elaborate historical or observational investigations (not even such a careful and thoughtful work as Peter Galison's account [1987] of experimentation in high-energy physics) definitively identifies a model for deciding when to stop investigating possible alternatives to a theory. These sources tell us, instead, that it all depends, that every answer to where I should call it quits on this research arises out of specific organizational and historical circumstances, and no amount of logic or philosophy of science gives an answer that is, logically speaking, better than semiarbitrary.

So there aren't any good, logically defensible answers. But everyone eventually does find an answer because, after all, everyone eventually stops. Sometimes, when someone asks me to speak to a group of sociology students, and I'm not sure what will interest them, I use an all-purpose title that almost any working scholar or scholar-in-training wants to hear more about: "The Three Things Every Sociologist Must Know." The first time I gave this lecture I really had no idea what I was going to say, but on the way to the lectern, I was inspired and began by telling them, "The first thing you have to know is how to start. The second thing is how to stop. And the last thing is: what to do in between."

I told them not to worry about starting because, whatever they chose to do, they had certainly already started working on it. They'd been thinking about and exploring all sorts of possibilities and had finally decided on one. But, having decided, they realize that they don't know what the next step is and think some kind of major preliminary exploration has to be done before they can "really" begin. I told them they'd been exploring for quite a while already, whether they've knew it or not: reading about their topic, thinking up clever ways to do the work, daydreaming about the finished product. (Much of the content of this book, it should by now be obvious, discusses matters that go on in this first stage.) Now they just had to start, which only required them to do the first thing that came to mind: read another book, look for more sources of information they could turn into usable data, write down everything they already knew and thought about the topic to see what they had already decided on without knowing they'd done that. . . . In other words, I told them, it doesn't really make any difference what you do . . . as long as you do something and get moving.

What to do after that, the second big question (though I mentioned it last), has an equally obvious answer. Do something and see what happens and keep on doing that as long as you can think of things to do.

Will a similar answer serve to tell you when to stop? Do colleagues agree on the E (what amount of an answer will be enough to answer every possible suggestion that you should have done "this" too)? No, someone will always want more. So "stop anywhere" really is the best answer. It may seem (this being the end of the road, after which you can't do any more) that you need a more logical and convincing reason than that. But since

the community of your colleagues has never come to a working agreement about this, you can't find O, the accepted "good reason" to stop here
or there or anywhere in particular. But you don't have to keep on doing
the project forever, though people sometimes act as though they do have
to do that. If there's no good reason to stop in any particular place, you
might as well stop for whatever bad reason is most pertinent: you've spent
all the money from the grant you got, or your fellowship has come to an
end and you have to start working at a real job. If you feel very comfort-
able doing what you've been doing and don't want to start on a new stage
of this enterprise, there's an endless list of bad reasons to stop. Choose
one and you're through. (This is, in fact, the working consensus of every
scientific community. If that wasn't true, no science would ever get done.)

You can find, if you think about it, the best of the bad reasons when you
(incorrectly, but you don't know that) see that, to "really understand" the
topic you've been investigating, you'd have to undertake some final investigation that now looks essential to answering the one question that, if
not answered, will make everything you've done till now useless. There's
always another question. That's how scientific and scholarly investigation
works. A friend of mine had almost finished her dissertation, for which
she had interviewed a large number of people about their experiences
with a particular disease. But now, she decided, she couldn't really understand their experience unless she also interviewed family members who
had helped them during the crises the disease provoked. That would require at least as many interviews as she had already done, and probably a
lot more. I couldn't talk her out of it, and her dissertation took a lot longer
to finish.

Was she just being "neurotic"? That's the usual diagnosis faculty and
friends apply to people who think there's still something else they *must*
do before their thesis or article or book is done. But they aren't neurotic.
They're just being logical, having run into the impossibility of estab-
lishing a *logically* proper stopping place, and being unwilling to stop for
some practical, therefore intellectually unjustifiable, therefore less than
morally acceptable, reason.

More experienced researchers recognize this peril and usually deal
with it more forthrightly, evaluating O (the desirable outcome) as "getting it done" and E (the price to be paid) as "what my colleagues will not
complain too much about if I stop here." My colleagues Blanche Geer and
Marsh Ray and I, who collaborated in doing the fieldwork for the project
that produced *Making the Grade* (1968), spent three years on the campus
of the University of Kansas, interviewing and, for a lengthy period, participating with and observing people from every part of the undergraduate school's student body. When we had come to a large number of pro-

visional conclusions and tested them out in all the ways we could think of; when we had written rough-draft versions of the final book; when it seemed like we were definitively through—we had a project meeting and gradually began discussing a topic that had come to seem very interesting to all three of us, something we had begun calling "Kansas culture." A large number of smart students from "good families" all over the state came to the university for their undergraduate education. Many of them had grown up in one of the smaller cities in the state—Hays, Dodge City, Leavenworth, Salina—and many others had grown up in larger conglomerates like Kansas City and its suburban ring, or Wichita. These young people would probably furnish some of the elite that would come to power in the state in the years to follow (so we reasoned) and then they would have available to them a network of acquaintances, a lot of understandings and perspectives that collective action could be based on, in other words, a culture, what one of us named, as we started excitedly talking about these possibilities, "Kansas culture."

As soon as someone said that out loud, and we all sat there imagining the grant proposal we could collectively write to support this new extension of our work, I said, "OK. That's it. This project is officially over." And we all agreed we'd had a close call.

That's how easy it is not to stop, even when a convenient stopping point presents itself.

Almost all the people who arrive at this impasse finally realize that the solution acceptable to their professional community is to accept the unavoidable and just finish the damn thing, with all its flaws. Everett Hughes used to tell the story of Don Roy's final oral examination on his dissertation (Roy 1952b, a masterful study of machine shop workers, later published in several articles [Roy 1952a, 1953, 1954] that most sociologists would give a lot to have written). As is well known, after the members of a faculty examining committee finish their questions, they ask the candidate to step out of the room while they discuss the work and decide whether its author has passed or not. So the faculty committee, having questioned Roy at length about his research, excused him to go wait in the hall while they deliberated his fate. On the way out he leaned over and whispered to Hughes that he didn't know if he should let them go ahead with their deliberations, because "there are a lot of holes in this thing that you guys never even got near." In Hughes's version of the story, he told Roy to keep quiet and take care of whatever he thought needed taking care of on his own time, after he had the PhD. That's the realistic, grownup thing to do, and almost everyone (Roy included) eventually does it.

The insistence on "one more thing" to be done occasionally gets just plain absurd. All but one of the main actors in this next (true) story aren't with us any more, so I've used their real names. Ned Polsky wrote a wonderful book called *Hustlers, Beats, and Others* (1967), which began with a long essay on pool hustlers. He knew all about pool hustlers, having earned pocket money, sometimes more than that, for a long time by hustling people who played worse than he did, getting them to bet on games they couldn't win because they weren't good enough, a fact he didn't feel required to tell them or give them enough evidence to figure out for themselves. He offered the book to the Aldine Publishing Company, for which I edited a series of observational studies it fit right into. Alexander Morin, the president of the company, was eager to have the book, but the final manuscript never arrived. Polsky kept missing deadlines (being in the publishing business, an editor for the Free Press of Glencoe at the time, he knew they were artificial).

Polsky insisted that these delays were essential because he had to consult some important historical documents before he could properly consider the book done, and they were buried in an English university library. The documents contained a full description, written by a member of a British noble house, of how he had ravished one of the female servants— on a *pool table* in the *billiard* room of the estate! Polsky couldn't rest easy until he had inspected these documents with his own eyes. This explanation didn't convince anyone else, but he insisted and would not deliver the manuscript until he satisfied this self-imposed requirement.

In the end, Morin was in New York, where Polsky lived, on other business. He went to Polsky's apartment on the Upper West Side. Ned wasn't home, but his wife was. Morin asked her if she knew where the manuscript was. She said she did, and he asked her to get it. She did. Morin inspected it, put it in his briefcase, and left. And so, as the result of a kidnapping, the book was published after all.

8 *IOUs, Promissory Notes, and Killer Questions: What About Mozart? What About Murder?*

Imaginary cases have their uses, mainly in suggesting dimensions of something we're interested in that rarely or never appear in reality. They find a different use when social scientists disagree with each other about the kinds of questions they usually call "theoretical," questions about what kinds of ideas someone can appropriately use to describe social phenomena. When discussants want to discredit ideas they disagree with, they often deploy imaginary cases in order to use the rhetorical device called the reductio ad absurdum, described this way by the Encyclopedia Britannica: "In logic, a form of refutation showing contradictory or absurd consequences following upon premises as a matter of logical necessity. A form of the reductio ad absurdum argument, known as indirect proof or reductio ad impossibile, is one that proves a proposition by showing that its denial conjoined with other propositions previously proved or accepted leads to a contradiction. In common speech the term reductio ad absurdum refers to anything pushed to absurd extremes."

To put it in the language of this chapter, social scientists sometimes argue about a theoretical point by presenting as conclusive evidence a truncated imaginary story posing as a scientifically established case, the bare bones of a set of facts (or even just an allusion to such facts) for which there's no real evidence. We might call these cases "scientific IOUs" (promissory notes, to be a little more formal, or markers, in gambling slang). They present conclusions in just a few words, implicitly promising that behind these words, buttressing the conclusion they suggest, lie a full complement of observations, data, and logical reasoning that conclusively demonstrate a contradiction between their opponent's argument and the details the case alludes to—but doesn't present. The language suggests that the case has already been proved and now has the status of something "everybody knows," needing no more than a one- or two-word allusion to destroy the opposition. Like an IOU in the sense that it promises, like a banknote, that on demand the promised value can and will be produced for inspection.

So these scientific debaters allude to something as though it were so obvious as to require neither logical argument or empirical proof. They present a hypothetical case as though it were stuffed with concrete information about the workings of some social organization, containing the wealth of observed events and verified data a serious case study contains, though it isn't and doesn't. They expect that the story the IOU alludes to will force their opponent either to concede defeat or to agree to a totally absurd proposition. Presenting the case by allusion, they leave out the complications serious research would inevitably introduce, that would, were they taken seriously, reveal the multiple branching possibilities underlying real cases of the kind their invention presents as so well-established as not to need presentation. Their rhetorical questions allude to the results of complicated causal thickets, the inputs and outputs the term *black box* gives a home to, but in no way demonstrate that anything that complicated is going on.

These debaters use the "killer question," an interrogative formula that reduces the empirical case promised in the IOU to a few evocative words, as a way of invoking the reductio ad absurdum, expecting most listeners or readers to accept an allusion to the hypothetical case as all that's necessary to support that logical argument. On a number of occasions, people used that tactic to combat ideas of mine they thought pernicious. To explain what happened, I'm going to refer to some personal experiences I found irritating and have always wanted to convert to an educational purpose. The cases promised by the killer questions addressed to me in fact led to a more comprehensive understanding of the development of some fields of sociological work, so I guess I have nothing to complain about. (If I sound a little irritated, it's because I consider this argumentative tactic illegitimate and sneaky and still resent having it used against me.)

THE KILLER QUESTION IN ACTION: REASONING FROM STRATEGICALLY INCOMPLETE CASES

I've been involved, to varying degrees and over many years, with three fields that on the surface seem to have little to do with each other—the sociologies of deviance, art, and science—but in which I see a deep underlying similarity, which surfaces as a chronic fight over definitions. Participants in these arguments often employ the reductio ad absurdum tactic and deploy the killer question. Two examples from my own experience in such discussions give some body to these generalities.

KILLER QUESTIONS. When I published *Outsiders: Studies in the Sociology of Deviance* in 1963 I was living in San Francisco, convenient to the University of California at Berkeley, which had, among its many appendages, the Center for the Study of Law and Society, then directed by the deservedly well-known scholar Philip Selznick. Selznick harbored in his center a cluster of researchers (among them Jerome Skolnick, David Matza, and Sheldon Messinger) in the developing field of "deviance," at the time a brand new name for the study of what had earlier been called "social disorganization" or criminology. A proponent of natural law, Selznick himself had grave doubts about this radical redefinition of a conventional field of sociology that rested on conventional ideas of right and wrong. As one of several writers who had popularized "deviance," and living close by, I was invited to talk to the center's members about the "labeling" theory of deviance, of which *Outsiders* served as a prime example.

I remember the occasion vividly. I laid out the ideas contained in the first chapter of the book—that deviance was not an innate or "natural" quality of someone's actions but rather resulted from the joint activity of such an actor and of the people who responded to his or her activity by labeling it as deviant. ("Deviant" was a general term that some of us had begun to use to encompass the various kinds of negative categories that arose in specific areas: "criminal," "crazy," "abnormal," "perverted," "unethical," "impolite," etc.) This ran counter to the common idea that such categories described things people actually were, essential aspects of their being, and thus easily defined. In this view, a person called a criminal really did commit crimes and, similarly, someone called unethical violated agreed-on standards of ethical conduct, an abnormal person did things normal people didn't do, and so on. That's how you could tell them from "normal" people.

When I finished the exposition, there was the usual time for questions and discussion. And I remember Phil Selznick, the director of the center, standing in a doorway at the back of the room, smoking a cigar, looking at me quizzically, and saying, mildly, "Well, Howie, I see what you're getting at; it's very interesting." And then coming in for the kill: "But, after all, what about murder? Isn't that *really* deviant?" He settled back, smiling, convinced that he had made a devastating point, had asked a killer question that boxed me into a rhetorical corner. What made it a killer question, of course, was that no one in their right mind would say murder was not a terrible thing. But that formulation of the problem cheated, because it confounded "deviant," which I had used as a technical term to denote the result of an act of labeling, with "evil" or "immoral," which seemed neither to have nor to require an empirical warrant. If you thought something was evil, you made a moral argument showing that such a position derived from a general ethical position. You couldn't prove murder was evil by doing research. That's what I was talking about.

So I didn't think Selznick had made such a devastating point, and countered with familiar counterarguments: that reasonable people differed over which acts of killing were murder and which were other things like "justified homicide," that these differences varied depending on what kinds of people did the killing or were killed, the historical era, and so on. He considered such arguments logic-chopping and didn't think I'd answered his question. I thought I had.

Before getting into the meat of this example, I'll add a second one. Some years later, when I was teaching at Northwestern University, the then dean of the College of Arts and Sciences inaugurated a series of "Dean's Lectures" and asked me to give one of them on the subject of my new book, *Art Worlds*. Although I hadn't put it this way in the book, *Art Worlds* presented what you could reasonably call a "labeling" theory of art. One component of the idea was to approach art as a collective activity, something people did together. The labeling component had to do with the problem of defining art as an object of study, a problem that had perplexed aestheticians for millennia and showed no signs of solution. I had solved it somewhat cavalierly by refusing to attempt a definition, instead treating the definition of objects or performances as art as itself a form of collective activity—so that "art" and the definition of something as art became the result of a lot of people agreeing that some things were art and some other things weren't—and I was interested in studying those occasions when people did define things as art and argued over the definitions, as well as in the kinds of arguments (arguments, of course, being a kind of collective activity) that philosophers (the dean was just such a philosopher) and others got into over what was or wasn't art. I didn't think it was possible to develop a foolproof definition of art that would settle all the arguments that had gone on for roughly two thousand years and showed no signs of being settled soon.

As I presented these ideas in my lecture, the dean fidgeted in his seat, increasingly and visibly upset. He could hardly wait to ask the first question, which not surprisingly took the form of a killer question: "Well, Howie, that's all very interesting but, after all, what about *Mozart*?" After my experiences with killer questions about deviance (Selznick was the first but not the only proponent of the "what about murder" ploy), I had an appropriate though unresponsive answer for him: "What *about* Mozart?" That question took advantage of the truncated, promissory form of the case alluded to. Because just saying "Mozart" doesn't present a fully formed case, complete with arguments and evidence. Saying "Mozart" seems to promise to do that, using the name to point to what would necessarily be a much more complex argument (if anyone were to actually make it) linking Wolfgang Amadeus Mozart to definitional quarrels in the field of aesthetics. "What about Mozart?" challenged him to provide the full case, to make the implicit argument explicit. He looked surprised (he thought the meaning of his question perfectly clear to any reasonable person) and said, "Well, isn't Mozart really a musical genius?" And I made what seemed to me the obvious answer: if you accepted all the premises of a particular approach to art, a specific and by no means universally accepted set of premises about what constituted great music, then Mozart certainly was a genius. But people sometimes rejected those premises and, if they did, might well not agree with the conclusion he had presented as self-evident. The dean, like Selznick, felt that he had asked a killer question and made a devastating point that I hadn't answered acceptably; I thought my answer took care of the problem.

I can't present an example from the sociology of science based in my own research or personal experience, but you can find examples everywhere in that field, which enemies sometimes call "antiscience" because it recognizes that it takes more than experiments and reasoning for scientific theories to be accepted by a scientific community. The enemies misread that recognition of social processes producing consensus among a group of colleagues as saying that scientific results, ideas, and theories are, after all, "just a matter of opinion." The killer question, as put to sociologists of science, takes two slightly different forms. The positive version is "What about airplanes?" If you use the form I used with the dean to ask for a full presentation of the promised case—"What about airplanes?"—the answer is, "Well, don't you believe in the science that says they will fly? If you don't, why do you ever get in one?" Since all the contemporary scholars involved in such arguments constantly fly here and there, that's a serious challenge: aren't they being inconsistent by flying, if their own research and thinking imply that the science supporting aviation is "merely" a matter of consensus?

The negative form of the killer question in the sociology of science is "What about astrology?" If you say "What about it?" the follow-up asks whether, thinking that science is just consensus, you think astrology was true back when all learned men believed in it. Sociologists of science respond that, being reasonable contemporary people, they believe that airplanes will fly and don't bother to read their horoscopes in the daily paper. But, they add, scientists have often collectively believed things that later generations of scientists no longer believe (e.g., the theory of phlogiston, described in chapter 6 of Kuhn 1970), so they also think it likely that scientists in years to come will treat many things contemporary science takes as obviously true the way we now think of astrology.

These quarrelsome uses of IOUs to replace fully presented cases arise when some group thinks its beliefs are under attack. While sociologists seldom attack other groups directly, their work often poaches on territory long held by other disciplines. And, most especially, by academic philosophy.

EMPIRICAL INVESTIGATION REPLACES SPECULATION. In all three of these cases, a field of empirical research (a science) has replaced a field of philosophical discourse. (In what follows, I have no intention of, to use Nathalie Heinich's [1998] phrase, "dethroning" philosophy, only noting what has observably been happening to fields of philosophical work.) In this process, what was once a realm of argumentation based on canonical examples and logical reasoning has been replaced by an enterprise in which scientists arrive at conclusions based on systematic investigation of the empirical world, assuming much less than philosophical discussions usually assume and requiring proof taken from empirical investigations of observed phenomena and from passing what Latour (1987, 180–95) calls "trials of rationality." That is, presenting evidence that no possible invalidating flaws exist in the supporting evidence and reasoning.

This kind of replacement by other disciplines has happened often in the history of philosophy. Physics and other natural sciences were once philosophical topics, but their discussions of physical and biological phenomena long ago gave way to the findings and theories of hard-nosed empirical physicists and biologists.

Beginning in the late nineteenth century, psychology changed from an introspective philosophical activity to an empirical practice carried on in a laboratory. Many classical topics in psychology remain for philosophers to talk about, at least for the moment—the nature of consciousness, for example—but many others have been superseded by empirical scientific investigation. More importantly, many older questions have been reformulated, sometimes quite drastically, in a new language, getting their meaning from a new paradigm, as Thomas Kuhn (1970, 190–95 and elsewhere) taught the world to see.

Similarly with the field of aesthetics, in which the question of what art is has changed from a search for unalterable philosophically established principles by which we can recognize "art" when we see or hear it to an investigation of the way participants in a world of people who collaborate to produce something called art deploy the term as they go about their business (Becker 1982). Ethics has turned into the sociological investigation of how both professionals and ordinary lay people make and enforce moral judgments. Epistemology has given way to "science studies," a mélange of sociology, anthropology, and history. The old questions of morality and ethics and knowledge don't go away. Aestheticians and epistemologists and ethicists continue to debate them. But much of their territory has been colonized by social scientists, covering the same ground from a different standpoint.

RELATIVISM. Since I've appealed to empirical investigation as the touchstone that helps us distinguish what to believe and accept from what to reject, I should make a small side trip and clarify my position on the vexed problem of relativism, which underlies all three of these examples. Are there "real" things out there we can appeal to when we want to settle our disagreements? Or is it just a matter of who can shout the loudest and recruit the most allies? Can we find out what's true by appealing to that reality? That's obviously what Selznick and the dean and the scientists in whose mouths I put questions about airplanes and astrology were doing. Here's what I think, and I believe this is what most sociologists and, in fact, most working empirical scientists think too, when they aren't engaging in polemics aimed at securing money and turf.

Something is "real," a statement about that thing is "true" and therefore has to be taken seriously, when what I say about it withstands all the criticisms and questions people can bring up to discredit it. I've always thought that's how sociologists should work. You anticipate what serious critics—people who really don't want your conclusion about whatever-it-is to be true, people who have a stake in showing you are wrong in any way they can do it—would say. Then you do whatever you have to do to counter those criticisms, so that those critics can no longer make those criticisms, because you have answered them so well that they have to accept your conclusions. This is not the same as shouting louder or having greater political skills. Instead, it refers to the agreement between you and your critics that their complaint isn't, by their own standards, logically or empirically tenable anymore and therefore they will stop making it.

This position has two antecedents in the social science literature on method (I'm sure there are others, but these are the ones that influenced me). I've referred earlier to the work of Donald Campbell and his collaborators (Campbell and Stanley, 1963; Shadish et al. 2001), who argued that working scientists establish the truth of what they say by dealing with "challenges to the validity" of their hypotheses. Which I translate as "countering the things people could say that would make it possible for doubters to dismiss my conclusions." He accompanied his argument with the important proviso that you could never, in research on human beings, deal with all possible criticisms, and so you had to choose the ones most likely to occur and not worry about the rest. This analysis can be applied fruitfully to all the kinds of work social scientists do—field research, historical studies, survey research, and so on.

The second antecedent occurs in Bruno Latour's (1987, 21–62) discussion of how scientists validate their findings and so gain their colleagues' acceptance for them. Two ways are relevant here. They subject the prospective finding, as noted above, to tests of various kinds, "trials of strength," which it must withstand. Other scientists accept a finding that has withstood all the tests that can be brought to bear on it, has taken the worst the opposition can offer and emerged victorious.

Scientists who want their colleagues to accept their results as true also control potential critics' moves by cutting off promising avenues of criticism with convincing answers before a critic even starts down that path. (Latour 1987, 56–9, adopts the rhetorical term "captation" for this purpose.)

In other words, I accept as "true" not what is just someone's opinion, but a statement that no one has criticized in an unanswerable way, a finding that has withstood all the trials friends and foes have subjected it to. I'm not proposing a criterion for what truth "really" is, simply saying what in practice has to happen so that other people who work in your field will accept what you say as true, or true enough for now.

Which adds another dimension to the analysis, a different way of seeing the question of truth. For me, that question is not an eternal problem of epistemology, but rather one that arises for people in a multiperson, usually multiorganizational, setting, where what is true is a practical matter that working scientists deal with. Instead of asking whether they deal with it "properly," in some ultimate sense, I want to know if they deal with it well enough to shut their critics up. The analysis consists of looking at a situation and asking who criticizes who, with what consequences. A likely and common result is that a statement later proved, to everyone's satisfaction, false will be taken as true until that later contradictory evidence arrives. But until then, for that scientific community, it's true. It's in that sense, that astrology was once taken as "true." (See the interesting brouhaha about the causes of King Rameses II's death in Latour 1998a and 1998b, and my discussion of this in Becker 2010.)

So, for me, what I say is true when no one asks me a doubting critical question I can't answer to their satisfaction, forcing them to shake their heads and say, in effect, "Well, I hate to admit it, but I guess you're right." If all or most members of a scientific community make that admission, it's good enough for me to treat the proposed result as true. There's a tricky aspect to this, because of course I wouldn't treat all questions from all people as worthy of such a serious answer. So: whose questions does the community to which the proposed idea is addressed accept? For me, here and now, it's the community of working social scientists, and maybe not all of them because, after all, this is not chemistry, where you might imagine that all the members of the community share standards of proof that no one argues about. Remember that Kuhn's field observations showed him (1970, 7) that social scientists spend a lot more time arguing about these epistemological difficulties than natural scientists do.

Similar answers to questions about relativism can be made with respect to the aesthetic questions art raises and the moral problems ethics investigates. Note that agreement on results in these fields isn't as necessary to the continuation of work in them as is true in science. Ethicists and aestheticians can and do continue to work quite happily even though they disagree on fundamental principles. Having disagreed for two thousand years at least, they'll probably continue to do so, but their disciplines don't suffer as a result.

We can agree that art objects exist independent of any observer. But we don't have to agree that a painting is art for the object to exist. That's true, but not in a way that's very interesting for a social scientist, and anyway, we immediately have to qualify such a remark. Because in fact artworks change (and people change them) all the time. Paintings deteriorate, music is performed by different people in different halls, and isolating what constitutes "the work" you want to talk about can only be accomplished by agreement among discussants about some convention that says when the work is the work we will talk about: for instance, we'll talk about the composer's work as the written score rather than the aural experience we have when someone plays it; or vice versa. Once that kind of agreement is reached, however provisionally and temporarily, discussion can go on perfectly well about "the work" thus isolated. Of course, the changes in the work that do occur will create anomalies that will produce problems for the discussants. (See the discussion in Becker 2006.)

The assessment of artistic value goes on continuously in communities and networks of working artists. Since artists never agree on all these questions, the agreement on value really works best in smaller subcommunities, although even there such disagreements as whether Baroque music should be played on contemporary instruments or on instruments from the period in which the music was written produce differences that can't be resolved in any universally accepted way. Disagreements on value don't, however, prevent working artists from agreeing to cooperate on more practical matters, like the creation of venues for musical performance, or what works will be accepted, for practical purposes, as constituting an agreed-on set of Acceptable Works, good enough to be exhibited or performed. But this possibility is often not realized, and subcommunities, which accept different standards, exist side by side. Within these communities, members usually have no trouble experiencing works more or less in the same way and arriving at more-or-less similar judgments.

So, as long as we both live and work in the same communities and accept the same premises and share the same experiences, I can agree with the dean that a work of art really is wonderful and that Mozart certainly is a genius.

Similarly with ethical questions and problems. Rooted as these are in forms of collective life, as a lot of sociological research (especially on so-called social problems) has shown, they invariably lead to conflict and the inability to resolve questions definitely when the discussants don't all share moral premises and a way of life. Once a group shares such premises, social science research can investigate the allegations of fact, propositions about causal relationships, and inferences about patterns of influence that shape the application of the ethical standards in question. Insofar as I share the form of collective life the standards are rooted in, I probably share the ethical judgments that follow from them.

SOCIAL SCIENCE AND PHILOSOPHICAL INVESTIGATION COMPARED. Comparing empirical investigation and philosophical discussion—to return to the main road—makes clear that a fundamental aspect of such discussions is definitional, and definitional with a twist. The scholarly enterprises I've characterized as philosophical want to find the rules that ought to govern definitions of value. The terms being defined are honorifics: "Art" is good. Nonart isn't so good. "Real science" is good. "Bad" or "pseudo" science isn't. "Law-abiding" is good, "criminal" is bad. The application of these terms has real effects: whether you go to jail or go home, whether people believe your research findings or laugh at them, whether what you've done is art or trash. When people argue about these definitions, more than logical precision is at stake.

We can see the philosophical investigation of ethics as a primitive forerunner of the sociological study of deviance (that's, of course, a sociologist talking). Sociologists have increasingly reformulated problems of the way people should conduct themselves and judge their own conduct and that of others, defining them as the study of how people think others (and they themselves) should behave and, importantly, as the study of the organizations set up to create and enforce these judgments, and the consequences of that organizational activity. Philosophers still write about ethical problems and search for defensible arguments for one or another ethical system. But sociologists now occupy much of this terrain, discussing problems related to the ones philosophers discuss, but formulated differently and answered in a different way, the answers judged for their empirical adequacy. Not "how one should behave," but "who thinks what about how one should behave, and what do they do about it."

Similarly, aesthetics has always been a field of philosophical inquiry, though early versions had a distinctly empirical aspect. But the great questions of aesthetics have mostly been "What is art?" and "What is great art?" and the converse, what is mere trash and not art at all. It's been a characteristically negative enterprise, designed to prevent unworthy stuff—which has its own (pejorative) names like "kitsch" or "mass culture"—from being mistaken for the real thing (see the discussion in Becker 1982, 131–64). The sociology of art, at least in the versions I prefer, avoids that question and instead looks at how participants in the organizational life of art worlds use the term *art* and what they hope to accomplish when they deploy it. Who assigns this title, how they maintain and act on those assignments, how these practices are maintained and acted on and with what results—those are the standard questions in such an empirical inquiry.

Epistemology tells us what we should count as "real knowledge" and what we can dismiss as phony and unworthy of respect. The sociology of science doesn't tell us what "real" knowledge is, but rather what kinds of organized activities produce the results scientists prize as scientific. A good example is Latour's investigation (1995) of the way French soil scientists made the leap, in their study of the savanna-jungle margin in Brazil, from observed facts (like an unmarked patch of forest) to abstract ideas (like the succession from one ecological type to another). This classic epistemological problem is hard to solve if you put it that way: how do you get from observation A, over here, to general proposition B, unimaginably far away over there? Latour shows that working scientists do it by taking very small steps—from a marked-off piece of land, to a sample dug out of the ground, to a box full of such samples, to a chart based on this box, and finally (I've left out most of the steps) to a journal article punctuated with tables and graphs summarizing their observations and using them as proofs. Each step makes sense to the community they present the results to, and the epistemological conundrum becomes a solvable "normal" scientific problem.

I don't want, in making these summary characterizations, to be unfair to the field of philosophy. Philosophy is a more varied enterprise than most academic disciplines, and no summary statements of the kind I've just made do justice to that variety. Many philosophers engage primarily in normative analyses of the kind I've just criticized, but plenty of others do what most social scientists would recognize as perfectly respectable social science analyses. My undergraduate teachers taught me to see Aristotle's *Poetics* as an empirical treatise on the characteristics of Greek tragedies that had specific effects on their viewers, a kind of social psychology or maybe even, as we might say these days, a study in the reception of dramatic works. But in such philosophical subfields as ethics, aesthetics, and epistemology, the main thrust is not empirical but analytic and normative.

When philosophers do discuss social organization, they often do it in a hypothetical way, inventing examples to illustrate the categories they've developed in their analyses instead of, like a social scientist, investigating the varying cases real life presents us for analysis and understanding. They trace judgments of aesthetic worth to the operations of an entity called the "art world" but don't discuss any particular art world in its full organizational reality. Instead, they use imaginary events, things that might happen in some field of art, to bring out the distinctions they want to make. Dickie (1975) devoted himself to questions like this: suppose the keeper of an elephant in the zoo proposed his elephant as a candidate to be a work of art. Does that make the elephant art? Well, it's a question, but not one that participants in the contemporary worlds of, say, painting or sculpture or literature or theater spend any time discussing or arguing about (although contemporary art often produces works that might be hard to distinguish from these invented examples). Dickie concocted the question for rhetorical purposes, rather than as an investigative tool, and so the IOU form was all he needed. Danto (1964) made less silly but similarly unrealistic arguments, for the same kind of purposes.

When the operations of the art world began to appear in the discussions of aestheticians, they weren't talking about the art world Raymonde Moulin (1967) had observed and written about, the one chapter 5 is devoted to, in which participants' judgments of aesthetic worth were irretrievably mixed up with judgments of financial worth, not because the people involved were venal but because the organization of the world of contemporary painting made that unavoidable. Nor were they talking about the world of bargains and deals and very uncertain markets analyzed by the economist Richard Caves (2000). Or the world of Big Hollywood Robert Faulkner (1983) described, in which a few top players in the major occupational categories make, between them, half the films Hollywood distributes every year.

Aestheticians pursue the logic of how such worlds arrive at the collective judgments they eventually arrive at, but not the messy organizational reality of curators and dealers and collectors and critics and their multiple and conflicting motives as social scientists describe them. The art world is, for them, a logical device that helps to explain how a system of aesthetic judgments might work.

The same is true (another sweeping generalization with many exceptions) of epistemology, which looks for the criteria distinguishing real science from bullshit (Frankfurt 2005). Latour, approaching epistemological questions, doesn't look for the logical justification for a result, but rather at how scientists recast that question into a series of small, noncontroversial steps, which get to the result in a way acceptable to the community of scientists they operate in, the colleagues whose opinions matter to them. There's no ultimate logic of truth in such an analysis, only an understanding of the logic in use by people who do the science we all accept. But working scientists always accept the logic of these demonstrations provisionally, ready to reassess findings and theories whenever new evidence makes that seem like a good idea. They don't expect truth to be permanently true.

About now, someone is going to start wondering about the double game I seem to be playing. I argued strenuously in chapter 6 for the usefulness of imaginary cases. Now I'm complaining that philosophers, in these various fields, make use of imaginary cases. They allude to Mozart and airplanes and murder as though they are talking about real things, but they aren't speaking about specific murders or specific scientific findings or specific works of Mozart's played by a specific someone on a specific occasion. Instead, they create an imaginary file drawer filled with "that sort of thing," a generalized entity represented by the name of Mozart. Not the real Mozart who wrote all sorts of things that got played in all sorts of places by all sorts of people on all kinds of instruments for all kinds of audiences. Their cases don't try to include the variety of inputs and outputs found in the world Mozart lived and worked in or the world present-day artists live and work in. Instead, they strip all that away to get to what they take as the logical core of the phenomenon that interests them. I, on the other hand, didn't recommend imaginary stories to social scientists to use as "demonstrations" of the validity of their conclusions, but rather as cases to think with. It's an important difference. The stories I find useful and recommend to others to think about are imagined, but the imagining contains a lot of details, everything I can imagine. And I use them just like the stories I find when I do fieldwork: to elaborate the possibilities that situations like the ones I've studied might contain, by comparing them to detailed imagined cases.

Often enough, these two ways of doing things—aesthetics and sociology of art, ethics and deviance studies, epistemology and sociology of science—just exist side by side, each minding its own business, speaking to its own disciplinary audience, sitting in its own offices in its own part of the university. But sometimes they conflict with one another and sometimes they create conflict within one of the disciplinary homes.

INTERGROUP CONFLICT. This is what happened with me and the dean about Mozart. He had been an aesthetician and quickly saw that I was committing a heresy by suggesting that art and genius, and all the related concepts so central to some aesthetic approaches, were social conventions. (In a favorite ploy of philosophical discourse, he might have accused me of saying that they were "mere" social conventions.) He wanted me to admit that what people like him took seriously—art and genius and all that—were real, not just the outcome of some agreement between interested parties. Agreements can be changed, and that would mean that those sacred things weren't, in some important sense, "real." Not eternally and incontrovertibly "works of genius." To a sociologist nothing is more real than what people have agreed on, which we make central in our work as "the definition of the situation."

Why should an aesthetician care what sociologists think? I think the dean wanted an acknowledgement of the reality of those concepts. He wanted me, and by extension social scientists in general, to admit that some features of art objects aren't relative, not matters of opinion and consensus, but rather inherent qualities of those objects, *and* (this is the real point) he wanted to hear me say that these inherent features had been verified as such by Social Science.

If we social scientists agreed to that, then our research agendas would have to change. We would devote ourselves to answering such questions as "What are the conditions under which great art is created?" taking the adjective "great" as it is generally or commonly applied as a given of the research, rather than as something to be itself investigated. We wouldn't be so interested in the fluctuating reputations of works, one of the bases for social science relativism vis-à-vis the arts. That Shakespeare was once thought less well of than he is now (see Smith's 1968 history of the varying fortunes of Shakespeare's reputation over the centuries) would be of no real interest and could be written off to the blindness, prejudice, and ignorance of earlier generations.

In such cases, what the dean and people like him appeal to is the common sense of informed art lovers and critics, what my father, a devoted believer in these ideas, loved to call "the wisdom of the ages." My insistence that reputations fluctuate, that the features of a work arise from an interaction between an ever-changing object and a variety of constantly changing appreciators—all the processes that go on in the black box whose output is artistic reputation—seems a willful, perverse, and provocative ignoring of all that wisdom and knowledge.

The same thing occurs in quarrels over the meaning of morally charged concepts like crime and deviance, and of the ideas of science. In the study of deviance, the professional groups who own the territory—police, lawyers, politicians, psychiatrists and other physicians—create the common-sense understandings a sociological investigation makes the object of

study. When my colleague asked me, "What about murder?" he was presenting an IOU for a full case, demonstrating (rather than alluding to)
the common-sense understanding that murder *really is* different and requires a different explanation than "less serious" actions that might be
definitionally more ambiguous. The IOU consisted of an alleged fact—
A killed B—without any of the details that discussing any case that had
actually occurred would involve. He wanted me to recognize this difference *and* agree that such a characterization was scientifically founded.

With respect to science, scientists (many of them academics themselves) can't understand why fellow investigators of reality refuse to
recognize the superior quality of the knowledge they produce, and they
are particularly infuriated by what they (incorrectly) take to be an impli-
cation of sociological studies of science: that science is just a matter of
agreement among people, as though they could agree to any damn thing
and that would make it science. They want us, sociologists, to agree that
our own science, sociology, ratifies the claims made by the other sciences.

INTRAGROUP CONFLICT. I've talked as though these attitudes and approaches simply differed along disciplinary lines. They don't. The arts and
humanistic disciplines are filled with people every bit as relativistic as
the most dedicated social constructionist could ask for, often because
they are personally acquainted with the ups and downs of reputation—
it's one of the things many of them study—and know how easily reputations change and on what flimsy evidential bases these changes rest.
Their own perusal of the evidence has led them to a sociological conclusion. You could say that they are sociologists without knowing it. I find
inspiration and useful methods and results in the work of such people as
Barbara Herrnstein Smith (1968), Michael Baxandall (1972), Scott Deveaux
(1997), Paul Berliner (1994), and others from a variety of fields.

On the other hand, some sociologists accept that inherent features of
events, objects, and activities exist, which seem to survive all variations
of social and historical context and must be interpreted and understood
as possessing these unchangeable features. They agree that some artworks
are works of genius, that some science is the real thing while other activities are phony science, and that some activities are really deviant.

I don't remember everything I said to Philip Selznick on that evening
in Berkeley, but this is what I would say now and have said on similar
occasions since. I did remind him that people don't agree about what acts
constitute murder, that murder under one set of circumstances is justi-
fiable homicide, under other circumstances not; that in many times and
places murder, or something it would be hard to tell from it, has been in

fact the only available way of settling disputes; and so on. That didn't satisfy him, and it won't satisfy anyone who believes that murder is inherently wrong and therefore deviant.

Nor would such weaseling satisfy the people who, on later occasions, asked why I wasn't willing to say that capitalism or patriarchy or homophobia were "really deviant," as many people were ready to say they were.

So I would, finally, have said that, since I shared many of those opinions, I was perfectly prepared to say that those things were and are evil, disgusting, or almost any other invidious word they wanted to use. And I would have asked them why that wasn't enough. Because it wouldn't have been. No more would it have been sufficient for me to say to the dean that, being a musician myself, trained in some version of the music he so revered, I felt the way he did about Mozart. And also felt the same way about Dizzy Gillespie and Stan Getz and a lot of other jazz players (because I was and am a jazz player), opinions I doubt he would have shared. Just as my agreement (because, after all, I am a working scientist too) with all those who think astrology isn't science wouldn't have satisfied critics, because they wouldn't have accepted my addendum that I did so as long as others shared my local definition of what constituted science.

THERE'S NO GENERAL SOLUTION. What follows has a very general bearing on many social science problems. Why wouldn't critics accept such answers? My answers wouldn't work for them because they don't just want agreement with their judgments, which I'm often glad to give, but a declaration that this isn't "just" a matter of personal opinion. Not at all. They want it to be a scientific finding, fully warranted as certified, scientifically verified knowledge. The dean didn't just want me to agree with him that Mozart is terrific. He wanted me to admit that objective, irrefutable, scientifically based evidence proves that he is. Selznick wouldn't have been satisfied with my agreement that murder is terrible; he wanted me to agree that its terribleness was a scientific result, not an emotionally shared moral judgment.

Why would anyone insist on that? Because science, and the certified knowledge it's thought to produce, is the only basis on which anyone can win an argument anymore. If I say that my opinion on any of these matters is correct because, let's say, the religious truth that you shall not murder has been revealed to me in sacred writings, many of my readers, who don't accept religious revelation as a source of knowledge, won't accept that conclusion. And I have nothing more convincing to say to them. If I say that my gut tells me that Stan Getz is a better saxophone player than Kenny G will ever be, that only convinces people who already agree with me. These and similar subtleties don't provide the certainty and persuasive power that only science now provides.

Why won't I accept these judgments, which I actually accept in my life as a citizen, piano player, and working social scientist? First of all, of course, because the supporting argument and evidence consists of cases that are promissory notes, not real investigations of real artists or scientists doing what they do in the conditions they usually do it in. But also because if I did, I would be committing myself to a research program doomed to failure. An important step in research, as earlier chapters have illustrated, is finding classes of phenomena about which there is something interesting to say. If the members of the class aren't the same in ways relevant to what you want to generalize about, you won't find any interesting generalizations. But that's what we do when we create a class defined by how other people (judges, police, religious leaders, whoever they might be) have reacted. It's what criminologists do if and when they accept conviction of a crime as revealing something about the "real" nature of the person convicted, instead of something about the process of conviction. People convicted may have some other things in common besides being convicted, but that isn't proved or guaranteed. Or, rather, it's only guaranteed if the process that singles these people out does so infallibly, selecting only people who do have something else in common, such as having committed a certain act, which research on what's often called "the dark figure of crime" has demonstrated over and over is nothing you can count on.

This is a classic problem of good social science research. We can't create homogenous classes of activity for which we might be able to find reasonable causal processes—for which we can construct a good approximation of the inputs and outputs to that process—if we rely on the conventional definitions available in the worlds we study. Those definitions are made, as much research has shown, for purposes other than social science (see, for example, Desrosières 2002) and reflect organizationally rooted compromises and expedients that just impede our efforts to make some social science.

But, when we ignore "common sense," "conventional wisdom," or "the wisdom of the ages," we eventually run into opposition from the people who take those definitions as self-evident and then argue from what they regard as typical cases, IOUs for a full demonstration that can't be produced, whose persuasiveness comes from the dubious source known as "what everybody knows." That's our dilemma, and there's no easy solution.

9 *Last Words*

When I began working in sociology in the late 1940s, it was just beginning a love affair with Big Theories, the more abstract the better. Serious social scientists wanted very much to create the equivalent of what they imagined physicists were doing, highly abstract theories that covered Everything. I read some of this material but soon stopped. I didn't think I was learning anything I could use. The theories didn't give me much help in understanding the world I lived in, or any ideas about what I could do to further my knowledge. I couldn't see how to connect things like the pattern variables Talcott Parsons had invented to anything around me. More mundanely, his theories (and others like them) didn't give me any idea of how to write the master's thesis I had to write, the immediate obstacle I had to get over to keep doing sociology.

I did think sociology was pretty interesting. I was reading books like *Deep South* (Davis et al. 1941), the report of research done by an interracial team of anthropologists—Allison and Elizabeth Davis, Burleigh and Mary Gardner, and St. Clair Drake—in a semimythical (to me, a provincial Chicagoan) town I eventually learned was Natchez, Mississippi. Their report on relations of class and caste rested on meticulously analyzed observations made in the situations of daily living. I could get into that, see the point of it, see how simple questions about mundane things could lead to an understanding of complicated patterns of interdependent activity. William Foote Whyte's *Street Corner Society* did the same thing. I could see how Whyte had done his work, what he'd seen and how he'd connected that to his relatively simple but powerful ideas about how cities worked. He'd studied Boston, and Boston differed from Chicago, but I could see how to adjust some of his ideas to take account of those differences. It looked like a way of working I could imitate.

I got lucky and met Everett C. Hughes, a professor in my department who encouraged the fieldwork I did with local musicians for the MA thesis and helped me understand what I was trying to do, how to get from my crude field notes to a finished product that told readers something socio-logically interesting and, not incidentally, what was and wasn't sociologi-cally interesting.

I read other books like those, and articles in journals, and the disserta-tions older students were writing, and developed my own idiosyncratic, but not totally out of step, idea of what good sociological work looked like.

I developed my interest in the topics of this book when it came time to write a PhD dissertation based on my fieldwork with Chicago schoolteach-ers, a larger and more complicated story to tell than the relatively simple one of my MA thesis. I looked for help to a dissertation that had been done a few years earlier by Oswald Hall (reported in Hall 1948, 1949) on the organization of the medical profession in Providence, Rhode Island. He had organized his report around the idea of "career," the patterns of movement doctors followed between the hospitals, offices, and informal groups that made up their professional world, and especially dealing with the upward mobility, the movements to "better" hospitals and to associa-tion with the "better" physicians in patterns of patient-sharing that was central to ideas of success among these physicians. The teachers I had interviewed also made careers moving between organizations, in their case the schools that made up the Chicago public school system. I could copy the structure of Hall's analysis, substituting 'teachers" for "doctors" and "schools" for the hospitals, offices, and informal groups he had writ-ten about.

And that worked. But teaching isn't medicine, teachers aren't doctors, and, most complicating of all, teachers didn't think of their careers as in-volving upward mobility in a hierarchical system. They didn't think all schools were alike, but some thought this kind was better while others thought that kind was. I had to introduce some new ideas to take ac-count of this difference (see Becker 1952a, 1952b, 1953b). Nothing very spectacular, but I had to account for this difference. So I suggested that mobility in occupational systems didn't always consist of vertical move-ment (although previous literature on careers had pretty much followed Max Weber in using, as a chief example, careers in bureaucracies, where the emphasis was on upward mobility through the bureaucratic ranks). I turned what had been taken as a standard, unremarkable, and unvarying organizational element into something that could take different forms under different circumstances. That added a new dimension, direction, to studies of careers.

I followed that model repeatedly in later work. When I studied mari-juana use (Becker 1953a), I modeled my explanatory strategy on Alfred Lindesmith's (1947) highly original explanation of opiate addiction as a process in which casual users took enough of the drug to experience with-drawal symptoms when they stopped use, interpreted the resulting dis-comfort as due to absence of the drug, and took another dose to relieve it. That emphasized the role of the interpretation users made of their inner experience in shaping what that experience was, rather than regarding it as a simple physical (perhaps amplified by psychological problems) re-action.

My interviews and observations showed that the experiences of users with marijuana varied widely, depending on what they knew about the drug's potential effects. But, just as teachers weren't doctors, marijuana wasn't heroin. It didn't produce habituation and the characteristic with-drawal symptoms of addiction. Instead, users "got high," and being high took various forms, the variation depending on what users had learned to recognize as marijuana-induced differences in their inner experiences. Which meant that "drug effects" had to be treated as variable, which in turn opened up, as necessary topics for understanding the phenomenon of human drug use, the kinds of things chapter 3 introduced as elements of the input-output machinery involved in drug experiences.

That kind of analytic operation has always been at the heart of my own research and thinking. When I investigate a case, I look for elements that seem to resemble each other in many ways and then look for how they differ, using the differences to uncover new variables and dimensions of explanation. When I'm gathering data, I give up the security of a well-defined problem and plan of research for ways of working that maximize the possibility of running across things I haven't thought of, things that will bring new possibilities to consciousness where I can deal with them more systematically. The example of Everett Hughes's perpetual inquisi-tiveness, his never-ending search for new and different examples, his will-ingness to question everything, pushed me to search for new material to think with in unlikely places, places not ordinarily recognized as sources of "real" social science data (see the analysis of Hughes's methods in chap-ter 2, and my own explorations beyond the limits of conventional social science in Becker 2007).

This doesn't mean that I think "qualitative" methods are better than "quantitative" methods, or that studies of small, self-contained groups produce better results than larger studies based on surveys and official statistics of various kinds. I particularly prize well-researched cases con-taining both kinds of material, like Jane Mercer's classic study (1973), which combined survey instruments, official school records, and all sorts of interviews and observations in careful evaluations of what happened to specific children as a school system evaluated and labeled them as "mentally retarded." Stanley Lieberson's comparative study (1980) of mobility rates and routes in the United States investigated the variation within as well as between racial groups to uncover complex connections in his very large case of one country for nearly a hundred years.

I prize, in other words, research that has enough data on enough things—people, practices, outcomes—to let investigators go beyond guesswork in explaining what's going on in the cases they study. I think that when I learn about new inputs, new outputs, new dimensions that I can move from one case to another, I've learned something that will help me generate not only answers to some questions I already have but also some new questions to ask. When Mercer's careful poking into exactly when a school officially labels a child "retarded" reveals that the school psychologist, administering a standardized test, wipes out all the situationally based (and more accurate) assessments, based on many more data points, made by teachers and parents (see the chart in Mercer 1973, 98–99 and the accompanying text), I know that, in any case resembling this one, I can look for professionals importing standards from elsewhere into a local setting and producing the kinds of anomalous results Mercer detected. Am I sure to find that? No. Is that a good place to start? Yes. And if I don't find what I'm expecting, so much the better. I'm on my way to finding a new element to build into future work.

This is a long way from the abstract theories so many people would like to produce. OK. I can live with that. I think the real action is closer to the earth, down here where people are doing things with each other, creating what we like to call, not realizing we're speaking metaphorically, "social structure" and "organization," though what they're really doing is finding ways to collaborate in the day-to-day here-and-now, getting life done. That's where I like to work and think. The air isn't as thin down here.

A friend of mine once stayed for several days at a Zen Buddhist retreat center. Every morning, the monks assembled and sat *zazen* together, each one facing a blank wall and meditating for fifty minutes out of the hour, and then doing it again for a second hour. The first morning my friend did his best, though he hadn't acquired the discipline that let him empty his mind of random thoughts.

At the end of the meditation period, all the monks lined up and left the meditation room in an orderly line. The head monk stood in the back of the room, near the door, and as each person passed him he leaned over and whispered something in the person's ear. My friend thought probably he was passing on some gem of Zen thought and, being at the back of the line, he had plenty of time to think about what the head monk would say to him, when he got there. He got more and more excited as he got nearer and nearer to what he had convinced himself would be a moment of pure enlightenment.

Then he reached the door, and the head monk leaned over and whispered in his ear, "Go get a broom and sweep the porch." The monk knew. That's where the action is.

References

Aberle, David F. 1966. The Peyote Religion among the Navaho. Chicago: Aldine.

Adrian, Dennis. 1982. "A Brief Personal History." In Selections from the Dennis Adrian Collection, by Museum of Contemporary Art. Chicago: Museum of Contemporary Art.

Alpers, Svetlana. 1988. Rembrandt's Enterprise: The Studio and the Market. Chicago: University of Chicago Press.

Artner, Alan. 1982. "MCA Rounds up Dennis Adrian's 'Maverick' Herd." Chicago Tribune, Arts and Books section, February 7.

Aubert, Vilhelm. 1982. The Hidden Society. New Brunswick, NJ: Transaction Books.

Aubert, Vilhelm, and Harrison C. White. 1965. "Sleep: A Sociological Interpretation." In The Hidden Society, edited by Vilhelm Aubert, 168–200. Totowa, NJ: Bedminster Press.

Baker, Nicholson. 2001. Doublefold: Libraries and the Assault on Paper. New York: Random House.

Baker, Wayne E., and Robert R. Faulkner. 2003. "Diffusion of Fraud: Intermediate Economic Crime and Investor Dynamics." Criminology 41:1173–1206.

———. 2004. "Social Networks and Loss of Capital." Social Networks 26:91–111.

Barley, Stephen R., and Gideon Kunda. 2004. Gurus, Hired Guns, and Warm Bodies: Itinerant Experts in a Knowledge Economy. Princeton, NJ: Princeton University Press.

Barthes, Roland. 1980. La chambre clair. Paris: Editions de Seuil.

Baxandall, Michael. 1972. Painting and Experience in Fifteenth Century Italy. Oxford: Oxford University Press.

Becker, Howard S. 1952a. "The Career of the Chicago Public School Teacher." American Journal of Sociology 57:470–77.

———. 1952b. "Social Class Variations in the Teacher-Pupil Relationship." Journal of Educational Sociology, 451–65.

———. 1953a. "Becoming a Marihuana User." American Journal of Sociology 59:235–43.

———. 1953b. "The Teacher in the Authority System of the Public School." Journal of Educational Sociology 27:128–41.

———. 1963. Outsiders: Studies in the Sociology of Deviance. Glencoe, IL: Free Press of Glencoe.

———. 1967. "History, Culture, and Subjective Experience: An Exploration of the Social Bases of Drug-Induced Experiences." Journal of Health and Social Behavior 8:163–76.

————. 1982. Art Worlds. Berkeley: University of California Press.

————. 1998. Tricks of the Trade: How to Think about Your Research While You're Doing It. Chicago: University of Chicago Press.

————. 2006. "The Work Itself." In Becker et al. 2006, 21–30.

————. 2007. Telling about Society. Chicago: University of Chicago Press.

————. 2010. "Review of John Searle, Making the Social World, and Paul Boghossian, Fear of Knowledge." Science, Technology, and Human Value, 14 (online 14 November).

Becker, Howard S., and Robert R. Faulkner. 2013. Thinking Together: An E-Mail Exchange and All That Jazz. Los Angeles: Annenberg Press.

Becker, Howard S., Robert R. Faulkner, and Barbara Kirshenblatt-Gimblett, eds. 2006. Art from Start to Finish: Jazz, Painting, Writing, and Other Improvisations. Chicago: University of Chicago Press.

Becker, Howard S., Blanche Geer, and Everett Cherrington Hughes. 1968. Making the Grade: The Academic Side of College Life. New York: Wiley.

Becker, Howard S., Blanche Geer, Everett C. Hughes, and Anselm L. Strauss. 1961. Boys in White: Student Culture in Medical School. Chicago: University of Chicago Press.

Bennett, H. Stith. 1980. On Becoming a Rock Musician. Amherst: University of Massachusetts Press.

Berliner, Paul F. 1994. Thinking about Jazz: The Infinite Art of Improvisation. Chicago: University of Chicago Press.

Blackwood, Easley. 1986. The Structure of Recognizable Diatonic Tunings. Princeton, NJ: Princeton University Press.

Blum, Richard, et al. 1964. Utopiates. New York: Atherton.

Blumer, Herbert. 1951. "Collective Behavior." In New Outline of the Principles of Sociology, edited by A. M. Lee, 166–222. New York: Barnes and Noble.

————. 1969. "Fashion: From Class Differentiation to Collective Selection." Sociological Quarterly 10:275–91.

Bowker, Geoffrey C. 2004. "Time, Money, and Biodiversity." In Global Assemblages: Technology, Politics, and Ethics as Anthropological Problems, edited by Aihwa On and Stephen J. Collier, 107–23 Oxford: Blackwell.

Calvino, Italo. 1974. Invisible Cities. New York: Harcourt Brace.

Campbell, Donald T., and Julian C. Stanley. 1963. Experimental and Quasi-Experimental Designs for Research. Boston: Houghton Mifflin.

Cândido, Antônio. 1995. On Literature and Society. Translated and with an introduction by Howard S. Becker. Princeton, NJ: Princeton University Press.

Castaneda, Carlos. 1968. The Teachings of Don Juan. Berkeley: University of California Press.

Caves, Richard E. 2000. Creative Industries: Contracts between Art and Commerce. Cambridge, MA: Harvard University Press.

Cohen, Stan. 1988. Against Criminology. New Brunswick, NJ: Transaction.

Coleman, James S., Elihu Katz, and Herbert Menzel. 1966. Medical Innovation. Indianapolis: Bobbs-Merrill.

Conwell, Chic, and Edwin H. Sutherland. 1937. The Professional Thief, by a Professional Thief. Annotated and interpreted by Edwin H. Sutherland. Chicago: University of Chicago Press.

Cressey, Donald R. 1953. Other People's Money. New York: Free Press.

Csikszentmihalyi, Mihaly, and Eugene Rochberg-Halton. 1981. The Meaning of Things: Domestic Symbols and the Self. New York: Cambridge University Press.

Dalton, Melville. 1959. Men Who Manage. New York: Wiley.

Danto, Arthur. 1964. "The Artworld." Journal of Philosophy 61:571–84.

Davis, Allison, Burleigh B. Gardner, and Mary R. Gardner. 1941. Deep South: A Social Anthropological Study of Caste and Class. Chicago: University of Chicago Press.

Davis, Mike. 1998. Ecology of Fear: Los Angeles and the Imagination of Disaster. New York: Metropolitan Books.

Debary, Octave, and Mélaie Roustan. 2012. Voyage au musée du quai Branly. Paris: La documentation Française.

Desrosières, Alain. 2002. The Politics of Large Numbers: A History of Statistical Reasoning. Cambridge, MA: Harvard University Press.

Deveaux, Scott. 1997. The Birth of Bebop: A Social and Musical History. Berkeley: University of California Press.

Dickie, George. 1975. Art and the Aesthetic: An Institutional Analysis. Ithaca, NY: Cornell University Press.

Dudouet, François-Xavier. 2003. "De la régulation à la répression des drogues: Une politique publique internationale." Les cahiers de la sécurité intérieure 52:89–112.

———. 2009. Le grand deal de l'opium: Histoire du marché légal des drogues. Paris: Editions Syllepse.

Durkheim, Emile. 1951. Suicide, a Study in Sociology. Glencoe, IL: Free Press.

Edwards, Lyford P. 1927. The Natural History of Revolution. Chicago: University of Chicago Press.

Emerson, Richard M. 1966. "Mount Everest: A Case Study of Communication Feedback and Sustained Group Goal-Striving." Sociometry 29:213–27.

Faulkner, Robert R. 1983. Music on Demand: Composers and Careers in the Hollywood Film Industry. New Brunswick, NJ: Transaction.

Faulkner, Robert R., and Howard S. Becker. 2009. Do You Know . . . ? The Jazz Repertoire in Action. Chicago: University of Chicago Press.

Felt, Lawrence. 1971. "Opportunity Structures and Relative Deprivation among the Poor: The Case of Welfare Careerists." PhD diss., Northwestern University–Evanston.

Finnegan, Ruth. 1989. The Hidden Musicians: Music-Making in an English Town. New York: Cambridge University Press.

Fisher, Jill A. 2009. Medical Research for Hire: The Political Economy of Pharmaceutical Clinical Trials. New Brunswick, NJ: Rutgers University Press.

Frankfurt, Harry G. 2005. On Bullshit. Princeton, NJ: Princeton University Press.

Freidson, Eliot. 1960. "Client Control and Medical Practice." American Journal of Sociology 65:374–82.

———. 1961. Patients' Views of Medical Practice. New York: Russell Sage Foundation.

———. 1970a. Professional Dominance. Chicago: Aldine.

———. 1970b. The Profession of Medicine. New York: Dodd, Mead.

———. 1975. Doctoring Together: A Study of Professional Social Control. New York: Elsevier.

Gagneux, Renard, Jean Anckaert, and Gérard Conte. 2002. Sur les traces de La Bièvre Parisienne: Promenades au fil d'une rivière disparue. Paris: Parigramme.

Galison, Peter. 1987. How Experiments End. Chicago: University of Chicago Press.

Gilmore, Samuel. 1987. "Coordination and Convention: The Organization of the Concert World." Symbolic Interaction 10:209–28.

Gleick, James. 1988. Chaos: Making a New Science. New York: Viking.

Goffman, Erving. 1952. "On Cooling the Mark Out: Some Aspects of Adaptation to Failure." Psychiatry 15:451–63.

————. 1961. Asylums. Garden City, NY: Doubleday.

Granger, Bill, and Lori Granger. 1980. Fighting Jane: Mayor Jane Byrne and the Chicago Machine. New York: Dial Press.

Hall, Oswald. 1948. "The Stages of the Medical Career." American Journal of Sociology 53:243–53.

————. 1949. "Types of Medical Careers." American Journal of Sociology 55:404–13.

Halle, David. 1993. Inside Culture: Art and Class in the American Home. Chicago: University of Chicago Press.

Harris, R. 1964. The Real Voice. New York: Macmillan.

Haskell, Francis. 1963. Patrons and Painters: A Study in the Relations between Italian Art and Society in the Age of the Baroque. New York: Alfred A. Knopf.

Hazan, Eric. 2002. L'invention de Paris: Il n'ya pas de pas perdus. Paris: Seuil.

Hedström, Peter, and Peter Bearman. 2009. The Oxford Handbook of Analytical Sociology. New York: Oxford University Press.

Hedström, Peter, and Richard Swedberg. 1998. Social Mechanisms: An Analytical Approach to Social Theory. Cambridge: Cambridge University Press.

Hedström, Peter, and Petri Ylikoski. 2010. "Causal Mechanisms in the Social Sciences." Annual Review of Sociology 36:49–67.

Heinich, Natalie. 1991. La gloire de Van Gogh: Essai d'anthropologie de l'admiration. Paris: Editions de Minuit.

————. 1998. Ce que l'art fait à la sociologie. Paris: Minuit.

Hennion, Antoine. 1988. Comment la musique vient aux enfants: Une anthropologie de l'enseignement musical. Paris: Anthropos.

————. 1993. La passion musicale. Paris: Edition Métailié.

Hersh, Seymour. 1968. Chemical and Biological Warfare: America's Hidden Arsenal. Indianapolis: Bobbs-Merrill.

Hughes, Everett C. 1935. "The Industrial Revolution and the Catholic Movement in Germany." Social Forces 14:286–92.

————. 1941. "French and English in the Economic Structure of Montreal." Canadian Journal of Economics and Political Science 7:493–505.

————. 1942. "The Impact of War on American Institutions." American Journal of Sociology 48:398–403.

————. 1943. French Canada in Transition. Chicago: University of Chicago Press.

————. 1945. "Dilemmas and Contradictions of Status." American Journal of Sociology 50 (5): 353–59.

————. 1946. "The Knitting of Racial Groups in Industry." American Sociological Review 11:512–19.

————. 1947. "Principle and Rationalization in Race Relations." American Catholic Sociological Review 8:3–11.

————. 1949. "Queries concerning Industry and Society Growing out of Study of Ethnic Relations in Industry." American Sociological Review 14:211–20.

————. 1971. The Sociological Eye. Chicago: Aldine.

Jordan, David P. 1996. Transforming Paris: The Life and Times of Baron Haussmann. Chicago: University of Chicago Press.

Joyce, Michael. 1990. Afternoon, a Story. Hypertext edition. Cambridge, MA: Eastgate Systems.

————. 2006. "'How Do I Know I Am Finnish?' The Computer, the Archive, the Literary Artist, and the Work as Social Object." In Becker et al. 2006, 69–90.

Kendall, Patricia L., and Katherine M. Wolf. 1949. "The Two Purposes of Deviant Case

Analysis." In Communications Research, 1948–49, edited by Paul F. Lazarsfeld and Frank Stanton, 152–57. New York: Harper.

Ketchum, William L. 1982. The Collections of the Margaret Woodbury Strong Museum. Rochester, NY: Margaret Woodbury Strong Museum.

Kidder, Tracy. 1981. The Soul of a New Machine. Boston: Little, Brown.

Klinenberg, Eric. 2002. Heat Wave: A Social Autopsy of Disaster in Chicago. Chicago: University of Chicago Press.

Koch-Weser, Jan, et al. 1969. "Factors Determining Physician Reporting of Adverse Drug Reactions." New England Journal of Medicine 280:20–26.

Kornhauser, Arthur, and Paul F. Lazarsfeld. 1955. The Analysis of Consumer Actions. In The Language of Social Research, edited by Paul F. Lazarsfeld and Morris Rosenberg, 392–404. Glencoe, IL: Free Press.

Kraft, Eric. 1992. Where Do You Stop? The Personal History, Adventures, Experiences, and Observations of Peter Leroy (continued). New York: Crown.

Kuhn, Thomas. 1970. The Structure of Scientific Revolutions. Chicago: University of Chicago Press.

Latour, Bruno. 1987. Science in Action. Cambridge, MA: Harvard University Press.

———. 1988. The Pasteurization of France. Translated by A. Sheridan and J. Law. Cambridge, MA: Harvard University Press.

———. 1995. "The 'Pédofil' of Boa Vista: A Photo-Philosophical Montage." Common Knowledge 4:144–87.

———. 1996. Aramis or the Love of Technology. Cambridge, MA: Harvard University Press.

———. 1998a. "Ramsès II est-il mort de la tuberculose?" La Recherche 307:84–88.

———. 1998b. "Ramsès II est-il mort de la tuberculose?" La Recherche 309:6.

Latour, Bruno, and Emilie Hermant. 1998. Paris ville invisible. Paris: Les Empêcheurs de penser en ronde/La Découverte.

Latour, Bruno, and Steve Woolgar. 1979. Laboratory Life: The Social Construction of Scientific Fact. Beverly Hills, CA: Sage.

Lave, Jean. 1988. Cognition in Practice. Cambridge: Cambridge University Press.

Le Dain, Gerald, Heinz Lehmann, and J. Peter Stein. 1972. "The Report of the Canadian Government Commission of Inquiry into the Non-Medical Use of Drugs." Information Canada, Ottawa, Canada.

Lemov, Rebecca. 2006. World as Laboratory: Experiments with Mice, Mazes, and Men. New York: Hill and Wang.

Lennard, Henry, et al. 1972. Mystification and Drug Misuse. New York: Harper and Row.

Lieberson, Stanley. 1980. A Piece of the Pie: Blacks and White Immigrants since 1880. Berkeley: University of California Press.

———. 2000. A Matter of Taste: How Names, Fashions, and Culture Change. New Haven, CT: Yale University Press.

Lindesmith, Alfred. 1947. Opiate Addiction. Bloomington, IN: Principia Press.

Lodge, David. 2011. The Campus Trilogy: Changing Places; Small World; Nice Work. New York: Penguin Books.

Maffi, Luisa, ed. 2001. On Biocultural Diversity: Linking Language, Knowledge, and the Environment. Washington, DC: Smithsonian Institution Press.

Mears, Ashley. 2011. Pricing Beauty: The Making of a Fashion Model. Berkeley: University of California Press.

Menger, Pierre-Michel. 1983. Le paradoxe du musicien: Le compositeur, le mélomane et l'Etat dans la société contemporaine. Paris: Flammarion.

———. 2006. "Profiles of the Unfinished: Rodin's Work and the Varieties of Incompleteness." In Becker et al. 2006, 31–68.

Mercer, Jane. 1973. Labeling the Mentally Retarded. Berkeley: University of California Press.

Mergen, Bernard. 1997. Snow in America. Washington, DC: Smithsonian Institution Press.

Mills, C. Wright. 1959. The Sociological Imagination. New York: Oxford University Press.

Molotch, Harvey. 1994. "Going Out." Sociological Forum 9:229–39.

Moulin, Raymonde. 1967. Le marché de la peinture en France. Paris: Les editions de Minuit.

———. 1978. "La genèse de la rareté artistique." Ethnologie française 8 (2–3): 241–58.

———. 1992. L'artiste, l'institution, et le marché. Paris: Flammarion.

Myers, John Bernard. 1983. "The Art Biz." New York Review of Books, October 13, www.nybooks.com/. Accessed October 17, 2013.

Nolan, Kathleen. 2011. Police in the Hallways: Discipline in an Urban High School. Minneapolis: University of Minnesota Press.

Passeron, Jean-Claude, and Jacques Revel. 2005. "Penser par cas: Raisoner a partir de singularités." In Penser par cas, edited by J.-C. Passeron and J. Revel, 9–44. Paris: Editions de l'Ecole des Hautes Etudes en Sciences Sociales.

Perrenoud, Marc. 2007. Les musicos: Enquête sur des musiciens ordinaires. Paris: La Découverte.

Perrow, Charles. 1984. Normal Accidents: Living with High Risk Technologies. New York: Basic Books.

Polsky, Ned. 1967. Hustlers, Beats, and Others. Chicago: Aldine.

Ragin, Charles C. 1987. The Comparative Method: Moving beyond Qualitative and Quantitative Strategies. Berkeley: University of California Press.

———. 2000. Fuzzy-Set Social Science. Chicago: University of Chicago Press.

———. 2008. Redesigning Social Inquiry: Fuzzy Sets and Beyond. Chicago: University of Chicago Press.

Ragin, Charles C., and Howard S. Becker. 1992. What Is a Case? Exploring the Foundations of Social Inquiry. New York: Cambridge University Press.

Ross, Alex. 2008. The Rest Is Noise: Listening to the Twentieth Century. New York: Picador.

Roth, Julius. 1963. Timetables. Indianapolis: Bobbs-Merrill.

Roy, Donald. 1952a. "Quota Restriction and Goldbricking in a Machine Shop." American Journal of Sociology 57:425–42.

———. 1952b. "Restriction of Output by Machine Operators in a Piecework Machine Shop." PhD diss., University of Chicago.

———. 1953. "Work Satisfaction and Social Reward in Quota Achievement." American Sociological Review 18:507–14.

———. 1954. "Efficiency and the "Fix": Informal Intergroup Relations in a Piecework Machine Shop." American Journal of Sociology 60:255–66.

Schacter, Stanley, and Jerome Singer. 1962. "Cognitive, Social, and Physiological Determinants of Emotional State." Psychological Review 69:377–99.

Scott, Marvin B. 1968. The Racing Game. Chicago: Aldine.

Seaman, Barbara. 1969. The Doctor's Case against the Pill. New York: Peter H. Wyden.

Shadish, William, Thomas D. Cook, and Donald T. Campbell. 2001. Experimental and Quasi-Experimental Designs for Generalized Causal Inference. Stamford, CT: Wadsworth.

Shapiro, Reva. 1988. "Analytical Portraits of Home Computer Users: The Negotiation of Innovation." PhD diss., University of California–San Francisco.

Skocpol, Theda. 1979. States and Social Revolutions: A Comparative Analysis of France, Russia, and China. Cambridge: Cambridge University Press.

Small, Mario Luis. 2009. "'How Many Cases Do I Need?': On Science and the Logic of Case Selection in Field-Based Research." Ethnography 10:5–38.

Smith, Barbara Herrnstein. 1968. Poetic Closure: A Study of How Poems End. Chicago: University of Chicago Press.

Smith, Charles W. 1989. Auctions: The Social Construction of Value. New York: Free Press.

Smith, Roberta. 1982. "Schnabel the Vincible." In The Village Voice (New York), November 2.

Sudnow, David. 1978. Ways of the Hand: The Organization of Improvised Conduct. Cambridge, MA: Harvard University Press.

Sutherland, J. H. 1976. Victorian Novelists and Publishers. Chicago: University of Chicago Press.

Thézy, Marie de. 1998. Marville: Paris. Paris: Hazan.

Tompkins, Calvin. 1983. "Season's End." New Yorker, 80–83.

Vaughan, Diane. 1996. The Challenger Launch Decision: Risky Technology, Culture, and Deviance at NASA. Chicago: University of Chicago Press.

———. 2004. "Theorizing Disaster: Analogy, Historical Ethnography, and the Challenger Accident." Ethnography 5:313–45.

———. 2006. "NASA Revisited: Ethnography, Analogy, Public Discourse, and Policy." American Journal of Sociology 112:353–93.

———. 2009. "Analytic Ethnography." In Hedström and Bearman 2009, 688–711.

Veblen, Thorstein. 1918. The Higher Learning in America: A Memorandum on the Conduct of Universities by Business Men. New York: B. W. Huebsch.

Velho, Gilberto. 1976. "Accusations, Family Mobility, and Deviant Behavior." Social Problems 23:268–75.

———. 2002 [1973]. A utopia urbana: Um estudo de antropologia social. Rio de Janeiro: Jorge Zahar.

Vianna, Hermano. 1988. O Mundo Funk Carioca. Rio de Janeiro: Jorge Zahar Editor.

Whyte, William Foote. 1955. Street Corner Society: The Social Structure of an Italian Slum. Chicago: University of Chicago Press.

Zelizer, Viviana. 1989. "The Social Meaning of Money: 'Special Monies.'" American Journal of Sociology 95:342–77.

———. 1994. The Social Meaning of Money. New York: Basic Books.

Index

black box producing drug experiences
(*continued*)
79, 87; knowledge of effects and, 67, 68,
69, 82; as tool for investigating other
things, 91–93. *See also* drug effects
black persons: poor women dealing
with welfare bureaucracy, 17–18, 19,
58; young men and opiate addiction,
61–62, 63–64. *See also* race
Blackwood, Easley, 127–28
blocks. *See* spatial orientation in cities
Bolter, Jay, 130
Boulez, Pierre, 21, 131
Bourdieu, Pierre, 22
Boys in White (Becker, Geer, Hughes, and
Strauss), 138–39, 140–41, 143
Brazil: funk in Rio de Janeiro, 132–33;
international comparative experiences
involving, 9–11, 15, 16–17, 20; Latour on
soil science research in, 177. *See also*
Velho, Gilberto
Brown, Roger, 102
bullshit, 178
bureaucracy: Brazilian, 10, 11, 16, 17, 19, 20;
Challenger disaster and, 157; of Chicago
welfare system, 17–18, 19, 58; for schol-
arly or artistic support in France, 21;
Weber on careers in, 185
Byrne, Jane, 146

Cage, John, 125, 131, 132
Campbell, Donald, 161–62, 173
Cândido, Antônio, 16–21
captation, Latour on, 174
careers: of Chicago schoolteachers, 185;
direction of mobility in, 185; of illnesses, 47, 53; natural histories as, 85
Cartier-Bresson, Henri, 112
cases/case studies: art-related, 94, 95;
Campbell on validity of, 162; defined, 2;
gathering diverse range of, 66, 121; rule
of thumb for comparing, 19. *See also*
imaginary cases; reasoning from cases
Castaneda, Carlos, 78, 87
caste systems: in *Deep South*, 184; industries resembling, 34; middleman in,
122–23
causation: vs. correlation, 61; investigating mechanisms and, 107; laboratory

experiments and, 161; searching for
additional causes, 65
Caves, Richard, 178
Cefai, Daniel, 28
Challenger space flight disaster, 147, 157
change, in things studied, 1–2, 3. *See also*
stability of social organizations
chemical warfare, 67, 69, 74, 87, 88–89;
fluoridation seen as, 92
Chicago: heat wave of 1995, 144, 145;
schoolteachers' careers in, 185; street
grid of, 24–26; wartime industry in, 37;
welfare bureaucracy of, 17–18, 19, 58
Chicago Imagists, 102–4. *See also* Adrian,
Dennis
children, desirable number per couple,
154–55, 159
Chinese immigrants, in middleman role,
123
class: art market and, 114, 121; political
party and, 1–2; of social researcher vs.
person studied, 137, 138–42
classical music: compositional scene in
France, 131; stable world of, 125
"Client Control and Medical Practice"
(Freidson), 47
Cohen, Stan, 134–36, 141, 143
collections, 150–52, 155, 157–58, 159
colloques, 11, 22
colonies, industry in, 32–35, 36–38
Columbia space craft disaster, 147
comparative method, 5–6. *See also* cross-
national comparisons
comparative reasoning, 85; finding similar things for, 29–30; unconventional
forms of, 39
complexity: of model, 144–45; of social
world, 4, 14
computer problems, analogical reasoning
about, 47, 55–60
control of drug use: by external agents,
69–70, 74, 87–90; by user, 69, 74–78, 91;
by user's agent, 69, 74, 78–87, 91. *See
also* chemical warfare; medically prescribed drug use; recreational drug use
control of knowledge, 60. *See also* power
cooling the mark out, 35–36
correlations: vs. causation, 61; changing
with historical circumstances, 1–2;

mobility and racial groups in United States, 187

Molotch, Harvey, 39

moral division of labor, 8–9

Morin, Alexander, 166

Moulin, Raymonde: on attribution of artworks, 101, 113; comparison of various art markets, 107, 108–13; on confusion of values, 95–96, 97–99, 101, 107, 178; dimensions to add to explanatory system of, 113–14; on scarcity in art markets, 107–13; on taking work out of art market, 106

Mozart, Wolfgang Amadeus, 170–71, 176, 179, 182

murder, 169–70, 179, 181–82

Murdock, George Peter, 7

musicians: Becker and Faulkner's record of thinking about, 29; defining characteristics of, 125–26; disrespect for squares, 20; studied for author's MA thesis, 137–38, 141, 184–85

music world, stability and change in, 125–33

Myers, John Bernard, 114–15, 117, 120–21

natural history: of side effects from new drug, 85–86; sociological concept of, 84–85

Natural History of Revolution, The (Edwards), 5

Negro personnel man, 36–37

Nick, Fred, 56, 58

normalization of deviance, 147, 148

nuclear disasters, 147

nurses hating patients, 19–20

Nutt, Jim, 102

O (outcome of expenditure E), 148

"On Cooling the Mark Out" (Goffman), 35–36

opiate drugs: addiction to, 61–65, 185–86; interpretation of withdrawal from, 70

oral contraceptives, side effects of, 72, 83, 85–86

organizational culture, and allocation of resources, 157

organizational stability, 125–33. See also social organization

outputs, 62, 187. See also black boxes

Outsiders (Becker), 168–69

packages: of music world, 128–31, 133; in sociology of science, 128

parables, 124

paradigm, research, 160, 172

Paris: advanced system of public transportation for, 148; heat wave of 2003, 144, 145; mid-twentieth-century art market in, 95–96, 110; spatial orientation in, 26–29. See also France

Park, Robert E., 31, 140

Parsons, Talcott, 184

Partch, Harry, 126–27, 128–29, 133

Paschke, Ed, 102

patent medicines, 74, 77, 78

patient advocate, 18

patronage, 115

Peretz, Henri, 23, 25, 27, 29, 41

Perrenoud, Marc, 137

personal problem, organizational counterpart of, 100

Pessin, Alain, 11

peyote, 70

pharmaceutical companies, 81–82, 91

philosophical arguments, compared to empirical investigation, 172–73, 176–79

photography, 109, 111–12

physiological functioning, normal, sociology of, 93

placebo effects, 73

pollutants, forced administration of, 92

Polsky, Ned, 166

power: in art worlds, 114, 121; to define music, 132; of inertia, 131. See also control of drug use; control of knowledge

power differentials on university campuses, 141–42

power imbalance in social research, 137, 140–41

professional dominance, 80

professional referral system, 52

promissory notes, scientific, 167–68, 170, 183

psychiatrists: compared by Hughes to prostitutes and priests, 39; Goffman on cooling out by, 35–36